# DeKalb County, Tennessee

# Marriages

# 1848 – 1880

Byron and Barbara Sistler

JANAWAY PUBLISHING, INC.
Santa Maria, California

Originally Published:
Nashville, Tennessee
1985



Reprinted by

Janaway Publishing, Inc.
732 Kelsey Ct.
Santa Maria, California 93454
(805) 925-1038
www.JanawayGenealogy.com

2006, 2013




ISBN: 978-1-59641-053-4



*Made in the United States of America*

DEKALB COUNTY, TN MARRIAGES

1848-1880

Where two dates appear on an entry, the first one is the date license was issued, the second (in parentheses) the date marriage was solemnized.  If only one date, it usually means that the date of execution was the same as the date of license issuance.

Sometimes the execution of the marriage was not reported to the courthouse, and occasionally the clerk failed to note in the marriage book that the license was returned.  We would usually make a notation in the entry to indicate the non-execution of a marriage if the book so revealed.

We transcribed these marriage records directly from a microfilmed copy of the original county marriage books, so error, where it occurs, will usually be ours.  However, it should be remembered that entries in the books themselves were copied from the licenses by clerks, and it is obvious from examining the pages that many of them were not prepared with great care.  Sometimes, for example, the date of execution will appear in the book as a date prior to license issuance.  In such cases, as well as where we had to guess in deciphering the handwriting, a question mark or "sic" is inserted on the entry.

The notation (col) after a name means Colored (Black).

Byron Sistler<br>
Barbara Sistler

Nashville, TN<br>
August, 1985

Aamson?, Joseph to Jane Hinson 9-9-1852
Adams, George to Nancy Cantrell 3-27-1849 (3-?-1849)
Adams, Jacob to Canzada Williams 5-5-1879
Adams, Johnson to Frances Vick 5-7-1866 (5-16-1866) [B]
Adams, Johnson to Frances Vick 5-7-1866 (5-7-1866) [B]
Adams, P. C. to Jennie Overale 3-24-1871 (3-30-1871)
Adams, Thomas to Milly E. Warford 12-3-1864 (no return)
Adams, Thos. to Milly E. Warford 12-3-1864 (no return)
Adams, William H. to Malvina Rynolds? 11-?-1852 (11-3-1852)
Adams, William K. to Josiphene T. Mitchel 9-24-1874 (no return)
Adams, Wils to Mary Hayes 5-11-1866 [B]
Adams, Wm. H. to Malvina Rynolds 11-?-1852 (11-3-1852)
Adams, Wm. K. to Josiphene T. Mitchel 9-24-1874 (no return)
Adamson, Bethel A. to Mary Ann Bain 11-22-183?
Adamson, C. E. to L. A. C. Anderson 8-23-1870 (8-25-1870)
Adamson, Christopher E. to L. F. Spurlock 1-25-1867 (1-31-1867)
Adamson, G. W. to Nancy Ann Briant 12-30-1868 (12-31-1868)
Adamson, Henry to Mary Jane Gann 4-18-1877 (4-19-1877)
Adamson, J. C. to E. J. Gillahan 10-17-1877 (10-20-1877)
Adamson, James E. to Ellice Pugh 8-11-1864
Adamson, Joel to Mary Reeves 10-3-1874 (no return)
Adamson, John R. to Margarett Briant 8-14-1875 (8-19-1875)
Adamson, John W. to Rachal J. Adamson 1-21-1876
Adamson, Joseph to Lakey Deen 7-6-1854
Adamson, Lamon to Mary Smith 9-4-1865 (9-6-1865)
Adamson, Presly to Pheby C. Connor 4-11-1876 (4-13-1876)
Adamson, Thomas J. to M. F. Dirting 7-21-1876
Adamson, Thomas J. to Mary E. Cannon 4-8-1861
Adamson, W. L. to Nancy Vantrease 12-20-1875 (6?-20-1875)
Adamson, Wm. D. to Levina Williams 8-24-1853 (8-25-1853)
Adamson, Wm. to Parthena C. Truett 8-2-1861 (8-4-1861)
Adcock, Anthony P. to Ebaline Wright 11-15-1856 (11-16-1856)
Adcock, Charly to Faney Curtis 7-27-1867 (7-28-1867) [B]
Adcock, Crocket to Gabriala Green 10-21-1865
Adcock, Edward to Martha Ann Adcock 3-8-1852 (3-11-1852)
Adcock, H. P. to Emaline Thrue 11-28-1874 (11-29-1874)
Adcock, Henrey to Mary J. Picke 2-13-1873 (2-15-1873)
Adcock, Henry to Nancy Self 1-27-1880 (no return)
Adcock, Isaac to Laura Potter 8-11-1858 (8-12-1858)
Adcock, Jacob to Jane William 7-5-1867 (no return)
Adcock, James E. to Lucinday Adcock 4-21-1870 (4-22-1870)
Adcock, James K. P. to Sarah Phillips 3-13-1872 (3-14-1872)
Adcock, James T. to M. C. Luny 8-15-1877 (8-6-1877)
Adcock, James W. to Mary West 8-13-1853 (8-14-1852?)
Adcock, John B. to Martha J. Pennager 2-14-1861 (2-17-1861)
Adcock, Lafayette to Sary Cutlar 1-1-1858
Adcock, M. D. to M. J. Readmon 12-19-1871 (12-20-1871)
Adcock, M. E. to Sarah McAfee 10-10-1865
Adcock, Newton T. to Sarah C. Cantrell 1-7-1874 (1-8-1874)
Adcock, Perry to Mary N. Wynns 10-1-1860 (10-2-1860)
Adcock, Rufus to Mary Pineager 10-24-1868 (10-25-1868)
Adcock, Starkley to Rua Lassater 2-7-1876 (2-9-1876)
Adcock, Tilmon to Sarah Ann McManas 11-2-1854
Adcock, Tona to Catharine Adcock 2-1-1875 (2-2-1875)
Adcock, W. H. to A. T. Turner 10-16-1875 (10-17-1875)
Adcock, W. J. to America Delong 4-11-1874 (4-12-1874)
Adcock, Wm. H. to Elizabeth Hayse 10-14-1848 (10-18-1848)
Adcock, Wm. to America L. Statton 2-26-1852
Adcock, Wm. to L. Parish 4-8-1877
Adcock, Wm. to Sarah Willmouth 1-6-1876
Adcok, Welcum to H. E. Barnes 10-23-1876 (no return)
Aderson, Benjamon to Mary Duke 5-13-1878 (5-14-1878)
Adimson, E. Monroe to Lucinda Craddock 3-23-1875 (3-26-1875)
Adkins, Cristerfer to Elizabeth Banskan 10-12-1865 (no return)
Adkins, George W. to Elizabeth Gann 9-17-1855
Adkins, J. W. to H. T. Hatfield 7-7-1868 (no return)
Adkins, Wm. to Elizabeth Hayes 2-14-1872 (2-18-1872)
Adkinse, W. R. to Sarah E. Foutch 5-17-1879 (8-10-1879)
Agee, Jonathan to Mary Griffitt 2-19-1866
Agee, Wm. M. L. to Elizabeth J. Page 8-9-1879 (5?-18-1879)
Aggie, Wm. to Lucinda Beshears 11-13-1875 (11-17-1875)
Albert, Wm. to Eliza Felts 11-29-1871 (11-30-1871)
Alcorn, Harmon to Elvira Smith 6-7-1856 (6-8-1856)
Alcorn, Robert to Letha Johnson 11-29-1876 (11-30-1876)
Aldridge, Isaac B. to Nancy Night 4-10-1873 (4-13-1873)

Alen, Wm. to Adiline Bane 1-29-1867
Alexander, Andrew to Elizabeth Adkins 10-27-1867 (no return)
Alexander, George to Bell Pipkins 9-6-1878 (9-7-1878)
Alexander, Isaac to Susanah Noaks 9-12-1862 (9-3?-1862)
Alexander, James to Mandy E. Alexander 8-6-1873 (no return)
Alexander, James to Sarah Ann Greer 11-15-1855
Alexander, John to Caroline E. Vannatta 1-7-1860 (1-8-1860)
Alexander, N. I. to Susanah Goodwin 8-14-1862
Alexander, Thomas to Barbara Chain 12-5-1866 (12-6-1866)
Alexander, Wm. to Nancy Pack 3-4-1864 (exec. no date)
Alexandra, Wm. to Matilda Bennett 3-13-1878 (3-15-1878)
Alexandria, Isaac to Hellen Frazier 10-7-1871 (10-8-1871)
Alexandria, Wm. to Jane Hess 10-28-1870 (10-22?-1870)
Allen, Alfred O. to Hellen Williams 2-19-1874
Allen, Americus to Susan Johnson 11-11-1857
Allen, Amos to Hariet Dean 1-12-1865 (1-15-1865)
Allen, E. N. to M. P. Mullican 8-29-1872
Allen, Elijah to Frances Adcock 9-30-1851 (10-5-1851)
Allen, F. M. to Matildy F. McCullough 2-9-1874 (2-12-1874)
Allen, George to Loura Estis 11-25-1872 (11-28-1872)
Allen, Henry to Ann Johnson 4-2-1866 (4-6-1866)
Allen, Hesakiah to Lewisa Page 10-19-1853 (10-20-1853)
Allen, Hezekiah to Sarah Robinson 12-12-1857 (12-13-1857)
Allen, J. B. to J. D. Luna 5-13-1875 (5-20-1875)
Allen, J. F. to Della Wood 10-14-1879 (10-16-1879)
Allen, James L. to Elizabeth Brim 9-9-1854 (9-1?-1854)
Allen, James W. to Lucy Ann Farmer 9-6-1860
Allen, James to Nancy L. Bratten 10-29-1868 (10-30-1868)
Allen, James to Sintha Fuston 10-16-1866 (10-18-1866)
Allen, John H. to Eliza Evans? 11-12-1859 (11-13-1859)
Allen, John H. to Marthena Allen 9-21-1857 (no return)
Allen, John to Mary Page 12-27-1855 (12-29-1855)
Allen, John to Viney Ann Tennessee Jones 6-13-1866
Allen, M. M. to Margret Fuson 4-28-1877 (no return)
Allen, M. to Sarah M. Fuson 1-6-1878
Allen, T. C. to Roda W. Cheatham 1-17-1871 (1-21-1871)
Allen, Tom to Harriett Sims 8-25-1872 (9-2-1872) [B]
Allen, Wels to Mary Turner 5-7-1866 (5-23-1866) [B]
Allen, Winslow to Lucinda Norris 7-11-1854 (7-13-1854)
Allen, Wm. A. to Tennessee Trapp 3-16-1865
Allen, Wm. F. to Arraminta J. Hayse 9-11-1856
Allen, Wm. P. to Mary C. Thomason 8-12-1854 (8-15-1854)
Allen, Wm. to Mary F. Hamleta 3-24-1866 (3-25-1866)
Allen, Wood to Fanny Gordon 12-21-1868 (12-24-1868)
Allison, R. D. to Louisa D. Dowel 6-22-1858 (6-24-1858)
Allison, Thompson to Rebecca Jones 12-22-1858 (12-23-1858)
Amonet, Parker to Luvina Wilson 9-1-1859
Anders, Wm. to Hannasah Close 6-26-1875 (6-27-1875)
Anderson, Alvin R. to Catherine Adcock 9-18-1873 (9-19-1873)
Anderson, Bazzel to Mary E. Hall 3-13-1872 (3-14-1872)
Anderson, Caleb to Martha J. Cantrell 10-13-1852
Anderson, Calvin W. to Margrett A. Adcock 8-2-1871
Anderson, George H. to Charrity F. Stark 9-4-1872 (9-5-1872)
Anderson, George to Margret Robinson 12-19-1876 (12-16?-1876)
Anderson, Isaac to Annie Adcock 7-26-1879 (7-27-1879)
Anderson, J. M. to Missouria Patten 9-11-1875 (9-12-1875)
Anderson, John to Dednea Johnson 8-16-1866 (exec. no date)
Anderson, Richard to Mary Stark 12-20-1870 (12-29-1870) [B]
Anderson, Robert J. to Elizabeth Robinson 2-21-1857 (2-24-1857)
Anderson, S. to M. J. Ferril 11-6-1876 (11-9-1876)
Anderson, T. M. to Frances E. Certain 11-7-1859 (no return)
Anderson, Thos. J. to Nancy Ann Willis 7-24-1851 (7-26-1851)
Anderson, Walter to Parmilea Tucker 2-13-1869 (2-14-1869)
Anderson, Wm. M. to Elizabeth Cantrell 11-25-1867 (no return)
Arnal, Wm. to Nancy Everlin 10-18-1865 (10-19-1865)
Arnel, John to Lucia A. Dollar 8-23-1876 (8-24-1876)
Arnel, T. E. to N. A. Readmon 1-15-1876
Arnold, Jesse to Elizabeth A. Taylor 3-25-1868
Ashburn, J. H. to S. Glavans? 1-6-1876 (1-7-1876)
Ashford, John to Matilda Gann 1-28-1862
Ashworth, J. T. to Fanie Talley 10-24-1870
Atnip, Benjamin to Lucindy F. Bain 4-15-1868 (no return)
Atnip, E. R. to M. C. Buster 8-16-1875 (8-17-1875)
Atnip, Elisha to Amanda Treysand 8-11-1866 (9-17-1866)
Atnip, Enoch to Martha Ann Allen 7-12-1853

Atnip, Jacob to Susannah T. Watts 3-26-1851 (3-27-1851)
Atnip, James L. to Nancy O. Trapp 8-30-1855 (8-23?-1855)
Atnip, John to Mary M. Holly 4-1-1869
Atnip, Johnathan to Asenith McGinis 7-1-1863 (7-2-1863)
Atnip, Joseph to Martha Luna? 10-24-1848
Atnip, Richard to Mandelia McInturff 2-4-1858
Atnip, Ruben K. to Kezy J. Taylor 5-17-1855
Atrip, John to Mary Clark 10-24-1850
Atwell, E. K. to Susan M. Gowen 5-12-1877 (5-13-1877)
Austin, John to Margaret Williams 10-13-1852 (10-14-1852)
Austin, Wm. to Louisa Gardner 2-2-1855 (2-4-1855)
Austin, Wm. to Rebecca Tucker 6-7-1854 (6-8-1854)
Avant, C. C. to Bettie J. Berry 10-12-1872 (10-13-1872)
Avery, Newton to Nelly Cantrell 7-4-1866 (7-5-1866)
Awlguire, John O. to Martha New 10-5-1858 (10-8-1858)
Ayars, J. S.? to D. J. Robinson 4-10-1869 (4-1?-1869)
Ayrs, James to Nancy Coleman 2-16-1858 (2-18-1858)
Badger, F. A. to Oedema Cope 7-3-1866
Bailey, James to M. Smith 10-22-1876
Bailif, Thomas to Eliza Wimaid 9-8-1875
Baim, Isaac H. to Mary F. Farmer 4-19-1871 (4-20-1871)
Bain, Arch to Rachel Titsworth 3-26-1864 (no return)
Bain, G. M. to A. J. Sewell 1-8-1863 (2-25-1863)
Bain, Isaiah to Anna Walker 4-1-1861 (4-2-1861)
Bain, John to Sarah E. Parker 12-22-1869 (12-23-1869)
Bain, John to Thursey Pollard 12-19-1868 (12-20-1868)
Bain, Thomas to S. E. Johnson 2-23-1869 (2-25-1869)
Bain, W. A. to Nancy C. Alexander 1-5-1863 (1-8-1863)
Bain, Wm. to Barthena Smith 12-30-1865 (12-31-1865)
Baine, John M. to Martha Farell 1-18-1856 (1-20-1856)
Baird, James M. to Amanda R. Goodner 11-21-1848 (11-23-1848)
Baird, Samuel to Eliza Heaven 2-18-1868 (2-23-1868)
Baites, Allen to Paticents Hale 1-9-1869 [B]
Baits, M. A. to N. Marler 12-26-1868 (12-30-1868)
Baker, Alex to Hariet Chambers 3-4-1868 (3-7-1868) [B]
Baker, Alford to Martha Beanbush 4-18-1866 (4-22-1866)
Baker, Bengamin to Haley S. Frazier 10-3-1874 (10-4-1874) [B]
Baker, Danial to Nancy C. Pressly 6-13-1874 (6-14-1874)
Baker, Francis to Martha Blakship 4-18-1866 (no return)
Baker, G. E. to Phelee Bozarth 8-?-1857 (8-11-1857)
Baker, James M. to Barbery Robinson 3-22-1854 (3-20?-1854)
Baker, Samuel K. to Louisa Ann Shanis 4-6-1861 (4-7-1861)
Baker, Wm. H. to Cathrine Sykes 1-5-1857 (2-25-1857)
Baliff, Joab to Elizabeth Fouch 3-9-1853 (3-?-1853)
Baliff, W. R. to Eliza J. Jones 12-13-1862 (12-14-1862)
Balis, Nicholas to Susanah Stokes 9-21-1866 (9-2?-1866) [B]
Ballard, T. J. to M. J. Pack 12-22-1869 (12-23-1869)
Balliff, C. A. to Talitha C. Foutch 4-13-1870 (4-24-1870)
Ballinger, D. W. to M. C. Clark 12-29-1877 (12-30-1877)
Balue, John to Susan C. Foutch 2-28-1859 (3-3-1859)
Bandy, Phillip to P. F. Pack 8-17-1876
Bane, J. D. to Martha T. Jones 8-29-1867 (9-1-1867)
Bane, James A. to Parlee Fite 12-23-1848 (12-24-1848)
Bane, Larkin to Manerva Cantrell 1-1-1853 (2-2-1853)
Bane, Wm. to N. C. Tramal 10-7-1870 (10-9-1870)
Bankhorn, Wm. to Lela Mannon 10-17-1865
Banks, Enoch H. to Rachel Murphy 11-10-1853 (exec. no date)
Banks, F. L. to Mary Jane Dawson 12-31-1857 (1-4-1858)
Banks, John to Perthenia Tomblin 9-30-1874
Banks, Joseph L. to Mary E. Banks 2-16-1876
Banks, Joseph W. to Lucretia J. Taylor 1-25-1864
Banks, Lafayett to Harriett Wright 7-22-1871 (no return)
Banks, R. W. to Semantha Parsly 3-1-1865 (3-2-1865)
Bankston, Wm. M. to Elizabeth A. Lawrence 3-13-1854 (3-14-1854)
Baret, Wills to Rachel Briant 1-26-1855 (1-3?-1855)
Barge, John to Martha C. Fite 3-12-1850 (3-14-1850)
Barks, Samuel to M. J. Redmon 12-18-1865
Barnes, A. to M. C. Harp 4-14-1877 (3?-28-1877)
Barnes, Archable to Marth Cantrell 10-10-1878 (10-15-1878)
Barnes, Britten to S. C. Brown 4-27-1871
Barnes, Britton to Gincey Brown 1-20-1865 (no return)
Barnes, H. L. to Hariet Luna 4-15-1875
Barnes, J. A. to Margaret L. Koger 5-25-1858 (5-26-1858)
Barnes, J. F. to M. J. Johnson 10-31-1877 (10-30?-1877)
Barnes, James L. to Lyda Richmon 6-21-1853

Barnes, James to Elizabeth Jones 7-20-1860
Barnes, Peter to Thema Starkes 7-4-1876
Barnes, Wm. B. to Jane Braswell 8-28-1862
Barnes, Wm. to Margrett J. Bullard 8-1-1872
Barr, Jacob C. to Hixey A. Martin 4-28-1854
Barrett, James A. to Ema C. Smith 6-6-1867 (6-7-1867)
Barrett, Obediah to Jane Briant 10-6-1857 (1-3-1858)
Barry, J. P. to Helen West 2-9-1875 (2-11-1875)
Bartlet, Wm. E. to Mary G. Stacy 9-16-1857 (9-17-1857)
Barton, C. B. to M. B. Baird 2-1-1876 (no return)
Bary, Clay to Fany Cantrel 3-19-1866 (no return)
Bass, Antony to Dicy M. Lawrence 12-24-1863 (no return) [B]
Bass, Henderson to E. M. Trusty 8-6-1876 (8-20-1876)
Bass, John A. to Sary J. Robinson 10-15-1866 (10-18-1866)
Bass, John W. to Rachel C. Turner 3-10-1849 (no return)
Bass, Josiah L. to Paralee Williams 3-12-1851
Bass, Mason to Allice Plumber 6-27-1874 [B]
Bass, Serss? to Hariatt Smith 3-17-1866 (3-18-1866)
Bass, Thomas D. to Eliz. J. Turner 1-16-1861 (exec. no date)
Bates, Bird E. to Betty J. Spence 12-13-1871
Bates, Bird to Marthey R. Bates 10-28-1870 (10-30-1870)
Bates, Dock to C. Marler 12-1-1877 (12-12-1877)
Bates, General to Silvana Johnson 1-30-1875 (2-4-1875)
Bates, Gill to F. J. Sewell 1-31-1863 (no return)
Bates, Isaac to Delililia F. Warford 8-8-1872 (8-9-1872)
Bates, Isaac to Sarah A. Lamberson 5-20-1873 (5-22-1873)
Bates, John to J. S. Tisdal 11-8-1874
Bates, Joseph to Rebecca Kelley 9-11-1875 (9-12-1875)
Bates, W. B. to Sarah Manning 12-4-1875 (12-5-1875)
Bates, Wm. R. to Malissia Henesly 8-12-1871 (no return)
Bates, Wm. to Syntha Martin 1-16-1851
Batts, Walter to Sarah Capshaw 7-1-1874 (7-2-1874)
Batts?, Isack W. to Mary Pack 12-21-1865 (12-24-1865)
Baty, Gramison to T. M. Vantreace 8-23-1876 (8-24-1876)
Baty, James to P. Lawrence 2-11-1849
Bayn, John to Marth Adcock 10-6-1865 (no return)
Bayn, John to Marth Addcock 10-6-1865 (10-25-1865)
Bayne, Daniel C. to Elizabeth Evans 2-22-1852
Bayne, David to Veta Adcock 1-16-1860 (1-11?-1860)
Bayne, John to Pink Brown 9-8-1873
Bayne, Mathew B. to M. C. Braswell 12-28-1870
Baynes, Archibald to Hexy C. Ferrell 11-8-1853
Bayors, D. W. to Sarah Inland 5-30-1866 (6-3-1866)
Beaseley, Joseph to Delia A. Smith 5-7-1870 (5-12-1870)
Beasley, Thomas to Dicey Magness 5-12-1872 [B]
Beasley, Tom to Marth Allen 10-5-1867 (10-6-1867)
Beatey, James to Fanny Bota? 4-25-1873
Beckwith, James R. to Matilda Whaley 3-27-1849 (no return)
Belcher, Thomas to Anna McKisseack 12-15-1879
Belcher, Thomas to Jennie Acole? 4-28-1873 (no return) [B]
Bell, B. F. to Oppelia Baird 12-21-1875 (no return)
Bellow, Sanal to Mary Askew 12-25-1864
Benner, John W. to E. C. Coniecel 12-22-1879 (12-24-1879)
Bennet, N. M. to Candis Newson 10-2-1865 (10-5-1865)
Bennet, William to Mary Sandlin 1-29-1854
Bennett, A. J. to Susan S. Hendrixson 5-7-1856 (5-8-1857?)
Bennett, Henry to Nancy Alexander 10-4-1848 (10-6-1848)
Bennett, James J. to Mary Frances Bing 1-18-1866
Bennett, James to Nancy Anderson 12-18-1875 (12-19-1875)
Bennett, Jas. M. to Hannah Sandlin 10-14-1857 (10-19-1857)
Bennett, John to Katherine Roberds 4-24-1864 (4-25-1864)
Bennett, P. H. to Chance P. Ross 7-13-1860 (7-17-1860)
Bennett, Samuel to Sarah Thompson 11-11-1850 (11-12-1850)
Bennett, W. to Dianna Murdoc 4-12-1876 (4-16-1876)
Bennett, William to Mison Sanders 11-10-1875
Bennett, Wm. to Jane Crook 6-17-1878 (solem,no date)
Bennette, James J. to Malissa Neel 2-5-1856
Bennette, John C. to Elenor Garrison 10-13-1852 (10-14-1852)
Bennette, John to Martha Malone 2-6-1856
Bennette, Thomas to Martha Purkins 7-10-1856
Bennette, W. H. to Eliza Jane Chapman 11-4-1854
Bennette, William C. to Luisa Sandlin 10-21-1855 (10-22-1855)
Bennette, William P. to Elizabeth W. N. Smith 12-23-1858 (exec,no date)
Bennette, William R. to Mary Sandlin 3-31-1852

Benson, Wm. to Mary Cantrell 12-27-1864 (12-28-1864)
Bernet?, W. J. B. to P. E. Standlin 1-2-1866 (1-4-1866)
Bery, Georgea. to Mary E. Magniss 8-22-1866 (8-23-1866)
Besheares, Elias to Zelpha Lawson 11-17-1865
Beshears, Henry to Susanah Redman 6-8-1867 (6-9-1867)
Beshears, Stephen C. to Lucinda Sandlin 7-22-1858
Besheres, Alexander to Caroline Bess 7-18-1867
Bess, Wm. to Delina Edge 2-29-1876 (3-2-1876)
Bethel, Hiram to Nancy Pistole 12-14-1848
Bethel, N. B. to Omesa Mullenax 12-19-1856 (12-25-1856)
Bethel, W. L. to Fanney Calhoone 4-1-1859 (no return)
Bethell, C. F. to Martha Ann Daugherty 9-28-1848 (9-29-1848)
Bethell, Cantrell to Julia A. E. Rady 2-5-1862 (2-6-1862)
Betty, Ned to Parly McLaine 4-14-1875 (4-15-1875)
Biba, James M. to J. Marton 1-9-1878 (1-12-1878)
Bigs, William to Nancy Delong 9-12-1853
Bilings, Newton to M. J. Steel 4-10-1875 (4-11-1875)
Billings, James to Elizabeth Ceartin 2-10-1866 (2-11-1866)
Billings, James to Mary Culwell 3-27-1874
Billings, William R. to Sarah Young 11-6-1851
Billins, J. J. to Helan Anderson 8-28-1878 (no return)
Bing, George A. to Josephine Potter 9-23-1871 (9-24-1871)
Bing, L. G. to Martha A. Cantrell 2-3-1863 (2-4-1863)
Bins, P. G. to Aiseneth Potter 2-19-1866 (2-20-1866)
Bird, John to Delia Smitson 8-24-1878 (9-8-1878)
Black, Robt. to Ida Manaleburn 9-8-1875
Blackbun, Joseph H. to Eliza J. Barger 7-30-1861 (8-8-1861)
Blackburn, James H. to Jennie Ford 3-17-1865 (3-19-1865)
Blackburn, Thomas to Charity Youngblood 6-16-1878 (6-23-1878)
Blackburn, W.H. to May L. Braswell 9-14-1874
Blair, Abraham to Anna Rule 5-24-1869
Blair, Monroe to M. P. Parsley 11-13-1875 (11-14-1875)
Blair, Thomas A. to Nancy Ann Cantrell 4-23-1851 (5-1-1851)
Blankenship, George to Amandy L. Cotton 2-24-1873
Blankinship, Jas. R. to Susan Fisher 2-2-1874
Blankinship, V. D. to Eliza Calvert 9-30-1865 (10-1-1865)
Blare, Thomas to Talitha Cantrell 1-1-1852
Bley, James to Roweana Scott 4-22-1866 (no return)
Blughus, P. B. to M. E. Snow 1-28-1878 (1-29-1878)
Bluhm, F. J. to N. A. Patterson 1-3-1880 (1-4-1880)
Blunt, J. W. to Lucy Delong 12-15-1848 (12-17-1848)
Blunt, U. M. to Elizabeth J. Ray 12-27-1859
Bly, James to C. Scott 5-11-1850 (5-12-1850)
Bly, James to Elizabeth Sandlin 1-30-1864 (no return)
Blyth, Calvin to L. J. Jennings 2-17-1869 (2-18-1869)
Blythe, Monroe to Nancy Robinson 11-13-1873 (11-15-1873)
Bogle, Ben to Ann Tubbs 12-27-1870 [B]
Bogle, T. A. to N. E. Jones 9-2-1876
Bohannon, Robert to Sylvia Johnson 9-6-1873 (no return)
Bomer, Rubin C. to Josie Canady 4-20-1871
Bond, Alford M. to Palestrene Fisher 2-27-1875 (3-1-1875)
Bond, George W. to Permelia Cheatham 3-8-1855
Bonds, George to Roda E. Bryant 9-22-1870
Bone, John D. to Fanny L. Coffee 2-26-1857
Bonhan, Martin T. to Rebecca Trapp 11-26-1865
Borin, James M. to Salley Alcorn 3-20-1873
Borum, Isaac to Mary Ann Patterson 2-21-1874 (no return)
Boss, W. D. to Nancy A. Prichard 3-29-1871 (3-30-1871)
Bostick, J. P. to Laura Stone 3-30-1878 (3-31-1878)
Botts, John W. to Dosha Austen 12-11-1852 (12-13-1852)
Botts, Watler to Martha T. Frazer 11-14-1859
Botts, Wm. F. to Mary Lawson 12-7-1870 (no return)
Bowens, Elias C. to Margaret Tate 6-15-1854 (6-5?-1854)
Bowers, E. S. to Emandy Winfor 12-21-1868 (12-22-1868)
Bowers, G. M. to E. T. Eason 1-24-1868 (1-25-1868)
Bowman, T. F. to C. A. Wright 2-24-1877 (3-1-1877)
Bowndes, Noah to Caroline Vantreace 11-15-1877
Boyatt, James K. to Mary Smith 7-20-1854 (7-21-1854)
Boyd, John L. to Sarah Ann Cannon 3-13-1856
Bozarth, Isaac to Chernine League 9-13-1879 (no return)
Bozarth, James M. to Angaline Bozarth 7-13-1872 (7-14-1872)
Bozarth, James Munro to Lotta Susan Medlin 12-15-1874 (12-17-1874)
Bozarth, Jefferson to Martha A. Pettigoe 12-22-1879 (no return)
Bozarth, Joseph to Martha Puckett 5-29-1866 (5-31-1866)

Bozarth, N. B. to Mattie Martain 11-27-1878 (12-18-1878)
Bozarth, Phinas to Martha Masior 6-1-1869
Bozorth, Isaac to Caroline Murphy 3-23-1860 (3-28-1860)
Bradford, Nelson to Mary A. Fisk 2-10-1872 (2-12-1872)
Bradford, Thu? to Sarah Revis? 12-2-1860
Bradly, E. L. to Candis Jenkins 4-17-1880 (no return)
Bradly, N. B. to Martha Driver 5-22-1868 (5-24-1868)
Brady, N. E. to Mary E. Martin 3-14-1865 (no return)
Brady, Thomas J. to Lavina Cooper 12-19-1851 (12-23-1851)
Bran, John to Laura Redmon 12-25-1878 (12-26-1878)
Brann, William to Clara Smith 7-7-1858 (7-8-1858)
Brant, Elijah M. to Margarett Jane Williams 10-22-1859 (no return)
Brashars, Loranzo to F. C. Johnson 3-4-1879 (3-5-1879)
Braswell, Aaron to P. F. Norton 11-15-1877
Braswell, Dempsy to Paralee Allen 9-21-1872 (9-22-1872)
Braswell, J. M. to Amanda Kerley 3-10-1866 (3-11-1866)
Braswell, Jack to H. Melton 10-20-1876 (10-22-1876)
Braswell, Jefferson to Mary Mohatha 8-8-1865 (no return)
Braswell, L. D. to Martha An Cadd 4-1-1877
Braswell, Matthew to Sarah Turner 2-5-1856 (2-6-1856)
Braswell, P. L. to Martha Braswell 10-16-1858 (no return)
Braswell, Sampson to Harriet Wade (Sadler) 12-25-1858 (no return)
Braswell, Sampson to Martha A. Mozier 1-16-1864 (no return)
Braswell, Sampson to Susan Kerby 2-28-1861
Braswell, William to Mary Vier 10-10-1864 (no return)
Braswell, Wm. to O. E. Shehorn 11-2-1853 (11-3-1853)
Bratcher, B. F. to Jane Green 1-9-1878 (1-3?-1878)
Bratcher, James to Sefrona Hayes 12-15-1878
Bratcher, Samuel M. to Tennessee Jennings 5-23-1874 (5-24-1874)
Bratten, James E. to Elizabeth R. Moore 6-19-1849 (6-20-1849)
Bratton, Elijah J. to Elizabeth M. Garrison 9-20-1854 (9-21-1854)
Bratton, John A. to Amanda N. Lamberson 2-24-1857 (2-25-1857) [*]
Bratton, Lemuel J. to Mary L. Fite 12-26-1871 (12-28-1871)
Bratton, T. G. to J. A. Parker 7-19-1878 (no return)
Bratton, Thomas E. to Sarah W. Grindstaff 12-14-1868 (no return)
Bratton, Thomas to Martha T. Garrison 3-22-1854 (3-30-1854)
Breadlove, A. C. to Elizabeth Elkins 8-30-1878 (8-31-1878)
Brent, Thomas N. to Martha Corley 9-24-1858 (9-26-1858)
Brent, William M. to Mary Driver 1-22-1857
Brent, William to Elizabeth Crook 1-15-1859 (no return)
Brent, William to Lucia Crook 10-7-1865 (10-8-1865)
Brent, Wm. to Sarah Bayne 5-26-1880 (no return)
Brian, W. T. to Mary Adcock 2-16-1871
Brian, Wm. A. to Hattie A. Stokes 5-27-1862 (6-10-1862)
Briant, Wash to Marth Briant 1-24-1866 (1-25-1866) [B]
Bridges, James N. to Lee Lawrence 2-20-1861 (2-2-1861)
Brien, Nelson to Martha E. Ford 11-22-1859 (11-26-1859)
Brient, Monsol to Jocy Neel 2-23-1878 (2-24-1878)
Briges, W. B. to Amanda Luckey 12-25-1858 (exec,no date)
Briggs, G. W. to M. E. T. Sneed 7-9-1850 (7-11-1850)
Briggs, James A. to Manorvey Baker 12-3-1856
Brim, Huston to Hannah Haney 5-20-1856 (5-21-1856)
Brimer, Jackson to Algelira Batey 1-15-1859
Brimer, Jackson to Josephine Devease 9-14-1865 (9-20-1865) [*]
Brimer, James R. P. to Nancy A. Jones 2-11-1867 (2-14-1867)
Brimer, Wm. to Martha Young 8-6-1859 (no endors.)
Britt, S. T. to Catharin Cantrell 5-25-1871 (no return)
Brock, C. F. to Mary Christian 5-31-1879 (6-1-1879)
Brock, David to Charity Neal 6-10-1879
Brock, P. c. to Jane Felts 11-23-1859
Brown, Braswell to Hariett Hathway 6-22-1866 (solemnized)
Brown, Isaac H. to Elizabeth Fouch 9-14-1865 (no return)
Brown, Isaac to Polly Pettigo 7-24-1871
Brown, J. L. to Judia Lafever 6-19-1867 (6-20-1867)
Brown, James W. to Teley Broseley 8-28-1872 (no return)
Brown, James to Elizabeth Hill 4-26-1853 (4-28-1853)
Brown, James to Nancy King 5-20-1870 (5-21-1870)
Brown, John L. to Mary F. Conk 12-6-1875 (12-7-1875)
Brown, John W. to Elizabeth Rowton 7-29-1854 (7-30-1854)
Brown, Mark to Jaine Pleager 12-25-1866 (2-1-1867)
Brown, Peater to Jain Pleager 12-25-1866 (2-7-1867)
Brown, Sidney to Jinney Roberts 8-11-1866 (8-12-1866)
Brown, Sim to Sarah Crowder 9-24-1871 [B]
Brown, Thomas to L. J. Spurlock 6-4-1877 (no return)
Bryant, Joseph to Mary E. Cantrell 4-23-1879 (no return)

Bryant, Joshua L. to E. J. Wood 11-17-1870
Bryant, W. R. to Marthaan Williams 9-2-1875
Bryson, Bethel to Hennie Officer 7-25-1878 (7-27-1878)
Buck, D. A. to Martha Cartright 6-9-1866 (no return)
Buck, Wm. H. to M. M. Murphey 2-20-1878 (2-2?-1878)
Buckner, Fredrick E. to Evalina A. Vantrease 6-25-1850 (no return)
Buckner, James to Susan Carmicle 5-17-1873 (5-18-1873)
Buckner, R. H. to Elizia McCullough 10-14-1872
Buckner, Robert H. to Virginia Meritt 6-12-1867 (6-13-1867)
Buland, Wm. to Josephine Conor 7-12-1865 (no return)
Bulington, Charles H. to Lucindy Turner 11-11-1868 (11-12-1868) [B]
Bullard, Benjamin to E. Martin 1-2-1871 (1-5-1871)
Bullard, Benjamin to Mary Hammons 9-24-1858
Bullard, Henry to Juley A. Sullins 3-18-1871 (3-19-1871)
Bullard, Jasper Green to Armetta Parsley 12-1-1874 (12-4-1874)
Bullard, Jasper to Amandy Snow 1-30-1873 (2-2-1873)
Bullard, William to S. J. Martin 9-26-1867
Bullen, James M. to Rebeckey Parseley 8-11-1870 (8-14-1870)
Bullerd, William to Dortherly Pittey 1-23-1872 (1-25-1872)
Burks, Dock to Matta Mottley 5-18-1878 (5-20-1878) [B]
Burnett, Bransford to Amand Warford 7-22-1855 (7-24-1855)
Burnett, John to Sallie Bayne 10-2-1871
Burns, James B. to Emely Davis 1-22-1855 (2-1-1855)
Burton, Charles to Sarah League 6-19-1868 (6-21-1868)
Burton, E. D. to Nancy Whaley 3-13-1849 (3-15-1849)
Burton, H. C. to M. J. Short 8-14-1878
Burton, J. E. to Mary A. Palmer 4-5-1880 (no return)
Burton, James to Cariline Foster 7-1-1861 (7-2-1861)
Burton, John J. to Nancy Puckett 8-18-1869 (8-19-1869)
Burton, Samuel to Laura Parker 4-25-1878
Burton, W. S. to R. F. Bond 3-1-1877 (3-22-1877)
Burton, Wm. E. to Tossa Bond 4-3-1865 (4-17-1865)
Burtram, David to Josey Gilbert 8-12-1876 (no return)
Bush, James to Louisa M. Abner 6-3-1851
Bussell, Patrick to Emma Bennett 4-12-1876 (4-13-1876)
Butcher, B. W. to _____ Sandlin 4-11-1864 (no return)
Butcher, J. R. to M. E. Hale 12-13-1876 (10-14-1877)
Butlar, Isaac to Tenessee Cooper 4-13-1878 (4-14-1878)
Butler, J. M. to M. E. Hale 12-25-1865 (no return)
Butler, J. M. to M. E. Hale 4-28-1865 (3?-16-1865)
Butler, Jno. B. to Elizabeth C. Garison 8-20-1877 (8-21-1877)
Butterbough, Edmond to Mary A. Wilson 7-21-1873 (7-23-1873)
Button, J. L. to H. A. Cantrell 7-3-1877
Byars, Franklin P. to Sharlott B. Cantrell 3-12-1874
Byars, O. D. to H. A. J. Potter 12-15-1874 (no return)
Byford, G. W. to Caroline Hildreth 12-15-1873 (12-19-1873)
Cabery?, Joseph to Mary Jain Pain 9-13-1865 (no return)
Caldwell, Willis M. to Sarah Ellen Pistol 6-19-1872
Calhoon, H. to Jennie Dinwiddle 2-19-1877 (2-20-1877)
Calhoon, James N. to Hannah L. Stokes 11-10-1858 (11-11-1859?)
Calicut, Davis to Shelata Sellars 3-19-1866 (3-20-1866)
Callicoat, John J. to Ann H. J. Smith 10-11-1854 (10-13-1854)
Cally, John to Martha Coker 2-16-1877 (2-18-1877)
Calvert, Geo. H. to Mary Alice Driver 3-21-1878 (3-25-1878)
Calvert, James D. to Mary F. White 2-11-1879
Calvert, James L. to Martha M. Tyree 1-14-1858
Calvin, John W. to Parilee Sneed 3-31-1863
Calwell, Lusion to Sarah Hendrixson 5-15-1880 (5-16-1880)
Calwell, W. W. to Maliss Warner 3-20-1866
Came, Charles to Margret Bates 2-1-1867 [B]
Camoren, James H. to Mary E. Richardson 2-7-1880 (2-8-1880)
Camp, J. W. to M. A. Robinson 1-13-1868 (1-19-1868)
Campbell, Geor. M. to Parlee Parsley 2-22-1879 (2-23-1879)
Campbell, Taylor to Susan Parker 12-27-1877 (12-28-1877)
Camron, Samuel H. to Mary E. Byd 5-7-1856 (5-8-1856)
Cannady, John c. to Margrart Edwards 12-2-1851 (12-5-1851)
Cannon, Alexander to Mary Ann Hays ommitted (10-26-1843)
Cannon, J. H. to A. E. Staley 9-4-1868
Cantrell, A. J. to Catharine Wright 1-14-1879 (1-19-1879)
Cantrell, A. P. to L. V. Elkins 11-26-1864 (11-27-1864)
Cantrell, A. P. to M. J. Cantrell 12-21-1868
Cantrell, Abraham to Rebecca Reeves 9-6-1855
Cantrell, Allen to Emaline Hargis 7-13-1852
Cantrell, Aron to Sarah Loss? 3-17-1866 (3-18-1866)
Cantrell, B. A. to Dorkus Parsley 1-23-1872

Cantrell, Benjamin to Nancy Pitman 8-30-1849
Cantrell, Benjamin to Rody Whitlock 6-26-1862 (6-27-1862)
Cantrell, Benjamon to Martha Jones 12-15-1874 (12-16-1874)
Cantrell, Berry Y. to Elender J. Blare 1-15-1852
Cantrell, C. A. to Jane Anderson 11-20-1875 (11-21-1875)
Cantrell, C. B. to Amanda Lee 11-25-1870 (11-27-1870)
Cantrell, Cheslew W. to Lavina Cantrell 5-2-1850
Cantrell, Danial W. to Jane Walker 6-17-1874 (6-18-1874)
Cantrell, David to Rebecca McGuiness 9-13-1877 (no return)
Cantrell, E. F. to N. J. Redman 5-10-1866
Cantrell, Elial to Arteta Redman 3-9-1853 (3-10-1853)
Cantrell, F. C. to M. C. Mosier 10-20-1875 (10-21-1875)
Cantrell, F. M. to S. B. Moore 1-27-1875
Cantrell, Frank to Recey Potter 7-31-1878 (8-4-1878)
Cantrell, George B. to Mary Lack 8-9-1879 (8-10-1879)
Cantrell, Green to Mourning Potter 12-17-1868
Cantrell, H. H. to Malisy Atnip 3-27-1875 (3-29-1875)
Cantrell, Hillis D. to Mary Stout 8-9-1871 (8-10-1871)
Cantrell, I. D. to Nancy R. Emery 11-23-1878 (11-24-1878)
Cantrell, Isaac to Elizabeth J. Griffith 10-2-1855
Cantrell, Isaac to Morning Webb 7-22-1852
Cantrell, Isaac to Simantha Potter 11-30-1868
Cantrell, J. A. to Matilda Elkins 1-28-1869
Cantrell, J. B. to Elizabeth Cantrell 10-25-1876 (no return)
Cantrell, J. B. to Virginia Atnip 8-26-1868 (8-27-1868)
Cantrell, J. H. to Malvina Jones 12-21-1869 (12-22-1869)
Cantrell, J. M. to W. A. Moss 11-28-1874 (no date)
Cantrell, J. P. to S. Cope 11-28-1870
Cantrell, James L. to Sarah Cantrell 5-18-1871 (5-24-1871)
Cantrell, James to Martha Moore 10-12-1853 (10-13-1853)
Cantrell, Jasper to Rachell Piniger 1-11-1864 (1-12-1864)
Cantrell, Jehue to Talitha Farrell 3-8-1873 (3-9-1873)
Cantrell, Jerry to Caroline Womackj 12-31-1869 (1-1-1870) [B]
Cantrell, Jessee to Elizabeth Fuson 1-3-1853
Cantrell, Joe to Cintha Anderson 8-24-1875 (8-25-1875)
Cantrell, John J. to Sarah Ann Redmon 3-2-1854
Cantrell, John to Sarah Readmon 5-10-1872 (5-12-1872)
Cantrell, Julis to Delia Potter 1-12-1876 (1-13-1876)
Cantrell, L. D. to C. M. Cantrell 6-4-1866 (no return)
Cantrell, Lawson to Nancy E. Arnold 1-5-1864 (1-14-1864)
Cantrell, Lenard to Fannie Wright 10-5-1878 (10-6-1878)
Cantrell, Lenard to Mary Pendleton 2-2-1864 (2-4-1864)
Cantrell, Lenard to Susan Jones 9-29-1876 (10-1-1876)
Cantrell, Louis K. to Mary E. Cantrell 1-20-1868 (1-22-1868)
Cantrell, M. H. to Martha Potter 1-17-1877 (no date)
Cantrell, Martin to Mary Ann Griffeth 4-25-1861
Cantrell, Martin to Nancy Griffith 3-26-1868
Cantrell, Monroe to Martha A. Forrester 3-8-1860 (3-11-1860)
Cantrell, Moses to Delilea Clark 9-26-1866 (10-1-1866)
Cantrell, N. E. to Faving? Mason 7-9-1870 (7-10-1870)
Cantrell, O. D. to Caldonia Turner 7-19-1879 (7-20-1879)
Cantrell, P. F. to N. C. Murdock 8-8-1860 (8-9-1860)
Cantrell, P. G. to Amanda James 7-26-1864
Cantrell, P. G. to C. A. Mullins 12-4-1877 (12-6-1877)
Cantrell, P. G. to M. L. Catton 1-14-1875
Cantrell, Pery G. to Emaline Givan 2-14-1859 (2-15-1859)
Cantrell, Phelix G. to Aney Hayes 10-13-1865 (10-15-1865)
Cantrell, Pleasant to Mary Murdock 9-5-1857 (9-8-1857)
Cantrell, Preston F. to Sarah L. Reeder 1-17-1864
Cantrell, R. M. to Josie Estes 2-12-1880
Cantrell, R. to M. A. Trapp 11-30-1877 (12-2-1877)
Cantrell, Robert to Letty Ann Colrits? 12-15-1870
Cantrell, Smith to Mary Linder 10-9-1856 (10-23-1856)
Cantrell, T. A. to Moetta Adcock 12-13-1856 (12-14-1856)
Cantrell, T. D. to Elizabeth P. Close 12-20-1879 (12-22-1879)
Cantrell, Tilmon D. to Olive Atnip 11-17-1868 (11-21-1868)
Cantrell, Tilmon to Martha E. Titsworth 10-23-1855
Cantrell, U. E. to Elizabeth Reeves 10-26-1854 (10-27-1854)
Cantrell, W. K. to Mary Close 10-24-1878
Cantrell, Watson to Polly Pigg 4-20-1861 (no return)
Cantrell, William W. to Martha Green 1-22-1867
Cantrell, William to Jane Winchester 2-7-1859 (no return)
Cantrell, William to M. Bery 11-27-1866
Cantrell, Wm. C. to Martha J. Allen 10-7-1862 (10-17-1862)
Cantrell, Wm. to Jane McGinis 11-7-1862 (no return)

Caplianeo, John to Elizabeth Trusty 11-7-1865
Caplinger, Samuel to Martha A. Trustee 2-26-1864 (no return)
Caplinger, Wm. R. to Catherine Davis 5-4-1867 (5-5-1867)
Capshane, Wm. to Sarah Allen 2-27-1868 (2-28-1868)
Capshaw, D. W. to F. C. Capshaw 3-6-1875 (no return)
Capshaw, E. W. to Sophronia Goodson 11-27-1874 (11-29-1874)
Capshaw, H. L. W. to Lucindy McGuire 12-29-1860 (12-31-1860)
Capshaw, John to Elily Furgerson 2-25-1859
Capshaw, Wm. to Prissey Young ?-2-1859 (11-3-1859)
Carner, Lorance to Mary J. Dowlen 8-4-1858
Carnes, John to S. L. Dunton 6-28-1877
Carnes, W. B. to Bettie Allen 5-10-1877
Carnes, W. D. to N. W. Allen 8-29-1876
Carnes, Wm. D. G. to Mary Josefine Vick 11-15-1859 (11-17-1859)
Carol, John A. to Sopha J. Bratton 1-31-1850 (2-5-1850)
Carroll, W. J. to Delilah Lamberson 3-31-1876 (4-6-1876)
Carter, Abner to Caroline Brown 12-27-1875 (12-28-1875)
Carter, Abslom? to Morindy K. Brown 1-13-1873 (date omit.)
Carter, Asa to Mary Robinson 1-16-1873
Carter, Bartley to Julia Herrod 8-23-1854 (8-24-1854)
Carter, Jackson to Mary A. Crips 3-10-1858 (3-11-1858)
Carter, James to Elvira P. Scott 3-1-1861 (3-3-1861)
Carter, John R. to Martha N. Dollar 1-7-1880 (1-11-1880)
Carter, John to Frances Roberson 2-14-1864 (2-15-1864)
Carter, Samuel A. to Mary Jain Hellum 5-16-1865 (5-19-1865)
Carty, Stephen to Elizabeth Fuston 8-22-1873
Casey, John to Milbery Page 11-9-1850 (11-10-1850)
Casey, Samuel to Eliza Atwell 7-23-1857
Caskey, Joseph B. to Mary White 7-24-1855 (7-25-1855)
Casky, John to Mulvina Garrison 3-22-1854 (3-23-1854)
Casky, John to Sally Durham 8-18-1864 (no return)
Casty, John F. to Mary T. Moore 9-6-1877 (no return)
Cates, George to Elizabeth Rugle? 12-3-1870 (12-4-1870)
Cathcart, George to Demares Braswell 1-15-1856
Cawley, Lemuel to Marth Cheatam 2-24-1877 (9-28-1877)
Cawley, W. B. to Etter Coape 1-28-1876 (2-1-1876)
Celf, Elicia to Martha Joblose? 8-24-1875 (8-26-1875)
Certain, J. M. to R. H. Young 2-8-1876 (2-9-1876)
Certain, Jason J. to Rachel Fowler 10-14-1854 (10-15-1854)
Certain, Richard E. to Rebeca Love 10-14-1858 (10-16-1858)
Certain, William to Stacy Purtle 2-22-1850 (2-21?-1850)
Chambers, Elisha to Mary Ann Jane Johnson 11-19-1850 (11-20-1850)
Chambiss, John to Frances Swinford 12-26-1853
Chamlins, Elijah to Jane Argo 5-1-1851
Chapman, Benjamin to Mary H. Scott 3-14-1874 (3-15-1874)
Chapman, John to Rebekee Bayliff 12-18-1866 (12-24-1866)
Chapman, L. to Susannah Jones 1-17-1850
Chapman, Sampson to Mary J. Danford 10-6-1869 (10-10-1869)
Chapman, Wily to Emiline Boyd 1-16-1859
Cheatham, Archabald B. to Martha Conger 11-3-1852 (11-4-1852)
Chehane, James M. to Emaly Moris 9-30-1861 (10-9-1861)
Childres, G. W. to Gennie Estis 10-3-1867
Childress, G. W. to S. T. Cantrell 9-27-1877
Childress, Hiram to Susan Robinson 4-27-1870 (no return)
Childress, Hyram to Mary S. Gracy 2-26-1870 (2-27-1870)
Childress, William to Narcissa Hutson 2-6-1861 (no return)
Childreth, George to Tennessee Estes 9-21-1870
Chisam, William G. to Acksey Looney 8-16-1856 (8-17-1856)
Chrisman, Isaac T. C. to Sariah Irwin 1-8-1849 (1-9-1849)
Christen, Benj. to Nancy J. Holland 2-22-1865 (no return)
Christian, Samuel M. to Mary Malone 3-6-1861 (no return)
Christian, Thomas N. to Fanny Winfree 5-8-1854 (5-11-1854)
Christian, Thos. A. to Rebecca J. Windham 2-26-1871
Christon, Thomas to Salley Ann Whitley 4-12-1854 (4-13-1854)
Christphine, Francis to Martha Gilbert 4-5-1863 (no return)
Chumley, Thomas E. to Mary Jane Chapman 7-1-1874 (7-5-1874)
Claiborn, John B. to Mary Sandlin 1-4-1872
Claiborn, John B. to Roxanna Baliff 12-24-1879 (no return)
Clark, Isaac to Fanney Lawrence 6-19-1876 (6-22-1876)
Clark, Joseph to Martha A. Whaley 8-7-1874 (no return)
Clark, Peter to Eli J. Markum 11-16-1860 (11-18-1860)
Clark, Robert L. to Nancy Bratton 1-24-1852 (1-28-1852)
Clark, William to Carolina Truitte 11-19-1849 (2-2-1850)
Clarke, John to Cenith Pack 8-12-1869
Clarke, Thomas to Delila Dabbs 3-10-1857 (3-11-1857)

Clayborn, Ephriam to Sarah Hane Neal 7-25-1872
Clemmons, Ansell to Rachel D. Fish 7-2-1860 (7-3-1860)
Clemmons, Jeremiah to Catharine McGinness 10-11-1850 (10-13-1850)
Clemmons, John to Martha Ann Glover 12-14-1854
Clemmons, John to Sarah Hall 2-14-1874 (2-16-1874)
Clemmons, Shadrick to Voney E. Emory 1-14-1873
Clemsons, Ansel to Mary J. Lewis 2-5-1862 (no return)
Close, Francis M. to Malinda Selff 5-30-1867 (6-2-1867)
Close, George W. to Nancy Kelly 2-9-1870 (3-13-1870)
Close, George to Hariete Neal 7-28-1876
Close, George to Mary J. Foster 5-26-1870 (no return)
Close, J. S. to Sarah V. Burton 1-4-1869 (1-14-1869)
Close, James H. to Helen Lawrence 3-22-1851 (3-27-1851)
Close, John G. to Mary J. Pitmon 2-16-1864 (no return)
Close, Thomas N. to Nancy M. Caskey 2-24-1857
Close, William to Hariet Chapthorn 12-23-1874
Clouse, George W. to Jane Fowler 1-11-1855 (no return)
Clouse, Wm. T. to Sarah Certain 10-22-1857 (no date)
Cluson, John W. to Jane Allen 9-21-1857 (10-4-1875)
Cobb, N. J. to Marge Lecur 6-17-1867 (6-20-1867)
Cockrum, John L. to L. A. Cantrell 3-16-1878 (3-17-1878)
Coffee, Wm. to Sarah Chapman 8-31-1870 (9-1-1870)
Coggin, E. A. to F. M. McLellan 3-12-1862 (3-13-1862)
Coggin, John C. to Nancy R. Presley 3-5-1856 (3-6-1856)
Coggin, L. P. to M. L. Hale 3-15-1876 (3-31-1876)
Coggin, W. T. to Martha Bohanan 11-4-1875 (11-7-1875)
Coggins, Burrel to Elizabeth Roberts 10-21-1867
Coggins, W. R. to Parmelia Fite 2-22-1875 (no return)
Coggins, Wm. to Amandy Jane Fisher 2-21-1871 (no return)
Coleman, G. T. to Jane Mitchel 2-19-1869 (no return)
Coleman, G. T. to Jane Mitchell 2-19-1869 (2-22-1869)
Colewich, M. C. to Martha Barens 8-16-1856
Colley, W. W. to Sarah Bixley omitted (8-4-1866)
Collin, J. b. to S. A. Craddock 3-10-1860
Collins, Benj. to Susan A. Driver 8-6-1868
Colman, C. W. to Oma Hargret 8-7-1869 (no return)
Colvert, Daniel S. to Margaret McFarlen 10-25-1855
Colwell, Felty to P. F. Harper 12-30-1865 (12-31-1865)
Colwell, Isaac to Lucy Ann Piram 10-17-1854 (10-18-1854)
Colwell, John to Sarah Jane Pack 2-9-1860
Colwell, Wm. to Nancy M. Hicks 1-7-1863 (no return)
Compton, Thomas L. to Elizabeth Roy 1-3-1857 (no date)
Conger, Eli to Elizabeth Merit 7-24-1856
Conger, Isaac J. to Mary Greer 2-22-1873 (2-25-1873)
Conger, John to Almyra Lee 8-19-1868 (8-19-1868)
Conger, W. P. to Martha E. Foster 9-24-1878 (9-24-1878)
Conger, Wiley to Drucilla C. White 11-10-1870 (no return)
Congo, Wiley to Nancy M. Tibs 6-15-1859 (6-16-1859)
Connelly, Wm. to Susa Hass 3-9-1877 (3-11-1877)
Conner, Henry to Rachel Adamson 9-9-1874 (no return)
Conner, Patrick to Carolina Dennis 3-17-1851
Conner, Tarence O.! to Keton 10-16-1850 (10-17-1850)
Conner, Thomas J. to Mary E. Keeton 5-21-1861
Connor, Peter to Emaline Hale 12-12-1867 (12-13-1867)
Coole, Hiram W. to Jane Bussel 2-5-1850
Cooper, Isaac to Talitha Yeargan 11-15-1848 (11-20-1849?)
Cooper, James W. to R. E. King 3-16-1870 (3-24-1870)
Cooper, John C. to Catharine Turney 8-19-1854 (8-20-1854)
Cooper, W. R. to E. Bratten 3-17-1876 (3-19-1876)
Cope, H. B. to Elizabeth Lowrey 11-8-1872 (11-10-1872)
Cope, James to Mary Preston 4-15-1876 (4-20-1876)
Cope?, Wm. to S. J. Magnes 1-12-1876 (1-13-1876)
Copehardt, B. H. to Amanda S. Driver 10-1-1878 (10-6-1878)
Copi, G. A. to C. d. Edge 6-25-1874 (6-28-1874)
Corley, Ambros to Sarah Fuson 7-13-1868
Corley, Coleman to Admonda Christian 8-26-1872 (8-21?-1872)
Corsel, George to Phillip Goodner 3-19-1866 (3-20-1866)
Cotten, J. P. to Artemisa Wilkerson 9-25-1858 (10-1-1858)
Cotten, John M. to Mary Cantrell 12-12-1848 (12-14-1848)
Cotten, John to Sarrah A. Wright 10-1-1873
Cotton, Starkey to Martha J. Cantrell 6-30-1857 (no return)
Cotton, T. L. to Mary Jane Lane 10-1-1864 (10-3-1864)
Cotton, Wm. A. to Mary Ann Looney 12-20-1859 (12-30-1859)
Cowen, Peter to S. G. Keeth 3-2-1878 (3-9-1878)

Craddock, S. S. to Harriett Frazier 5-1-1873
Cradoc, Nathaniel H. to Sintha J. Braswell 1-20-1864 (no return)
Crane, Charles E. to Amandy Seay 4-29-1861 (5-2-1861)
Crastie?, Lewis to M. E. McClellan 3-18-1866 (no return)
Crawford, W. A. to Amanda Hindsley 1-28-1880
Crickenson, James to Mary E. Smith 5-22-1865 (no return)
Cripes, John to Z. E. Cubbins 4-3-1878 (4-4-1878?)
Cripes, Wm. to Sarah E. Page 5-8-1878
Cripps, John to Luisa Trapp 3-2-1866 (no return)
Crips, Felix to Syntha Hendix 9-4-1879 (no return)
Crips, Henry to Samantha Milligan 2-26-1879 (3-2-1879)
Crips, Henry to Sarah Etheridge 9-11-1875 (9-12-1875)
Crips, John L. to Nancy C. Smith 2-1-1854 (2-2-1854)
Crips, Peter to Rebecca Womack 9-6-1869 (no return)
Crips, T. J. to Darthula Griffith 4-23-1869 (4-25-1869)
Crips, Thomas to Elizabeth Carder 11-4-1858
Crips, Wm. to Martha Boughers 8-22-1872
Crips, Zenith to Margaret Carte 12-5-1866 (12-6-1866)
Crook, J. W. to Mary J. Bradd 10-6-1869 (no return)
Crook, J. W. to Nancy J. Parker 10-6-1869 (11-2-1869)
Crook, Jerry to Catherine Gann 12-11-1867
Crook, John Monroe to Sarah E. Braidy 2-6-1867
Crook, John to Charlott Fry 12-17-1848
Crook, John to T. J. Natale 11-25-1865 (11-29-1865)
Crook, Mathew J. to Fanny Parker 12-26-1852
Crook, Sylvanus to Pheby A. Cleaborn 8-18-1871 (8-19-1871)
Crook, Tilmon to Malvina Parkerson 5-8-1855
Crook, Wm. to Didady Bates 10-27-1877 (10-28-1877)
Crook, Wm. to Martha Roberts 7-1-1858 (7-3-1858)
Crook, Wm. to Parale Driver 3-25-1858 (exec. no date)
Crook?, Thomas to Celia C. Jackson 3-22-1872 (3-23-1872)
Crouder, John to Martha Starke 12-16-1868 (12-17-1868) [B]
Crowder, Allen to Harriett Hunter 1-23-1872 (1-24-1872) [B]
Crowder, James M. to Emley Stokes 1-3-1873 (no return) [B]
Crowder, John to Supphonia Foutch 8-31-1869 (9-2-1869)
Crowder, L. D. to M. H. Lisk 12-24-1879
Crowder, Moffet to Nelly Cronk 12-24-1851
Crowder, S. M. to Caroline Williams 10-4-1867 (no return)
Crowder, S. M. to Nancy Williams 4-11-1874 (4-12-1874)
Crowder, Winson to Sarah Dennis 4-17-1851 (4-19-1851)
Crowley, Wm. G. to Rebecca M. Fouch 7-4-1853
Cubbins, Encory to Martha J. Marks 8-15-1841
Cubbons, Francis M. to Nancy Jane Conner 2-4-1851
Cubins, Leroy to Eles Robinson 1-26-1875 (no return)
Culwell, Harmon B. to Juley A. Foster 1-1-1874 (1-11-1874)
Culwell, J. P. to M. E. Cantrell 12-15-1877 (12-16-1877)
Culwell, Wm. R. to Calaferna Meggerson 1-1-1870 (no return)
Culwell, Wm. R. to California Meggerson 1-1-1870 (1-12-1870)
Culwell, Wm. to Elizabeth E. Hendrixson 5-8-1879
Culwell, Z. to S. C. Foster 12-11-1869 (12-2?-1869)
Cumins, Wm. to Lina Anderson 8-4-1879
Curley, Colman to Sarah Ann Christian 1-18-1855 (1-24-1855)
Curtice, Lee? to Mary Jacups 12-17-1874
Curtis, David to Nancy J. Johnson 4-27-1869 (no return)
Curtis, J. D. to Phroney Maloane 2-24-1875 (2-27-1875)
Curtis, Joseph to M. Maloane 1-9-1878 (1-13-1878)
Curtis, L. to Amanda P. McClellen 10-3-1866 (10-7-1866)
Curtis, Thomas J. to Armetine Williams 10-24-1866
Curtis, Thomas to Mahala Hale 2-15-1852
Curtis, Wm. T. to Elizabeth Halemontallar 1-24-1880
Curtis, Wm. to Elizabeth Teen 9-25-1850 (no return)
Cutchins?, James to Charity Braswell 12-12-1855 (12-17-1855)
Dabbs, George to Mary Clarke 9-21-1857 (9-24-1857)
Dables, Thomas to Samantha Hays 9-12-1877 (no return)
Dale, Isaac A. to Sinty J. Casper 12-19-1849 (12-30-1849)
Dale, James R. to Mary L. Kerby 1-19-1864 (no return)
Dale, James to Mary E. Tramel 10-2-1866
Daller, David C. to Martha E. Johnson 7-11-1874 (7-14-1874)
Dalton, Marton to Sarah E. Bussel 4-13-1853 (4-14-1853)
David, Henry C. to Mary J. Johnson
David, Thomas K. to G. F. Johnson 1-11-1873 (1-12-1873)
Davis, B. A. to R. G. Cantrell 2-24-1876
Davis, Benjamin F. to Lidy Griffith 9-9-1852 (9-16-1852)
Davis, Doctor A. to Amanda M. Maxwell 3-15-1860
Davis, Elias to Elizabeth Smith 12-10-1851

Davis, George W. to Malinda Griffith date omitd (exec.10-28-1852)
Davis, Henry to Frances Runels 6-8-1864
Davis, Isaac L. to Hannah E. Baty 10-23-1871
Davis, Isam to Frances Helen Neal 9-10-1872 (9-12-1872) [B]
Davis, J. B. to Sallie E. Stuart 5-28-1870 (5-31-1870)
Davis, J. H. to Verginia Braswell 11-25-1876 (11-26-1876)
Davis, Jack to Doke Baker 9-2-1878
Davis, James to Louisa White 9-22-1857 (9-20?-1857)
Davis, James to Sophrona Pittman 12-10-1879 (no return)
Davis, John Jr. to Martha Fite 1-25-1871 (1-26-1871)
Davis, John to Sarah Cantrell 3-2-1868 (3-3-1868)
Davis, John to Susan Ann Keath 8-22-1849 (8-24-1849)
Davis, John to Talitha Hull 3-22-1854 (3-24-1854)
Davis, L. N. to Mary Lee Turner 5-2-1876 (5-3-1876)
Davis, L. Y. to Susan Wade 7-4-1863 (no return)
Davis, Logan to Elizabeth Duke 6-27-1877 (6-29-1877)
Davis, Melvin to Mary Potter 10-17-1864 (no return)
Davis, Nelson C. to Parasetta F. Lee 8-5-1864 (8-6-1864)
Davis, Peter to A. M. Williams 12-18-1865 (12-21-1865)
Davis, Reuben to Elizabeth Griffith 9-17-1855 (exec. no date)
Davis, S. B. to E. J. Cantrell 10-18-1876
Davis, S. M. to Sefilia ----- 2-1-1875
Davis, T. J. to Avaline Fuson 5-4-1878 (5-5-1878)
Davis, T. J. to Tennessee Robinson 12-4-1879
Davis, T. P. to Lillie Luckey 4-27-1880 (4-29-1880)
Davis, Thomas J. to Micy Simpson 10-15-1868 (10-?-1868)
Davis, Thomas to Dela Lawrence 12-28-1861 (12-29-1861)
Davis, Thomas to Mary Little 5-15-1871
Davis, Thomas to Nancy Keef 5-5-1877
Davis, W. to S. J. Kirk 10-12-1870 (10-16-1870)
Davis, Wm. to Luisa Page 8-28-1867 (8-29-1867)
Davis, Wm. to Thena A. Trusty 3-29-1879
Davis, Zack to Mary E. Curtis 6-30-1868 (no return)
Davise, G. S. to Mary Kidwell 10-10-1878
Day, Lewis W. to Mary Ann Goodman 12-1-1859
Deadgrave?, M. L. to Julia Ann Davies 10-9-1861 (no return)
Deadman, Wm. F. to Mary J. Potter 10-23-1867
Deadman, Wm. to Elizabeth Corley 1-12-1872
Dearmon, James to Harriet C. McGuire 11-25-1873
Deeks, David J. to Matilda J. Sullivan 11-4-1852
Deling, George to Sarah Neal 7-22-1868 (7-25-1868)
Delong, David to Hannah Cantrell 2-11-1875
Delong, James to America Redmon 2-7-1861
Delong, Martin to Paralee Cummons? 7-3-1858 (7-4-1858)
Delong, W. J. to Narcica Stone 9-3-1877
Denbey, Wilson to Sophia Preston 9-27-1866 (10-4-1866)
Denby, J. S. to M. J. Alexander 10-19-1869 (10-24-1869)
Denney, Charles to Mary Presley 3-27-1878 (3-28-1878)
Denney, Charles to Syrenia A. Duse? 1-25-1872 (1-28-1872)
Denney, J. W. to M. J. Walker 10-12-1876 (no return)
Dennis, A. C. to Mary A.. Vandergrift 1-28-1873 (1-30-1873)
Denton, Isaac to S. J. Trapp 2-24-1876
Dewease, Dime? to Lucy Lafevers 11-1-1869 (no return)
Dewese, Francis M. to Frances Maxwell 11-19-1859 (11-23-1859)
Dier, W. C. to Mahaly Franklin 7-23-1866 (7-24-1866)
Dildein, George to Mary Medlin 9-4-1864 (9-5-1864)
Dingno?, W. D. to Boneta Marton 12-9-1877 (12-12-1877)
Dinwiddie, James L. to L. C. West 5-14-1873 (no return)
Dirting, David A. to Elizabeth Davis 11-29-1870 (12-1-1871?)
Dirting, John A. to Alcey E. Adamson 12-17-1873 (12-18-1873)
Dobbs, George R. to Mandy C. Albert 12-6-1871 (12-7-1871)
Dodd, H. C. to A. M. Griffith 1-11-1866 (1-14-1866)
Dodd, J. H. to Mary Smith 1-23-1866 (1-25-1866)
Dodd, J. R. to S. C. Mathey 7-8-1876 (7-9-1876)
Dodd, James to Nancy Vanhoozer 9-11-1862
Dodd, Milton C. to Rebeca Turney 9-28-1858 (9-29-1858)
Dodd, R. M. to Sarah Hall 1-22-1870 (1-23-1870)
Dodd, Thomas W. to Jane Cubbins 4-16-1863 (no return)
Dodson, John to Mary Robinson 12-8-1868 (12-10-1868) [B]
Donnell, J. N. to S. A. Cantrell 12-27-1875
Donnell, John to Virginia C. Durham 12-25-1852 (12-26-1852)
Dood, R. M. to J. C. Turner 11-16-1878 (11-20-1878)
Dorsey, J. W. to M. A. James 8-16-1879 (8-21-1879)
Doss, Bejamon to Mina Gorss 6-6-1877 (no date)
Doss, James P. to Julia A. Vantreese 1-14-1858 (1-20-1858)

Doss, James P. to Mary N. Bone 1-19-1866 (1-29-1866)
Doss, Monroe F. to Matta Botts 12-27-1857 (12-28-1857)
Doss, Tobe? to Lizy Preston 3-11-1871 (3-12-1871)
Dougherty, Leander to Malvina F. Keaton 9-5-1873 (9-7-1873)
Dowel, Burgis to Anna Rice 2-5-1866 (no return) [B]
Dozier, Matthew T. to Erun Camron 5-28-1856 (5-29-1856)
Drake, Isaac to Elenora Allen 3-11-1861 (no date)
Dreese, Samuel to Mary C. Madelly 6-14-1873 (6-26-1873)
Drew?, J. M. to M. A. Petty 8-9-1866
Drewery, Jacob to Susan Atwell 3-16-1870 (no return)
Drewrey, Jas. E. to Sarah Drewrey 2-5-1874 (no return)
Drewry, George to Susan Hendricks 10-5-1849
Driver, A. D. to Gabell? Kelley 12-24-1870 (12-29-1870)
Driver, Asa to Tabitha Hickman 9-25-1850 (10-1-1850)
Driver, Asiah to Mary J. Hooper 1-4-1858 (1-6-1858)
Driver, Berry to Elizabeth Vannatta 6-19-1861 (no return)
Driver, Berry to Pheby C. Sandlin 10-16-1867 (10-18-1867)
Driver, D. D. to Kissie Powel 8-9-1877
Driver, D. D. to Mary Jane Hickman 5-25-1861
Driver, Giles Sr. to Mary Johnson 7-15-1855
Driver, Giles to Malina Jane Threwet 11-25-1849 (11-25-1849)
Driver, H. K. to M. E. Haney 4-5-1880 (4-6-1880)
Driver, J. M. to F. J. Bridges 3-7-1877 (3-15-1877)
Driver, J. T. to Fannie Hallum 5-13-1879
Driver, James M. to Arminty Driver 3-9-1871 (3-11?-1871)
Driver, John A. to Mandy P. Roberts 6-4-1870 (6-5-1870)
Driver, Licurgus to Tennessee Stokes 11-3-1873 (11-4-1873)
Driver, Miles W. to S. E. Johnson 9-26-1876 (9-28-1876)
Driver, Solomon to Amanda J. Purkins 8-31-1859
Driver, Thomas D. to Sarah Roberts 12-27-1857
Driver, William L. to Nancy M. Briant 1-23-1856 (1-24-1856)
Driver, Wm. M. to Nancy E. Wanford 8-28-1869 (no return)
Druels, B. B. to Ethelinda Folles 10-7-1875 (no return)
Drury, A. B. to Vina Adimson 10-26-1866 (no return)
Drury, W. B. to Mary Newly 12-30-1868 (12-31-1868)
Drury?, John E. to Josie Buttram 1-20-1880
Duff, W. C. to A. E. Turner 10-20-1875 (10-21-1875)
Duke, Charley E. to Oleevy L. Loggin 12-20-1859 (no date)
Duke, James M. to Cansada Vannatta 8-6-1866 (8-4?-1866)
Dulaney, James M. to Nancy Cantrell 4-8-1869
Dun, John R. to Elvira Martin 4-3-1849
Duncan, Robert to Jane Neale 8-2-1872 (no return) [B]
Duncan, Samuel C. to Sary P. Bethell 9-4-1870 (9-5-1870)
Dunham, David L. to Drusilla Wilkerson 1-12-1856 (1-17-1856)
Dunham, David to Teresa Smith 12-26-1868 (12-30-1868)
Dunham, Elijah H. to Anny Pitman 2-26-1852
Dunham, John to Margaret Pitman 8-15-1849
Dunham, William to Nancy Adcock 3-29-1849 (ret,no cert.)
Dunlap, James M. to Elizabeth Davis 12-24-1854
Dunlap, W. A. to Harriet A. Easham 10-9-1867
Dunlop, J. S. to Emma Canady 6-11-1871
Dunn, Henry to Frances Runnels 6-4-1865 (no return)
Dunn, Hiram to Jane Redmon 2-8-1851
Dunn, Sirus to Vilet Love 1-15-1853 (no date)
Durham, Elial? to Elizabeth Johnson 11-6-1849 (12-6-1849)
Durham, George W. to Elizabeth Veer 12-11-1856 (12-15-1856)
Durham, J. B. to Sarah Cantrell 6-22-1871
Durham, Lewis to Paralle Lewis 4-6-1850 (4-11-1850)
Durham, M. J. to Louisa Warren 1-14-1876 (1-15-1876)
Durham, Riley to Thona Melton 9-10-1874
Durham, Thomas to Frances Smith 11-2-1878 (11-3-1878)
Durlin, James M. to Amanda J. Anderson 12-29-1866 (no return)
Duvault, Francis J. to Eveline Parsly 9-19-1861
Dyer, G. F. to Lizza Seawel 5-15-1877
Dyer, Jefferson to Martha Burton 8-7-1848 (8-17-1848)
Dyer, John H. to Bettie Steel 1-1-1879 (1-2-1879)
Dyer, John M. to Louisa C. Mills 11-17-1852 (11-18-1852)
Ealsy, Henry to Cora A. League 7-11-1872 [B]
Eam, Wm. J. S. to Evelin Rose 5-21-1857 (5-22-1857)
Earheart, Alexander C. to Martha J. Gambell 4-27-1872 (4-28-1872)
Earheart, Joseph to Sarah J. Maynard 6-20-1872
Eason, T. W. to Esnoria H. Blackburn 4-26-1873 (4-27-1873)
Eastham, Henry C. to Hellen Dunlap 8-6-1872
Eastham, William S. to Nancy Allen 9-13-1854
Easthan, H. C. to Susan Allen 2-23-1861 (2-24-1861)

Eastrage, Wiley P. to Mary M. Smithson 3-19-1853 (3-24-1853)
Eastus, Thomas J. to _____ 5-31-1871 (no return)
Eaton, Isaac A. to Martha McMillon 9-5-1874 (9-6-1874)
Eaton, William to Calista Traswell 1-24-1871 (1-25-1871)
Eavens, Lambered to Amonet Clark 4-2-1866 (4-7-1866) [B]
Eavins, Eli to Talmy Maginest 12-29-1874
Ebre, Thomas to Julia Ann Watson 6-25-1853 (6-26-1853)
Eddings, Monroe to Melviney Malone 1-18-1873 (1-19-1873)
Edge, Edward W. to Elizabeth Braswell 8-1-1877 (8-5-1877)
Edge, Elem to Feby Watson 12-23-1853 (no date)
Edge, Henderson A. to Mahala A. Martin 8-20-1855 (9-2-1855)
Edge, Todivora to Sarah E. Cripps 7-31-1872 (8-1-1872)
Edge, William to Harriett A. Braswell 2-23-1871
Edge, Wm. J. to M. C. Fowler 8-29-1878
Edmons, Joshua D. to Sarah M. Glenn 12-15-1853
Edwards, A. to Amanda E. Davis 6-28-1860 (no return)
Edwards, Albert J. to Minnie Williams 12-24-1873
Edwards, Henry C. to Mary J. Melton 4-20-1854
Eledge, Isaac W. to Mary Barens 1-5-1855 (1-11-1855)
Eledge, James B. to Mary Turner 2-6?-1849 (no return)
Eles, Monroe to Elizabeth Hunt 7-31-1876 (8-6-1876)
Elexander, Samuell to Ritta Elexander 7-7-1877 (7-8-1877)
Elkins, John M. to Martha Cantrell 3-20-1869
Elledge, J. F. to Mollie Sellars 1-16-1880 (1-18-1880)
Elliott, William to Syntha Roberts ?-7-1851 (8-7-1851)
Ellis, Benjamon to Kanzady Bradly 8-22-1879
Elrod, B. S. to Tennessee James 12-14-1853 (12-15-1853)
Elrod, James to America Frisly 4-5-1879 (4-6-1879)
Elrod, John to Elizabeth Warren 1-1-1868
Elrod, Owen to M. C. Medlin 12-21-1878 (no return)
Elrod, William to Mary Lefever 1-24-1850 (11-24-1850)
Elrod, Wm. to Nancy Childers 1-9-1851
Emery, David to D. E. T. Dinnes 9-1-1865 (no return)
Emory, Andrew to Sarah Hicks 2-10-1850
England, Archibald D. to Martha Jane Martin 12-16-1850 (12-17-1850)
English, A. to Canzady Cantrell 10-2-1852
English, John to Canzady Hildrith 4-24-1880 (4-26-1880)
Ervin, Wm. to Malinda P. Pack 12-29-1867
Eskew, Russel to Martha D. West 12-21-1854 (12-24-1854)
Estes, Bracket L. to Drusilla Willis 2-3-1857 (2-4-1857)
Estes, Jno. to Sarah P. Hildrith 8-4-1877 (8-5-1877)
Estes, John to Rebecca George 10-22-1864
Estes, Wm. to Elizabeth Bridges 11-11-1854
Estis, B. L. to Amondy Patton 1-?-1873 (1-9-1873)
Estridge, Simpson to Mary A. Smithson 11-13-1861 (no return)
Estridge, Simpson to Rachel Bullard 1-27-1855
Etherage, James P. to Eliza Carter 8-25-1873 (8-28-1873)
Etherage, James to Martha J. Crips 6-10-1869
Etherage, John to Sarah M. McIntire 1-2-1873
Etheridge, John to Rebecca Rusan 9-25-1859 (9-26-1859)
Etheridge, Wm. to Annie J. Banks 12-4-1872 (12-5-1872)
Ethridge, Francis M. to Sarah H. Hendrixon 1-21-1873 (1-24-1873)
Ethridge, Isham to Mary Snider 1-7-1851 (1-9-1851)
Ethridge, John to Samantha Jane Hendrickson 3-16-1853 (3-18-1853)
Ethridge, W. G. to Parlly Reaves 3-22-1877 (no return)
Ethridge, Wm. E. to Nancy Snider 6-14-1867
Ethridge, Wm. G. to Lucretta Crip 11-23-1854 (11-24-1854)
Evanes, J. G. to Sarah Skerlock 3-4-1866
Evans, Bransford to Mary Bunton 4-3-1866 (4-6-1866)
Evans, E. J. to Eugenia Webb 6-22-1875 (6-23-1875)
Evans, Edward to Martha Barger 10-14-1851
Evans, J. C. to M. C. Barger 10-18-1876 (10-19-1876)
Evans, J. D. to S. C. Hibdon 3-24-1877 (3-25-1877)
Evans, J. E. to M. J. Warde 12-25-1876 (12-28-1876)
Evans, James to Martha Colwell 6-22-1854 (6-21?-1854)
Evans, John H. to Narcissa Cantrell 7-9-1874
Evans, John to Narcissy Cantrell 10-8-1853 (10-10-1853)
Evans, Moses A. to Julia E. Measles 2-22-1860 (2-23-1860)
Evans, R. S. to M. E. Roberts 9-26-1876 (9-29-1876)
Evans, W. L. to Sarah Pistole 9-15-1876 (9-17-1876)
Evans, W. P. to E. V. Robards 7-27-1879 (7-31-1879)
Evans, Wm. D. to Paralee Clark 1-21-1852 (1-22-1852)
Evans, Wm. D. to Sarah Neale 8-11-1871

Evans, Wm. to Elizabeth Wilder 3-9-1854
Everett, John to Setty Tubb 6-3-1869 (7-4-1869)
Evins, George to Susanah Tramol 1-4-1873 (1-5-1873)
Evins, Wm. P. to Mary J. A. Murphy 1-16-1873
Ewell, James A. to Nancy L. Hall 12-10-1875 (12-12-1875)
Ewing, Gustavus to Irena S. Williams 4-23-1873 (4-24-1873)
Exum, John to Mary Conger 5-12-1874 (4-13-1874)
Exum, Joseph to Judia Christen 7-22-1875 (7-23-1875)
Fanan, J. to H. Cantrell 7-15-1865 (no return)
Fanes?, Wm. H. to N. A. C. Ward 4-22-1869
Fannes, W. L. to E. M. Scott 1-21-1867
Farell, J. H. to W. A. Mass 12-23-1874
Farkirson, Olever to Sarah Sewel 10-17-1855
Farler, Wm. B. to Elizabeth Parker 1-18-1864 (no return)
Farley, Henderson P. to Fancy Warren 5-5-1856 (no return)
Farller, J. P. to Twendy Ashford 3-24-1866 (3-25-1866)
Farmer, Horrace L. to Elizabeth F. Stanford 5-9-1874 (no return)
Farmer, Wm. J. to Martha J. Williams 12-19-1879
Fautch, Amous to Nancy Jackson 2-5-1849 (2-8-1849)
Felts, Edmon H. to Elizabeth Elrod 1-2-1851 (1-7-1851)
Fergerson, Francis to Frances M. Bigsby 6-14-1851 (exec. no date)
Ferrel, James to Nancy Pack 12-21-1865 (no return)
Ferrel, M. P. to Manervy Sullens 11-20-1858 (11-21-1858)
Ferrell, A. J. to Mary J. Cheatham 1-16-1850
Ferrell, Alex E. to Martha Foster 4-3-1862 (4-5-1862)
Ferrell, C. to Mary J. Graham? 3-29-1862 (3-30-1862)
Ferrell, Charles to Sarah Goodson 1-29-1861 (1-30-1861)
Ferrell, James to Lucy Jane Durham 2-1-1851 (2-9-1851)
Ferrell, James to Nancy Dunn 5-8-1877 (5-10-1877)
Ferrell, James to Rachel Durham 12-31-1862
Ferrell, John to Mary Barens 11-10-1856 (11-13-1856)
Ferrell, M. D. to Sophia Holly 10-3-1877 (10-4-1877)
Ferrell, T. L. D. to Sarah M. Horney 1-27-1880 (1-29-1880)
Ferril, Enoch to Lidia Green 6-27-1865 (6-29-1865)
Ferrill, J. R. to Catharine Johnson 8-6-1877
Ferrill, Wm. E. to Bettie Smitson 2-4-1876 (2-9-1876)
File, Henry M. to Mary Barger 9-30-1851 (10-1-1851)
Findley, George to Mandy Gogin 12-14-1853
Finley, Jesse F. to Marta James 3-31-1852
Finley, Thomas J. to Elizabeth F. New 10-17-1849 (10-30-1849)
Fish, E. H. to Nancy M. Hendrickson 1-27-1857
Fish, James to Mary J. Joins 11-2-1862 (no return)
Fish, Jordon to Mary E. Taylor 7-28-1864
Fish, Samuel to Mary J. Fuson 12-9-1872 (12-22-1872)
Fish, Wm. B. to Elizabeth C. McIntire 7-7-1860 (7-8-1860)
Fish, Wm. to Dilila Allen 8-29-1873 (9-5-1873)
Fisher, Bery to Susan Dunham 3-13-1850 (3-15-1850)
Fisher, Ferdinand P? to Louisa Wright 2-8-1872 (no return)
Fisher, J. D. to Lizzie Evertt 9-16-1878 (no return)
Fisher, James to Cyntha Calwell 1-7-1862
Fisher, Jerrymiah to Hellen Standford 10-25-1871 (10-26-1871)
Fisher, John to Elizabeth Fisher? 10-11-1866
Fisher, John to Lucinda Aldrige 10-17-1865 (10-11-1865)
Fisher, John to Polly Ann McDaniel 2-20-1859 (no return)
Fisher, John to Rebecca Capshaw 10-23-1862 (10-24-1862)
Fisher, Joseph J. to Susan Wright 11-15-1854 (11-161-1854)
Fisher, L. B. to Varnetta Boyd 6-1-1863 (no return)
Fisher, S. to M. A. Bailif 12-24-1877
Fisher, Thomas to Catharine Meirs 9-1-1859 (no return)
Fisher, Thomas to Mary Saunders 12-16-1851 (12-19-1851)
Fisher, William to Sophrona Adcock 2-11-1874 (2-12-1874)
Fisher, Wm. J. to Mary Calwell 3-22-1861 (3=24=1861)
Fisher, Wm. to Mournin? Fisher 10-3-1859 (10-5-1859)
Fite, Isaac M. to Madre Bethel 9-6-1856 (no return)
Fite, Isaac N. to Mary E. Fuson 11-24-1875 (no return)
Fite, Isaih D. to M. E. Prichard 12-20-1876 (12-21-1876)
Fite, J. H. to Virginia A. Measels 10-17-1874 (no return)
Fite, James L. to Alaminta Ralley 8-9-1850
Fite, John A. to Sintha Coble 7-11-1872 (7-14-1872)
Fite, John H. to M. S. David 8-18-1874 (8-19-1874)
Fite, L. D. to Carolina Tubb 8-3-1849 (8-9-1849)
Fite, L. H. to Malcina Bowers 10-21-1862 (10-26-1862)
Fite, Lemuel H. to Malcina Bascum 10-21-1862 (10-26-1862)
Fite, T. H. to S. T. Meash 3-28-1874 (3-30-1874)
Fite, Thomas to K. Vick 11-?-1866 (no return)

Fite, Thomas to Margat R. Vick 11-5-1866 (no return)
Fite, Wm. M. to Sarah C. Given 7-29-1861 (7-30-1861)
Fitspatric, John to Susan Higgins 6-29-1858 (7-1-1858)
Fitts, M. to Elizabeth Allen 2-20-1869
Fitts, W. L. to Susan Hutchins 10-6-1869 (no return)
Fitts, Wm. G. to N. A. E. Stewart? 12-23-1868 (12-24-1868)
Flanders, B. F. to F. M. Cantrell 5-15-1863
Fletcher, Aaron to R. A. Durham 10-13-1861 (no return)
Flippin, H. C. to Sarah P. Foutch 10-8-1869 (no return)
Floid, Thomas to Eliza Green 11-17-1877 (11-28-1877)
Floide, Charly to Genarvie? Stenson 3-25-1875 (3-27-1875)
Floide, Robert to Mary Biggs 1-10-1876
Florida, Samuel to Nancy Jane Foster 11-24-1874 (11-25-1874)
Floyd, M. M. to Sarah A. Blackburn 3-29-1865
Floyd, Thomas to Eliza Preston 4-12-1876 (4-15-1876)
Floyd, Wm. to Elizabeth Briggs 7-12-1862 (7-13-1862)
Floyed, Wiat F. to Lean Reynolds 4-5-1869 (4-8-1869) [B]
Ford, Brown to Fannie Wright 9-30-1879 (10-2-1879) [B]
Ford, Green B. to Mary Rackley 11-29-1852 (12-2-1852)
Ford, J. C. to N. C. Turney 12-13-1869 (12-16-1869)
Ford, James to Isibella Mixen 11-25-1869
Ford, John H. to Marthena Allen 9-?-1857 (9-22-1857)
Ford, Moses A. to Mary Jane Ray 1-2-1850 (1-3-1850)
Ford, W. W. to Susanah Goodson 1-8-1859 (1-9-1859)
Ford, Willis to Matilda C. Meggerson 9-21-1861 (9-22-1861)
Foster, A. L. to Mary E. Cancin? 2-5-1860
Foster, A. to Elizabeth Hill 10-6-1866 (no return)
Foster, B. F. to Mary L. Steel 7-22-1857 (no return)
Foster, Charley to Sarah Moore 6-17-1876 (6-18-1876)
Foster, E. H. to Elizabeth Flordia 1-5-1874 (1-11-1874)
Foster, F. G. to M. C. Irvin 1-9-1878 (1-10-1878)
Foster, G. J. to N. L. Moore 12-27-1875
Foster, J. J. to Nancy Whaley 2-13-1849
Foster, J. S. to Sarena Parsley 12-18-1875 (12-19-1875)
Foster, Jackson to Bethany Culwell 11-23-1870 (11-26-1870)
Foster, Jackson to Cason Florda 10-29-1857
Foster, John C. to M. M. Mayge? 11-30-1864 (12-2-1864)
Foster, John F. to Sarah H. Williams 10-30-1879
Foster, John to M. M. Mayge? date omitd (exec.12-2-1864
Foster, S. M. to M. P. Patterson 6-21-1868 (6-22-1868)
Foster, Tilman L. to Eliza J. McHood 11-2-1872 (11-17-1872)
Foster, Tilmon H. to Marinda Smith 12-19-1877 (12-20-1877)
Foster, Wm. E. to Blanchy Ann Lane 10-18-1848 (10-19-1848)
Foster, Wm. G. to Judah Ann Boatwright 10-2-1861 (10-3-1861)
Foster, Wm. to Susan P. Aalsup no date
Fouch, James M. to Mary Askew 6-10-1872 (6-16-1872)
Fouch, Jason to Caladonia Cheek 9-20-1867 (9-22-1867)
Fouch, John A. to Sarah Washer 3-10-1852 (3-14-1852)
Fouch, Samuel to Delila Sims 3-4-1850 (no return)
Fouch, Wm. to Adonorindey Curtice 9-28-1870 (9-29-1870)
Foutch, F. M. to Belvina Rowland 4-1-1876 (3-2-1876)
Foutch, George to Julia Anderson 8-24-1878 (9-8-1878)
Foutch, J. A. to Nancy Johnson 2-9-1875 (exec. no retrn)
Foutch, John C. to J. E. David 9-9-1862 (9-10-1862)
Foutch, Levi to Amanda Bennett 3-11-1876
Foutch, N. T. to J. R. Hearn 5-24-1870 (5-26-1870)
Foutch, Shay to Cynthia Deadman 2-10-1870 (no return) [B]
Foutch, Thomas to Becca Washer 8-8-1876 (8-10-1876)
Foutch, Wm. W. to Eliz. Jane Eaton 10-2-1868 (10-22-1868)
Fowler, Daniel to Elizabeth Young 10-2-1866
Fowler, J. C. to Martha J. Redmon 11-27-1860 (no return)
Fowler, Jasper to Eliza Mangrum 8-27-1868
Fowler, John G. to Elizabeth E. Hathaway 11-19-1851 (11-20-1851)
Fowler, John to Paralee Johnson 11-1-1863
Francis, Thomas to Eliza Fuson 10-30-1867 (10-30-1867)
Frazier, Almon L. to Martha Alexandria 1-28-1874
Frazier, Charles S. to Mary A. Tyree 1-19-1871
Frazier, Jacob to Mary Daulton 1-28-1851 (1-29-1850?)
Frazier, Jessee to Ellen Tyree 12-31-1873 [B]
Frazier, Wm. to Sarah Shields 10-6-1877 (10-7-1877)
Frazor, Aaron to Paralee Evans 8-21-1854
Frazor, John to Mary Brown 2-25-1854
Frisly, R. T. to Julia Bozarth 12-4-1864
Fry, A. J. to Jane Catnrell 3-29-1856 (3-20?-1856)
Fry, T. C. to L. A. Hamilton 4-13-1870 (4-23-1870)

Fugerson, Wm. to Martha J. Smith 6-29-1860 (7-1-1860)
Fuller, Join to Louizah Braswell 5-23-1866 (5-29-1866)
Furgerson, L. D. to Mary Webb 5-7-1877 (5-9-1877)
Fusan, A. J. to Elizabeth Williams 2-25-1864 (no return)
Fusan, James to Martha Sellars 12-25-1864 (12-24?-1864)
Fusan, Thomas to Elizabeth Hendrix 7-21-1864 (no return)
Fuson, Allen to Fanny Barnes 7-25-1871 (7-30-1871) [B]
Fuson, G. M. to M. E. Gothard 12-20-1877
Fuson, James G. to Eveline Trammel 11-21-1874 (11-22-1874)
Fuson, James H. to Mary J. Henrixon 10-5-1862
Fuson, James H. to Parmelia Cathcart 6-29-1875 (exec. no date)
Fuson, James L. to Malissa Cantrell 8-3-1857 (9?-3-1857)
Fuson, James R. to Tavelee Cubbins 7-31-1862 (8-3-1862)
Fuson, John A. to Mattie Berry 12-3-1872 (12-19-1872)
Fuson, Rufus to Jane Fowler 2-10-1857
Fuson, Samuel to Catharine Pistole 5-8-1853
Fuson, T. J. to M. C.? Hathaway 1-27-1875 (2-4-1875)
Fuson, T. J. to Mary Hathaway 1-27-1875 (no return)
Fuston, Elias to Alice J. Pope 2-1-1879 (2-2-1879)
Fuston, Samuel to Hixey Donley 5-20-1875
Fuston, Wm. to Mary Warren date omttd (exec 4-30-1839
Fuston, Wood to Mary Plumly 6-21-1873 [B]
Gain, Reny to Jane Allen 5-13-1866
Gambrell, Wm. to Sarah Cardwell 1-3-1850
Gandy, Wm. F. to Elizabeth Neil 12-31-1862 (no return)
Gann, John W. to Kizeah Reeves 7-19-1866
Gann, John to Mary Hunt 8-7-1862
Garenhier, Jasper to Sarah Mass 1-7-1867 (1-10-1867)
Garham, John K. to Sarah J. Cantrell 4-28-1863 (4-30-1863)
Garison, A. L. to Nancy Flippin 5-10-1868 (5-11-1868)
Garison, Henry to Mariah Bottums 6-16-1863 (6-18-1863)
Garison, Riley to Susan Keaton 2-1-1865
Garner, Curtis to Ora Marcrum 6-29-1849 (no return)
Garner, Jessee to Fanny Anderson 4-5-1869 (4-16-1869)
Garner, John to Leathey Smith 1-2-1871 (1-5-1871)
Garner, Peter to Elizabeth Robinson 8-10-1870 (8-11-1870)
Garner, W. H. to Angeline Smith 4-7-1873 (4-15-1873)
Garner, Wm. to Martha Conger 1-3-1854 (1-5-1854)
Garrett, Thomas to Luisa Smith 1-29-1866 (no return)
Garrison, Calvin to Mary N. White 1-16-1856 (2-7-1856)
Garrison, E. M. to Rebecca Carter 9-11-1850 (no endorsmnt)
Garrison, Jackson to Narcissy Pridy 11-8-1848 (no return)
Garrison, James to Nancy Bradley 7-16-1857 (7-17-1857)
Garrison, Lafayette to Frances Wright 12-24-1864 (no return)
Garrison, Logan to Elizabeth James 1-13-1860 (no return)
Garrison, Thomas to Eliz. R. Winfrey 12-15-1879 (12-16-1879)
Garrison, Wm. to Caroline Goodner 1-16-1873 (1-19-1872?)
Garritson, John C. to Amandy J. Hall 9-15-1872 (9-24-1872)
Gasaway, George to Harriett Hays 10-6-1869 (10-7-1869) [B]
Gay, D. M. to Rachel L. Gilbert 3-6-1880 (3-7-1880)
Gay, James M. to Rachel E. Taylor 12-13-1872 (12-15-1872)
Gay, John W. to Rebeca Lockheart 12-10-1870 (12-11-1870)
Gay, Samuel to Mary Haines 5-14-1864 (no return)
Gayin, Kay to Jane Allen 5-3-1866 (no return)
George, Enoch to Paralle Dade 6-27-1857 (6-28-1857)
George, James N. to Manorvey Robinson 3-5-1855
George, Martin to Sophronia N. Rodgers 12-28-1853 (no return)
George, Wm. H. to Jane Biford 1-18-1864 (no return)
Gibbs, Isaac to Elizabeth Martin 2-28-1874 (3-4-1874)
Gibbs, Isaac to Mary Wooden 1-24-1857
Gibbs, James to Martha A. Martin 12-16-1872 (12-18-1872)
Gibbs, John to Nancy Looney 10-20-1858 (10-21-1858)
Gilbert, Daniel to Elizabeth M. Caskey 1-13-1851 (not executed)
Gilbert, G. W. to Arrena Gilbert 12-28-1862 (12-29-1862)
Gilbert, George to Easter York 8-6-1879
Gilbert, J. C. to M. F. Ferrell 9-25-1869 (9-25-1869)
Gilbert, J. M. to Malinda Steps 9-5-1874 (9-6-1874)
Gilbert, J. M. to N. C. McGee 4-3-1879 (no return)
Gilbert, J. M. to Tolla McAfee 12-29-1866 (12-30-1866)
Gilbert, J. W. to H. E. Bryant 12-15-1856 (12-18-1856)
Gilbert, John M. to Oliva Kerby 6-24-1868 (6-25-1868)
Gilbert, Robert V. to Mary Cotten 4-24-1861 (4-25-1861)
Gilbert, W. A. to J. E. Stiles 11-14-1877 (11-15-1877)
Gilbert, Wm. A. to Margat J. Martin 12-18-1874 (12-19-1874)
Gilings, Edly H. to Mary Turner 3-15-1871 (3-16-1871) [B]

Gill, Huston S. to Frances R. Smith 9-20-1878 (9-22-1878)
Gilly, Wm. C. to Sarah Miller 9-8-1860 (no return)
Givan, Robert J. to Eliza Meazles 8-27-1850 (9-5-1850)
Givans, L. B. to Kizey Potter 3-2-1857 (3-4-1857)
Given, T. M. to Helen Vanatta 12-11-1879 (12-24-1879)
Given, Thomas to Sarah Whaly 5-5-1866 (5-6-1866)
Glen, Wm. M. to Frances A. McClure 7-18-1873 (7-20-1873)
Glenn, Andy to Emily Cammeron 5-19-1871 (5-18?-1871)
Glenn, Wm. to C. Starks ?-?-1866 (9-6-1866)
Glenn, Wm. to Childa Starks 8-25-1866 (no return) [B]
Gleson, John to M. A. Starke 3-21-1870 (3-23-1870)
Glover, Benjamin H. to Eliza Maxfield 8-29-1868 (8-3?-1868)
Goff, Franklin to Nancy Elrod 5-2-1856
Goggin, J. W. to Virginia F. Givan 9-12-1873 (9-14-1873)
Goggin, John G. to Martha C. Vandgrift 12-21-1872 (12-22-1872)
Goggins, Jorden W. to Nancy F. Allen 1-6-1872 (1-7-1872)
Goin, Jackson to M. A. Goin 11-14-1876 (11-5-1876)
Goodman, John C. to Frances Redmon 12-30-1856 (12-31-1856)
Goodman, Solomon to Elizabeth Johnson 12-22-1856 (12-25-1856)
Goodman, Wm. R. to Catherine Baty 5-20-1869
Goodner, George to Mary Britten 2-25-1868 (no return) [B]
Goodner, John F. to Nancy C. Floyd 3-5-1849 (3-7-1849)
Goodner, Stephen to Mary Williams 3-11-1871 (3-12-1871)
Goodner, Thomas W. to Angelea Bradly 2-26-1867 (3-10-1867)
Goodson, Champ to Lesita Titsworth 5-12-1862
Goodson, Champion to Mary Jane Tittsworth 11-14-1853 (11-24-1853)
Goodson, Greenbery to A. Felphs 1-5-1867 (no return)
Goodson, O. D. to Johannah Crowder 7-16-1858 (8-19-1858)
Goodson, Peter to Rebecca Wright 3-22-1849
Goodson, Thomas R. to Lucinda Smith 2-11-1857 (2-12-1857)
Goodwin, Jackson to Eliza Bullard 8-6-1852 (8-7-1852)
Goodwin, Marion to Vinia Dale 3-15-1873 (3-16-1873)
Gorden, David to Ann E. Thompson 1-10-1874 (no return) [B]
Gorden, George to Mary Foster 6-11-1859 (6-14-1859)
Gorman, G. W. to Sarah Bozorth 10-20-1864
Gosset, Wm. G. to Mary E. Lamberson 8-20-1854 (no return)
Gothard, Edward to Talitha Givans 2-8-1854 (2-9-1854)
Gothard, James to Nancy C. Fuson 12-19-1860 (12-20-1860)
Goulsby, Jaswa to Isabell Fisher 9-27-1876
Gowen, W. D. to Mattie E. Woods 9-24-1873 (9-25-1873)
Gowins, Spencer to Edith Morison 2-11-1859 (exec. no date)
Graham, Wm. J. to Hixey C. Ferrell 3-2-1861 (3-3-1861)
Grammer, Joseph to Hester Capshaw 2-5-1852
Gray, John H. to Lou Allen 10-2-1875 (10-3-1875)
Gray, Samuel H. to Matilda Driver 7-16-1851 (7-17-1851)
Greeb, Wm. to Arena Rowland 8-18-1874 (8-19-1874)
Green, Amno to Anna Todd 11-6-1877 (11-7-1877)
Green, Amos to Amandy Tubb 4-20-1872 (no return) [B]
Green, Archable D. to Sarh Liles 9-26-1872
Green, Coleman to Angelina Haley 4-22-1876 (4-23-1876)
Green, Elias N. to Martha Cantrell 5-3-1864 (5-5-1864)
Green, Francis M. to Mary A. Taylor 8-21-1860
Green, James N. to Mary Ann Keton 4-3-1852 (4-4-1852)
Green, James W. to Gabriella Edons 5-17-1853 (exec. no date)
Green, James to B. A. McDowell 3-13-1876 (3-14-1876)
Green, James to Eveline Davault 12-26-1866 (12-27-1866)
Green, James to Hixey McGinis 8-25-1870 (8-27-1870)
Green, James to Isabella Meggeson 4-21-1869 (no return)
Green, Jessee to Ellen Parcly 9-6-1876 (9-7-1876)
Green, John S. to N. E. Herd 10-3-1867
Green, M. C. to Haret Mulican 2-28-1868 (3-1-1868)
Green, M. L. to M. J. Baine 10-21-1867 (10-24-1867)
Green, Mathew to Mary H. White 2-3-1863
Green, Monroe to Martha Lyles 12-4-1872 (12-5-1872)
Green, Ranse to Ellen Young 10-16-1879
Green, Wm. C. to Serena Carter 6-6-1866 (no return)
Greer, James P. to Nancy Cantrell 9-19-1873 (9-24-1873)
Gregory, Silas to Sarah Rigsby 7-6-1854 (7-12-1854)
Griffeth, D. to Roxa Wright 10-6-1874 (10-11-1874)
Griffeth, W. H. to M. J. Friffith 10-14-1875
Griffeth, Wm. T. to Famia Cantrell 10-30-1866 (10-31-1866)
Griffin, J. W. to Eliza Jane Vick 7-24-1860 (not endorsed)
Griffin, Jacob to Catharine Martin 6-7-1858
Griffin, Lafayette to Eliza J. Thomason or White 12-30-1850
Griffith, David to Lucey Cantrell 2-2-1879

Griffith, E. G. to S. S. Ward 9-23-1878 (9-26-1878)
Griffith, George to Tennessee Smith 12-22-1877
Griffith, Isaac D. to Sallie Cope 9-11-1871 (9-13-1871)
Griffith, J. J. to Sarah An Jones 5-13-1869 (no return)
Griffith, J. M. to Allis Chapman 7-14-1877 (7-15-1877)
Griffith, James to Math F. Hix 1-22-1867
Griffith, James to Santhia? C. Griffith 8-10-1872 (8-18-1872)
Griffith, Johnathan to Margaret Williams 1-5-1874 (1-7-1874)
Griffith, Johnathan to Sarah Arnold 11-4-1872 (11-8-1872)
Griffith, Josiah to Susanah Scott 7-22-1855 (7-26-1855)
Griffith, Ozious D. to Maring Wall 1-9-1868 (1-12-1868)
Griffith, W. C. to Bettie Durham 4-6-1880 (4-8-1880)
Griffith, W. T. to Josephina Close 8-13-1874 (8-15-1874)
Griffith, Wm. W. to Nancy Ann Davis 11-20-1852 (11-25-1852)
Griffith, Wm. to Elizabeth Bass 1-11-1872 [B]
Grigston, Ishmael to Mahala J. Foutch 7-9-1855 (7-12-1855)
Grindstaff, Benjamon to Sallie Thomas 11-27-1876 (12-7-1876)
Grindstaff, J. D. to Tempy Fite 3-31-1862 (4-2-1862)
Grindstaff, N. H. to Jenna Griffith 4-30-1877 (5-6-1877)
Grindstaff, Nathaniel H. to Margarett T. Fite 9-13-1872 (9-19-1872)
Grindstaff, Pleasant to Easter Lamberson 1-31-1874 (2-1-1874) [B]
Grindstaff, W. J. to Mary J. F. Smith 10-4-1879 (10-5-1879)
Grinstaff, Samuel to Araminta J. Hays 7-30-1860 (7-31-1860)
Grissam, R. H. to Sophy Tyree 1-7-1863 (2-18-1863)
Groomes, G. M. to N. C. Turner 7-24-1879
Groomes, J. B. to Molley Hayes 11-14-1877 (11-18-1877)
Groomes, James to Mary Barry 9-4-1876
Grooms, John W. to Amanda F. Vick 1-12-1864 (exec. no date)
Grooms, Thomas to Mary Truette 3-27-1855 (3-28-1855)
Guinn?, J. D. to Elizabeth Redmon 12-4-1862
Guthard, Edward to C. A. Self 2-25-1870 (2-26-1872?)
Guy, G. D. to Mary A. Gilbert 10-19-1878 (sol. no date)
Hackette, Peter to Sarah Williams 6-21-1849
Haggard, Jessee to Elizabeth Smith 3-23-1859
Haggart, P. T. to Roxy Robinson 12-27-1879 (1-5-1880)
Hail, Jefferson to Mary Bone 5-7-1866 (5-10-1866)
Hail, John to Mary Bond 5-7-1866 (5-13-1866) [B]
Haile, James T. to Delila Frances Rich 2-26-1875 (2-28-1875)
Hailes, James C. to Virginia L. Martin 4-7-1874 (4-9-1874)
Haim, S. to Matilda A. Robinson 10-24-1865 (no return)
Hale, A. J. to Sarah Norton 1-23-1849 (1-22?-1849)
Hale, B. F. to Mary Rich 10-27-1869 (10-28-1869)
Hale, David H. to Malissie Neel 10-14-1853 (no return)
Hale, Elijah to B. Z. Watson 10-2-1877 (10-8-1877)
Hale, H. L. to Emaline Bain 10-21-1865 (10-22-1865)
Hale, Henry to Sarah J. Johnson 12-8-1849 (12-9-1849)
Hale, J. L. to M. E. Garner 1-31-1877 (2-1-1877)
Hale, J. M. to L. M. Cole 3-24-1876 (3-30-1876)
Hale, J. M. to Mary H. Goggin 12-16-1879 (12-18-1879)
Hale, Joal D. to Susan Scribner 1-24-1854 (1-26-1854)
Hale, John R. to Cintha Martin 4-16-1856 (4-17-1856)
Hale, John to Martha Vine 2-21-1865
Hale, John to Phebe Scott 12-26-1860 (12-25?-1860)
Hale, L. G. to Elizabeth Fite 9-6-1851
Hale, Lafayette to Malissa Wines 8-23-1854 (8-24-1854)
Hale, Lemon to Mary E. Allen 7-1-1859 (7-3-1859)
Hale, Pleasant to Elizabeth Hunty 9-6-1852
Hale, Purtilas A. to Julia Neal 3-27-1878 (3-31-1878)
Hale, Reuben B. to Catharine Vantrease 8-17-1853
Hale, S. C. to Mary E. Anderson 10-3-1866 (10-5-1866)
Hale, Thomas J. to Mary George 12-18-1858 (12-19-1858)
Hale, Thomas to Sary Chinly 9-21-1866 (9-22-1866)
Hale, W. J. to Parilee Lillus 6-8-1861 (6-9-1861)
Hale, W. T. to Lula B. Lewis 4-4-1876 (4-6-1876)
Hale, Wm. L. to Kesiah George 10-17-1857 (10-18-1857)
Hale, Wm. M. to Malinda M. Hallum 2-14-1870 (2-19-1870)
Haley, Jessee to Nancy Young 9-30-1870 (10-2-1870)
Hall, B. F. to N. P. Dale 2-14-1865
Hall, David E. to Sarah Deney 8-22-1865 (no return)
Hall, David to D. J. Hegwood 6-11-1870
Hall, Francis to Parilee Griffith 1-13-1860 (1-15-1860)
Hall, George to Julia Tittle 1-28-1876
Hall, H. L. to Martha A. Smith 8-21-1876 (exec. no date)
Hall, J. M. to Elizabeth Bradley 2-18-1862 (2-20-1862)
Hall, J. M. to Lucy J. Dinwiddy 2-24-1868 (2-2-1868)

Hall, John E. to Matilda C. Finley 6-15?-1850 (6-13-1860?)
Hall, Robert S. to Mary P. Dennis 9-18-1869
Hall, Robert to Elizabeth Martin 8-2-1865 (no return)
Hallerin, John T. to Tennessee Bond 11-23-1872 (11-24-1872)
Hambleton, Wm. J. to Sarah C. Terney 4-15-1871 (4-16-1871)
Hamelton, James F. to Mary F. Garner 10-11-1858 (10-13-1858)
Hamilton, James F. to Nancy Congar 10-8-1859 (10-12-1859)
Hamilton, Micajah to Martha J. Cumings 12-24-1859 (12-25-1859)
Hammons, Joseph to Mary Parrish 5-12-1853 (12-7-1853)
Hammons, Joseph to Spica Taylor 9-25-1858
Hancock, Henry to Catherine Viesz 6-3-1866
Hancock, John to Sarah Higgins 7-5-1870 (no return) [B]
Hancok, Joseph to Lue Wood 2-22-1878 (2-27-1878)
Hanes, Wm. to Tennessee Hendrixson 11-9-1874 (2-9-1875)
Haney, H. L. to Mary Gilbert 9-12-1874
Haney, Levi to Elenor Capshaw 3-24-1857
Haney, Tilman to Mary Rolland 10-1-1862 (10-2-1862)
Haney, Wm. to Paralee Capshaw 10-13-1853
Hanford, Samul to Helon Hays 9-12-1866 (no return)
Hardcastle, H. L. to Nettey New 2-2-1874 (2-15-1874)
Hardcastle, Pallis M. to Mary J. Malone 9-27-1869
Harden, Wm. to Mary Grindestaff 11-9-1876
Hardin, David C. to Narcissus? Spurlock 3-9-1871 (3-23-1871)
Hardin, Wm. to Josephine Parish 8-15-1872
Hardison, L. H. to Chrisasis? Etheridge 7-18-1878 (7-1?-1878)
Hargis, F. C. to C. J. Rigsby 5-20-1876
Haris, Jesse to Louiza Herington 4-4-1868 (4-5-1868)
Harmon, Sterling B. to Margret J. Haile 9-10-1873 (9-11-1873)
Harmon, W. P. to E. L. Bullard 8-24-1870 (9-11-1870)
Harney, J. J. to Mical Allen 11-20-1867 (11-21-1867)
Harper, Abner S. to Martha Winfree 8-11-1856 (8-14-1856)
Harper, James M. to George Ann Bond 4-14-1880 (4-15-1880)
Harper, Thomas C. to Sarah Jane Hales 1-21-1852 (1-22-1852)
Harps, Jasper N. to Malvina Griffith 7-14-1853
Harris, Alexander to Minerva Gamble 9-4-1869 (9-5-1869)
Harris, J. W. to M. L. Fare 8-2-1860
Harris, Thomas R. to Mahaly Smith 9-5-1849
Harris, Willims to Nancy Pack 4-10-1856
Harrison, John S. to Julia E. West 12-22-1856 (exec. no date)
Harrison, W. B. to Jane Robinson 5-1-1871 (5-3-1871)
Hart, Thomas to Nancy C. Alexander 10-11-1855
Hartwell, James to Sarah Lafever 10-17-1874
Hatfield, James to Mary Martin 7-21-1864
Hathaway, Elijah to Jane Pistole 6-19-1860 (exec. no date)
Hathaway, George to Saliny Yeargin 12-7-1868 (no return)
Hathaway, H. S. to Kizy Parish 1-29-1858
Hathaway, James A. to D. A. Badger 10-29-1876 (exec. no date)
Hathaway, Joseph to Dempsy W. Howard 7-14-1871 (7-15-1871)
Hathaway, Levy to Mahaly Pitman 10-9-1870
Hathaway, Westly to Judah King 10-16-1873 (10-17-1873)
Hathaway, Wm. L. to Martha Sea 10-17-1864 (10-19-1865?)
Hathway, A. D. to Adline Caphshaw 9-7-1866 (8?-15-1866)
Hathway, Lenard to Laury Roland 2-9-1864 (2-11-1864)
Hawker, Wm. P. to Eliza Jane Alexander 9-16-1858
Hawker, Wm. to Nancy Bean 6-19-1876 (6-21-1876)
Hawkins, H. T. to Mary Malone 1-11-1878 (1-13-1878)
Hayes, Asbury N. to Tennessee Cooper 2-20-1872 (2-22-1872)
Hayes, G. W. to Druciler Clark 9-1-1879 (9-4-1879)
Hayes, I. N. to Elizabeth Exum 3-8-1880 (3-29-1880)
Hayes, J. B. to Mary Evans 11-19-1877 (11-21-1877)
Hayes, J. H. to M. A. Atnip 1-16-1869
Hayes, J. R. to Sarah F. Fitts 5-5-1877 (no return)
Hayes, J. T. to Farasetta Jones 12-15-1864 (12-16-1864)
Hayes, James M. to A. E. Hall 4-3-1874
Hayes, James M. to Edith Griffith 11-3-1864
Hayes, James T. to Virginia Richardson 11-30-1867 (12-1-1867)
Hayes, James T., Jr. to Sarah A. Curtin 12-23-1871 (no return)
Hayes, James to Manervy Parker 5-27-1876 (5-28-1876)
Hayes, James to Susan Cameron 12-22-1865
Hayes, Jasper N. to Sarah J. Given 5-26-1880
Hayes, M. C. to Rebecca Bluhm 2-4-1880
Hayes, Marion to Rebecca Holly 12-20-1879 (no return)
Hayes, Monro to Amanda Hayes 5-8-1866 (no return) [B]
Hayes, N. E. to Zorof Berry 11-14-1877 (no return)
Hayes, Seazer? to Sarah Buson 8-23-1876

Hayes, Thomas to Sinda Hancock 2-26-1877 (2-29-1877)
Hayes, Wm. H. to Molly M. Parker 6-2-1868
Hayese, John H. to Honriah B. Cantrell 9-27-1873 (9-29-1873)
Haynes, Joshua to Mary Narceny 7-26-1861
Hays, A. J. to Tennessee King 2-3-1876
Hays, Alexander to Rebecca F. Clark 10-30-1849 (2-2-1850)
Hays, John W. to Elizabeth Compton 7-22-1865 (no return)
Hays, R. C. to M. M. Martin 9-19-1860 (9-20-1860)
Hays, Samuel to Rebeca D. Ferrel 2-23-1866
Hays, Thomas to Mary Mason 7-11-1867 (7-18-1867)
Hayse, F. H. to July Ray 11-7-1865 (11-9-1865)
Hayse, Isaac H. to Eleener Fuson 8-21-1849
Hayse, Isaac M. to Nancy J. Moore 10-17-1872
Hayse, Isaac to Eliza H. Robinson 12-18-1852 (12-23-1852)
Hayse, Jackson B. to Liley Boyne 7-28-1873
Hayse, Jasper N. to Sarah E. Patterson 5-13-1856
Hayse, John W. to Elizabeth J. Turney 1-24-1855 (1-25-1855)
Hayse, John to Matilda Pack 7-10-1852 (7-11-1852)
Hayse, Sampson to Louisa Jane? Dougherty 8-27-1849 (8-29-1849)
Hayse, Thomas to Jane Adams 12-23-1872 (12-25-1872) [B]
Hayse, Wm. T. to Luella Woolridge 12-11-1872 (12-12-1872)
Heagon, Hiram to Sallie Qualls 10-11-1872 (?-11-1872)
Hearn, Joseph L. to Susan F. Laurence 12-21-1863 (12-22-1863)
Hearn, M. P. to Bethenia P. Rollins 11-17-1873 (11-23-1873)
Heath, Rufus to Susan Rankhorn 11-15-1853 (11-16-1853)
Heflin, Wm. to Elizabeth Stokes 10-10-1877 (10-11-1877)
Helm, F. D. to Fannie Oakley 1-3-1877 (1-4-1877)
Helton, Christerfer C. to Elizabeth Pollard 12-30-1868
Henderson, Thomas to Mary Hill 3-27-1864
Hendrexan, W. to Mary Bennett 3-30-1863
Hendricks, Allen to Jane Roberds 7-25-1849 (7-26-1849)
Hendricks, John to Charlotta Redmon 8-14-1856
Hendrickson, David to Eliza Simpson 1-31-1855
Hendrickson, John to Martha T. Martin 7-9-1859
Hendrickson, Joseph to Sarah Huggins 7-16-1853 (7-17-1853)
Hendrickson, Lemuel D. to Mary J. Clayborn 4-28-1852 (4-29-1852)
Hendrickson, Richard to Rebecca Smith 8-3-1864
Hendrickson, Wm. C. to Elizabeth E. Burnette 12-7-1851
Hendrix, B. G. to A. E. Alexander 12-23-1866 (no return)
Hendrix, Wilson to Frances Taylor 8-8-1866 (8-9-1866)
Hendrixon, Farris to Nancy Adkins 6-5-1869 (6-6-1869)
Hendrixon, Henry to Elizabeth Taylor 7-13-1861 (7-18-1861)
Hendrixon, Jeremiah to Sarah Taylor 10-5-1861 (10-6-1861)
Hendrixon, Wiley to Martha Hendrixon 1-13-1870
Hendrixson, Alexander A. to Mary Ann Taylor 11-5-1865 (11-10-1865)
Hendrixson, F. M. to Mary A. Stewart 4-9-1872 (4-11-1872)
Hendrixson, Haris to Sarah Hayse 4-10-1872 (4-11-1872)
Hendrixson, Hiram to Zantry P. Turner 8-17-1870
Hendrixson, Smith to Nancy A. Curtis 1-28-1868 (no return)
Hendrixson, Wm. C. to Samantha J. Robinson 12-26-1872 (1-2-1873)
Hendsley, John to Ready Denny 11-24-1875 (11-26-1875)
Henesley, James to Nancy Ellis 10-4-1871 (10-5-1871)
Henley, Almon to Malinda Herron 4-14-1870
Henley, Samuel to Mary Grifeth 1-2-1866 (1-4-1866)
Henly, Amon to Mary Robards 7-28-1869 (no return)
Henly, George to Susan Fouch 1-16-1872 (no return)
Henly, James to Nancy E. Foutch 9-22-1873 (no return)
Henly, Wm. to Martha Franklin 5-20-1874 (5-28-1874)
Hennafree, J. P. to M. E. Cantrell 7-19-1866
Hennsley, William to Nancy Bates 1-29-1872 (1-30-1872)
Hensley, Harden to Lucinda Ellis 8-28-1867 (no return)
Heptanstall, William to Emily Acuff 1-7-1875
Herd, George to Sarah Milligan 8-31-1872 (no return) [B]
Herd, James W. to Emma Davis 1-4-1870 (1-5-1870)
Herd, James W. to Emma Davis 1-4-1870 (no return)
Herenton, M. F. to Lucy McEntire 10-5-1878 (no return)
Heriman, S. B. to M. H. Hibdon 5?-8-1880 (no return)
Heron, Samuel to Sarah T. Buckner 5-22-1855 (5-24-1855)
Herren, Thomas D. to Palina F. Moses 2-11-1851 (no return)
Herriman, Josiah to Jane Wiliams 8-9-1865 (no return)
Herrin, William to Jane Barks 3-6-1854 (3-7-1854)
Herrondon, Wm. to Margaret Williams 10-4-1855
Hibden, Elisha to Nancy Harmon 10-24-1869 (10-29-1869)
Hibden, Joseph to Rachel P. Bullard 4-3-1869 (4-4-1869)

Hibdon, A. E. to Sallie Rutledge 3-16-1871 (3-17-1871)
Hick, Horas to Louvina Hays 5-7-1866 [B]
Hickey, Samuel to Rachel Bass 6-27-1874 [B]
Hickman, J. H. to S. A. Ethridge 9-24-1868 (9-25-1868)
Hickman, Wm. to Sarah J. Down 1-19-1872? (1-25-1870?) [*]
Hicks, A. B. to Matildy Measle 9-1-1873 (9-4-1873)
Hicks, Benjamin F. to Emsy Webb 1-2-1869 (1-3-1869)
Hicks, Elijah to Elizabeth Hibden 7-7-1875 (7-8-1875)
Hicks, H. F. to Paralee Youngblood 12-26-1855
Hicks, J. S. to Elizabeth Parkerson 7-2-1867 (7-3-1867)
Hicks, James to Jane Heddrick 9-25-1869 (no return)
Hicks, James to Nancy E. Shields 10-16-1875 (10-17-1875)
Hicks, Samuel to Mary E. Forgerson 1-24-1849 (1-25-1849)
Higenbottom, Wesley to Elisabeth Foutch 7-30-1868 (7-31-1868)
Hilaritt, S. J. to Delila J. Bane 12-2-1861 (12-3-1861)
Hildreth, Alexander to Alyin Williams 4-2-1866 (no return)
Hildreth, H. H. to V. L. Worley 11-16-1877 (no return)
Hildreth, Hiram to Melvina Bain 8-16-1862 (9-17-1862)
Hildreth, Samuel J. to Martha Ann Wooldridge 3-13-1850
Hildrith, John to Sarah Johnson 6-23-1880 (6-24-1880)
Hile, Randle to Mary Baty 1-16-1869
Hill, C. to Lucinda Pope 9-24-1868
Hill, C. to Susan Pitman 2-4-1867 (2-6-1867)
Hill, Daniel G. to Elizabeth Caskey 3-16-1852 (3-18-1852)
Hill, Fedrick J. to Martha Drury 6-24-1853
Hill, George H. to Harriet Beckwitt 11-30-1852
Hill, Henderson to Matilda Bennette 3-14-1853
Hill, James R. to Martha E. Tramel 9-6-1871 (9-7-1871)
Hill, John D. to Charity Cantrell 9-18-1851
Hill, John to Anisa M. Trammell 7-25-1864
Hill, John to Elizabeth Meggerun 4-19-1862
Hill, John to Sarah Herrin 1-17-1857 (no return)
Hill, Joseph Irvin to Fanny Thomas 10-17-1874 (no return) [B]
Hill, Monroe to Mary Bethel 9-22-1875 (9-23-1875)
Hill, Pleasant to Mary Trammel 9-2-1856
Hill, Toney to Sallie McGuines 8-22-1879
Hill?, William R. to Elizabeth Tramel 8-29-1855 (8-28?-1855)
Hilliard, John to Frances Bullard 9-18-1855
Hindsley, Joseph to Delia Denny 2-16-1877 (2-17-1877)
Hirendon, Henry to Mary Ann Wilson 1-18-1871 (2-19-1871)
Hirendon, Y. L. to Margrett Banks 2-14-1871 (2-20-1871)
Hobson, F. W. to M. F. Wasker 12-5-1865 (12-6-1865)
Hodge, James C. to Susan Haney 3-11-1853
Hodge, John to Mary Files 3-17-1870 (3-18-1870)
Hodge, John to Nancy Hendrix 5-25-1876 (5-26-1876)
Hodge, Levi to M. J. Forde 10-8-1876
Hodge, Nuton to Sarah M. Pleger 12-28-1865 (no return)
Hodges, Wm. to Mary Gilbert 9-24-1862
Holder, S. K. to L. Adcock 3-15-1875 (3-18-1875)
Holder, Thomas F. to Mary Ann Quillin 12-17-1852
Holis, James M. to N. J. Johnson 2-16-1865 (2-19-1865)
Holland, Alex to Sarah Alexandria 6-11-1873
Holland, J. W. C. to Mary S. Cantrell 4-7-1875
Hollansworth, Joshua L. to Mary E. Clarke 1-15-1856 (1-16-1856)
Hollay, William to Knector? C. Exum 11-13-1857
Hollemen, A. B. to Mary A. Briggs 9-6-1854 (9-7-1856?)
Hollensworth, James to A. Williams 1-28-1878 (1-29-1878)
Holley, John S. to Casander Foster 2-17-1869 (2-18-1869)
Holley, John S. to Elizabeth Batts 9-30-1862 (10-2-1862)
Hollinsworth, Josiah to Sarah Bradford 1-9-1868 (1-9-1868)
Hollinsworth, L. D. to Elisabeth Spurlock 1-23-1875 (1-24-1875)
Hollinsworth, Obediah to Allice Smith 1-2-1874 (1-3-1874)
Hollis, Jessee F. to Huldy B. Turner 3-10-1860 (3-11-1860)
Holly, Wm. to Spicy Hammons 11-23-1863
Holt, Calvin to Charlotta Redmon 12-27-1878 (no return)
Holt, Robert to Mary Colwell 6-16-1859
Hooper, A. B. to Edney Wilson 9-22-1875 (9-23-1875)
Hooper, James F. to Margaret F. Bennett 9-25-1860 (9-26-1860)
Hooper, S. W. A. to Nancy R. Trapp 10-26-1867 (10-21?-1867)
Hooper, T. M. to M. D. Fish 8-2-1866 (8-3-1866)
Hoover, Wm. to Elizabeth Fitts 11-14-1864 (12-23-1864)
Hopkins, John W. to Elizabeth J. Hayes 8-9-1872 (8-11-1872)
Horton, Littleton to Susan Webb 9-8-1852
Hoskins, Bunk to Corilee Smith 10-27-1875 (10-28-1875)
Hoskins, William P. to Sophronia C. Floyd 1-17-1853 (1-18-1853)

Hoskins, William T. to Malisa Jane Stokes 11-10-1855 (11-11-1855)
Hoss, John to Anis Mahaly Trammell 10-5-1864 (no return)
Hoss, Thomas J. to Martha Banks 7-19-1870 (7-21-1870)
Houston, John G. to Mary E. Lawrence 6-2-1856 (6-3-1856)
Howard, James to Harriet Finley 3-4-1856 (3-6-1856)
Howard, Thomas to Peggy Scott 8-10-1876
Howell, B. F. to Sarah J. Moss 7-4-1872
Huchins, James to Sarah Childress 9-12-1864 (no return)
Huddleston, W. R. to Amanda W. Burton 7-16-1879 (7-20-1879)
Huddleston, Wad to Adline Ray 8-21-1879 [B]
Hudelston, George to Ann Johnson 2-3-1877 (2-4-1877)
Hudleston, Wade to Jennie Shields 12-4-1871 [B]
Huggins, S. J. to M. E. Smith 2-5-1865 (no return)
Huggins, Thomas R. to Matilda Evans 4-3-1855 (7-3-1855)
Huggins, W. H. to Matilda Foster 1-23-1862
Hulet, John W. to Paralee Sims 11-17-1856 (no return)
Hull, James M. to Bathena Rodgers 6-17-1854 (6-18-1854)
Hullet, Josiah to Sarah E. Driver 12-23-1864 (no return)
Hullet, William to Mary Jane Hale 11-11-1852 (11-12-1852)
Hullett, William to Nancy Hess 6-18-1871
Hunroe, Peter J. to Huldy J. Adkins 8-20-1860 (8-24-1866?)
Hunt, Archabald to Emiline Simpson 9-1-1852 (9-2-1852)
Hunt, Levi B. to Martha A. Payne 8-14-1851
Hunt, Malshel to Mary E. Evans 11-5-1851 (11-6-1851)
Hunt, Mattha to Margaret Dunlap 9-13-1853
Hunt, Matthew to Kiza Ann Wooderd 10-22-1856 (no return)
Hunt, Matthew to Susan Harrington 11-29-1856 (11-30-1856)
Hunt, Simeon T. J. to Sarah Jane Adamson 5-14-1859 (5-15-1859)
Hunt, Wm. to Elizabeth Ashworth 5-21-1867 (no return)
Hunter, Jackson to Jane Calcot 9-7-1874 (9-8-1874) [B]
Hunter, John to Eliza Askew 9-27-1865 (9-28-1865)
Hutchens, Lawrence to Sary Jessee? 7-28-1866 (10-11-1866)
Hutcheons, Eli D. to Malissa Robinson 10-11-1854 (10-12-1854)
Hutcheson, Isaac to Nancy Botts 11-11-1852
Hutchings, Lawson to Sarah Jain Penegar 7-27-1866 (no return)
Hutchins, Charles D. to Nancy Dyer 8-10-1854
Hutchins, Isaac to Allis Whitman 7-6-1868 (no return)
Hutchins, J. S. to Julia A. Smith 8-29-1876 (no return)
Hutchison, E. to Amanda Love 10-12-1866 (10-15-1866)
Hutchison, Isaac to Allis Fults 3-18-1869
Hutson, James W. to R. J. Roy 8-8-1874 (8-9-1874)
Ingeram, J. J. to Sarah Ray 11-20-1848
Ingram, J. J. to Martha Pack 9-10-1867 (9-11-1867)
Ingram, James Eli to Emma Ethridge 1-11-1872 (1-10?-1872)
Irvin, James to Elizia Robinson 10-10-1872 (no return)
Irwin, A. P. to Elizabeth Cope 6-6-1864 (no return)
Isbell, David to Josey Cantrell 11-12-1868 [B]
Isbell, W. J. to Sarah M. Cameron 2-1-1861 (2-3-1861)
Isbell, Wm. J. to Adaline H. Starnes 7-27-1867 (no return)
Ivey, A. to Nancy Johnson 2-3-1856 (2-5-1856)
Ivins, Wm. G. to Sarah E. Smith 4-3-1865 (4-6-1865)
Jackson, Andrew to Mandelia Atnip 3-15-1867 (3-16-1867)
Jackson, J. F. to Rebecca Walls 9-24-1862 (no return)
Jackson, James B. to B. C. Corley 5-15-1880 (5-16-1880)
Jackson, Leander to Milley Kelley 7-26-1852 (8-2-1852)
Jackson, Wilson to Elizabeth Prentice 10-6-1848 (10-8-1848)
Jackson, Wm. to Carolin Oakley 1-10-1866 (1-11-1866)
Jaco, Erastus to Alice A. Adkins 1-21-1880 (1-20?-1880)
Jacobs, Clint to Elizabeth J. Malone 8-30-1876 (9-3-1876)
Jacobs, James to Tennessee Hathaway 6-18-1878 (6-30-1878)
James, Bartle to Eliza Magan 7-29-1865 (no return)
James, Berry to Darthula Stokes 12-23-1872 (no return) [B]
James, D. to M. F. Batton 2-10-1868 (2-11-1868)
James, E. P. to Amandy C. Batton 9-9-1867
James, George W. to Virginia Ann Lane 2-3-1859 (2-8-1859)
James, Hardwell to Eveline Maynard 1-3-1866 (no return)
James, Wm. to Jane Pedigo 5-25-1859 (5-26-1859)
Jared, Josiah to Edame Keith 8-7-1869 (no return)
Jarerel?, C. C. to M. L. Braswell 12-1-1873 (12-18-1873)
Jarvis?, John S. to Evaline T. Glover 2-17-1856 (exec. no date)
Jencinkins, Wm. to M. E. Fite 1-5-1875
Jenings, James to Nancy Keaton 2-26-1877
Jenkins, Obediah to Mahala Jones 12-17-1857
Jenkins, Obediah to Sarah Griffith 7-22-1850 (7-23-1850)
Jenkins, Wm. to Elizabeth Jones 12-21-1868 (12-25-1868)

Jenkins?, Nathan Z. to Elizabeth Cantrell 8-14-1855 (8-20-1855)
Jennings, J. S. to N. C. Sellars 8-10-1869 (8-11-1869)
Jennings, Jessee A. to Tennessee Ausbey 5-25-1872 (5-26-1872)
Jennings, Joshua L. to Martha Jane Doss 12-10-1850 (no return)
Jennings, W. C. to Amanda F. Allen 8-30-1861 (9-1-1861)
Jennings?, Jacob A. to Delila J. Haley 10-10-1862 (10-15-1862)
John, Lewis to G. N. Northcutt (6-22-1865)
Johns, Albert to Liza Stocklin 1-8-1878 (1-10-1878)
Johnson, A. R. to Milbary Pettey 2-7-1880 (2-8-1880)
Johnson, Allen to Lakey Adamson 10-13-1855 (11-18-1855)
Johnson, Andrew to Luca Cathcate 12-1-1877 (12-20-1877)
Johnson, B. L. to Sarah M. Givans 11-17-1850
Johnson, Barnibas B. to Nancy Mullin 7-8-1861 (7-9-1861)
Johnson, Carrel to Elisabeth Deems 12-16-1865 (12-17-1865)
Johnson, Carroll to Elizabeth Culwell 3-7-1874 (3-8-1874)
Johnson, Columbus to Liza Maloane 2-3-1877 (2-4-1877)
Johnson, Daniel to Sarah Shehan 1-4-1869 (1-6-1869)
Johnson, Dopson to Mary Pain 2-12-1864
Johnson, Dosson to Mary Pain 2-12-1864 (no return)
Johnson?, George to Caroline Maning 8-14-1873 [B]
Johnson, George to Mary E. Certain 10-15-1874
Johnson, Hardy to Matilda Alexander 9-11-1862 (9-12-1862)
Johnson, Henry to Malvina Pack 9-12-1871
Johnson, Hyram to Macy Ann Bullard 2-20-1868
Johnson, Isaac N. to Ellen Hunt 1-15-1873 (no return)
Johnson, Isaac to Martha H. Scott 9-18-1867 (9-19-1867)
Johnson, Isaac to Parilee Trammel 10-19-1865 (10-29-1865)
Johnson, J. C. to M. J. Keith 5-19-1877 (no return)
Johnson, J. W to S. D. Hathaway 2-12-1877
Johnson, James to Narcissa Neal 2-24-1876 (2-25-1876)
Johnson, John E. to Mary C. Lawson 3-17-1879 (3-20-1879)
Johnson, John T. to Elizabeth E. Garrison 6-20-1872 (6-30-1872)
Johnson, John to Cansady Colwell 1-28-1856 (no return)
Johnson, John to Elizabeth Dun 4-4-1857
Johnson, John to Hannah Pack 2-20-1858 (no return)
Johnson, John to Jane Merritt 12-17-1860 (12-23-1860)
Johnson, John to Mary Dobbs 3-31-1870 (4-7-1870)
Johnson, John to Sallie Melton 6-24-1872
Johnson, Jonathan to Lusinda Colwell 3-23-1854 (5-5-1854)
Johnson, Lazeris to Mary Dickson 3-13-1878 (3-16-1878)
Johnson, Levi to Mary Jane Lay 12-26-1859 (12-27-1859)
Johnson, Mathew to Visa Taylor 5-10-1854 (5-11-1854)
Johnson, Ples to Emeline Jones 11-24-1869 (11-26-1869) [B]
Johnson, Robert to Mary Ann Miller 11-24-1860 (11-25-1860)
Johnson, Robert to Sarah Bayne 9-24-1875 (9-26-1875)
Johnson, Rufus to Susanah Malone 10-16-1872 (10-20-1872)
Johnson, Thomas to Nancy Neale 8-14-1868 (no return)
Johnson, W. A. to M. E. Woolrige 8-27-1865
Johnson, W. A. to Mary McCarter 1-1-1880
Johnson, W. M. to E. J. Pickett 2-24-1865
Johnson, W. M. to Josie Avant 12-2-1878 (12-26-1878)
Johnson, W. N. to Mary Blye 12-19-1863 (no return)
Johnson, W. W. to M. L. Stocklin 12-24-1877 (12-26-1877)
Johnson, Wm. P. to Margaret Banks 8-3-1855
Johnson, Wm. to Mary Curtin 1-31-1872 (2-1-1872)
Johnston, Mathew to Sarah E. Styles 12-9-1878 (12-11-1878)
Joines, Henry to Elizabeth Young 7-13-1877 (7-15-1877)
Joines, Henry to Matilda M. Harget 6-19-1868 (no return)
Joines, Tilmon to Elizabeth Crips 10-15-1868
Joins, Henry to Mahaly Braswell 6-6-1870
Jones, A. C. to M. E. English 1-13-1868 (1-14-1868)
Jones, A. L. to Roceana Redmon 12-23-1874 (no return)
Jones, A. P. to Malisa Williams 9-28-1878 (9-29-1878)
Jones, Alfred to Elizabeth Nicles 2-16-1850 (2-24-1850)
Jones, Alfred to Julian Brand 3-18-1851 (3-20-1851)
Jones, Amasa to Sarah C. Adcock 9-12-1855
Jones, Archibald A. to Lusetta J. Wood 3-26-1850
Jones, Bird L. to Mary E. Dyer 7-24-1869 (7-29-1869)
Jones, C. T. to M. E. Jones 10-1-1875 (10-2-1875)
Jones, Columbus to Eliza Scott 6-23-1864 (no return)
Jones, Danel to Susan Fisher 12-18-1865 (12-24-1865)
Jones, George W. to Nancy Strowd 3-22-1850 (3-23-1850)
Jones, H. H. to Tennie Measle 2-9-1870 (3-10-1870)
Jones, Hezekiah to Hariet Jones 2-22-1865 (2-25-1865)
Jones, Isaac to Jane Mercer 2-14-1874 (no return)

Jones, J. C. to Jennie Cantrell 6-1-1880 (no return)
Jones, J. C. to Mollie Mergerson 12-18-1875
Jones, J. L. to Nancy J. Clemmons 10-27-1870 (10-28-1870)
Jones, J. R. to M. F. Mullican 10-28-1876 (11-1-1876)
Jones, Jackson to Dulsena Pellum 1-2-1852 (1-6-1852)
Jones, James E. to Malinda A. Wilson 8-15-1861 (no return)
Jones, James E. to Mary J. Griffeth 10-27-1866 (11-1-1866)
Jones, James R. to Marcy A. Robinson 9-28-1870
Jones, James R. to Nancy Bailiff 5-1-1855 (no return)
Jones, James to Mary F. Adcock 2-6-1875 (2-7-1875)
Jones, James to Mary P. West 12-11-1855 (12-12-1855)
Jones, James to Polly Mannan 11-20-1853
Jones, John A. to M. J. Woolridge 12-16-1871 (12-17-1871)
Jones, John M. to Anny Malone 5-4-1865 (5-7-1865)
Jones, John to Emily Reynolds 2-26-1850 (no return)
Jones, John to Harriet Foutch 12-18-1857
Jones, John to Isabel Harris 11-1-1851 (11-2-1851)
Jones, John to Winey Book 9-21-1865
Jones, Joseph to Anna Rigsby 3-18-1866 (no return)
Jones, Joseph to Mary Jane Malone 6-25-1852 (6-29-1852)
Jones, L. M. to Nancy A. Roberds 1-31-1868 (no return)
Jones, Martin to Martha Adkins 12-7-1851
Jones, Mathew to Frances P. Barnes 12-26-1853 (12-27-1853)
Jones, Matthew to Sarah Williams 2-17-1849 (no return)
Jones, Ohu to Elizabeth C. Dodd 1-5-1858 (1-7-1858)
Jones, R. F. to Eliza Whaley 3-15-1878 (3-17-1878)
Jones, S. C. to Nancy McDowell 12-29-1870 (12-30-1870)
Jones, Thomas to Frances Walker 2-17-1865
Jones, Wade to Martha Burton 1-2-1878 (1-3-1878)
Jones, Wiley to Artily Curtis 12-15-1860 (12-17-1860)
Jones, Wm. E. to Mary T. Price 10-31-1862 (11-7-1862)
Jones, Wm. V. to Nancy W. Stoner 8-29-1859
Jones, Wm. to Darthula Chapman 8-16-1860
Jones, Wm. to Eliza. Willmoth 5-31-1854 (6-1-1854)
Jones, Wm. to Winny Hicks 11-16-1864 (no return)
Jordan, John to Catharine Ferrell 9-29-1857
Judee, Zack T. to Callidoney Robinson 8-1-1872
Judkins, B. R. to Anjaline Elkins 11-3-1862 (11-4-1862)
Judkins, B. R. to Elizabeth Parker 5-12-1869
Judkins, Edmon to Rebecca T. Trapp 12-11-1868 (12-13-1868)
Judkins, Henry to Kenie Cantrel 12-21-1859 (12-30-1859)
Judkins, Wm. H. to A. H. Donnell 7-22-1865 (7-23-1865)
Julian, Dennis C. to Frances Walker 5-13-1856 (5-14-1856)
Karr?, Wm. to Mary Petty 5-21-1860
Kathcart, Henry to Martha Lack 1-17-1871 (1-18-1871)
Keaton, J. W. to L. L. Overall 8-12-1867 (no return)
Keaton, Madison to Tabitha Bracher 9-30-1858
Keaton, S. M. to Nilly E. Conner 8-6-1860 (no return)
Keaton, Wm. to Susannah Keath 9-6-1855
Keef, John F. to Martha Noakes 1-12-1876 (1-15-1876)
Keef, John to Nancy Barrette 4-30-1849 (5-1-1849)
Keel, Jermiah to Rutha Tromull 3-27-1878 (no return)
Keel, Joab to Jane Estus 12-28-1874
Keel, Wm. Thomas to Ellennora Cantrell 11-25-1871
Keele, James P. to Mary Hornes 4-3-1872
Keely, John to Rebecca Hoss 8-28-1869 (8-29-1869)
Keer, J. C. to Amandy Exum 2-3-1866 (2-5-1866)
Keeth, James to Elizabeth Connor 1-18-1872
Keeton, Cornelias to Julian Keath 8-22-1855 (8-26-1855)
Keeton, Isam to Mary Ann Adkins 7-29-1852
Keeton, Samuel M. to Nelly E. Cannon 8-6-1860 (8-7-1860)
Keeton, Thomas to Emley Garrison 4-7-1879 (4-9-1879)
Keff, Thomas to Elizabeth Estes 8-31-1855 (9-2-1855)
Kegle, Benjamin T. to Nancy Joines 9-25-1872 (10-5-1872)
Keil, John to Mary J. Young 12-23-1861 (no return)
Keith, Wm. to Eliza J. Chapman 2-18-1867 (2-20-1867)
Kelley, H. B. to Levona Clemmons 2-2-1880 (2-4-1880)
Kelley, John to Josephine Hayse 1-3-1856
Kelley, Richard to Areanah Robertson 4-29-1866 (no return) [B]
Kelly (Kerley?), Sidney to Elizabeth McInteer 9-21-1850 (9-23-1850)
Kelly, G. P. to Nancy Titsworth 2-28-1879 (3-2-1879)
Kelly, R. to A. Robertson 4-3-1866 (4-29-1866)
Kelly, Wm. J. to Louisa Hayes 5-14-1851 (5-15-1851)
Kelly, Wm. to Arcances Moss 9-7-1878
Keltey, Wm to Eliza Botts 10-19-1854

Kennedy, J. T. to M. C. West 12-28-1869 (12-29-1869)
Kennedy, J. W. to Philis? Allen 8-26-1849
Kerbey, Wm. to Mary Ann Haney 8-28-1856
Kerby, G. W. O. to Elizabeth Vanhooser 10-6-1873 (10-9-1873)
Kerby, Goolsbury to Erman Brooks 4-1-1858 (4-10-1858)
Kerby, John to Ellet Stephens 3-22-1870 (3-28-1870)
Kerklen, Joel to Martha Aldrege 3-15-1853
Kerklin, Wiley to Mary Ann Webb 6-23-1855 (6-24-1855)
Kerley, John to Elizabeth Thomas 11-14-1855
Kerly, H. G. to Elizabeth Lack 11-15-1859 (11-16-1859)
Kerr, John F. to Mary F. New 2-22-1854 (2-23-1854)
Kerr, Joseph S. to Susan F. Lawrence 12-21-1863 (12-22-1863)
Kersey, A. J. to Elizabeth Bottes 6-17-1876 (6-18-1876)
Kersey, Calvin to Adaline Staner 9-17-1862 (9-18-1862)
Kidwell, Henry H. to Elan Seay 1-6-1862 (1-12-1862)
Kidwell, James M. to July An Patton 8-14-1855 (8-16-1855)
Kife, J. B. to Samantha Fisher 12-22-1877 (12-23-1877)
Kile, W. B. to Kallie Grindstaff 12-19-1877
Killy, Harry to Elizabeth Braswell 10-9-1858 (no return)
Kimbrow, Jo. to Sarah E. Goreme 4-25-1879 (4-26-1879)
King, Jacob A. to Mary Braswell 9-19-1873
King, Spencer to Mary P. Pistole 8-29-1871
Kinnmon, Wm. to Mahala Stanley 2-19-1857
Kirby, Francis to Enicy Ferrell 1-11-1859
Kirby, Wm. C. to Susanah Hodges 10-31-1862 (9?-1-1862)
Kisshower, Harman to Samantha Petty 12-22-1869
Kitchens, James H. to Martha E. Dowell 1-30-1870 (2-2-1870)
Kithcart, George to Caroline Rich 1-27-1870
Knowles, F. P. to Oma Stout 2-7-1876
Knowles, John H. to Nancy C. Taylor 12-13-1869 (12-14-1869)
Kurr, Wm. S. to Nancy M. Carter 3-3-1871 (3-4-1871)
Kursey, Hanable to Mary Jane Youngblood 7-26-1854 (7-27-1854)
Lack, J. B. to Hannah N. Magness 4-12-1871
Lafeaver, L. D. to Marthar. Presley 1-11-1877 (1-22-1877)
Lafever, Andrew J. to Elly Ann James 12-17-1859 (12-20-1859)
Lafever, Franklin to Fanny Waren 6-17-1858 (6-20-1858)
Lafever, G. E. to Parly Carter 3-13-1877 (3-18-1877)
Lafever, Isaac to Sally L. Herrin 3-19-1861 (3-27-1861)
Lafever, Jessee F. to Catherine Becker 3-22-1860 (3-28-1860)
Lafever, John to Jeny A. James 3-16-1865
Lafever, Lee to Malinda White 2-11-1864 (no return)
Lamb, Kelly to Mary Presley 2-10-1869 (2-11-1869)
Lamberson, Dewitt C. to Matilda E. T. Preston 3-11-1851 (no return)
Lamberson, Isaac to Easter Crowder 5-24-1869 (no return)
Lamberson, James H. to Mary Bratton 9-2-1853 (9-8-1853)
Lamberson, T. J. to Delia Powell 1-28-1877 (no return)
Lamberson, Wm. R. to Amanda E. Richard 2-18-1867 (2-21-1867)
Lambertson, George W. to Dedama Bats 8-25-1866 (no return)
Lambertson, J. W. to E. W. Seay 2-1-1860
Lambrison, Richard to Tabitha Williams 4-18-1874 (no return)
Lancaster, B. F. to Josaphine Potter 3-28-1867
Lancaster, Henry to Eliza Exum 8-22-1878 (9-1-1878)
Landers, Richard W. to Texas Wright 2-6-1873 (2-9-1873)
Lane, E. E. to Ann Love 12-2-1875
Lane, Elias to Fanney P. Hall 1-3-1873 (1-5-1873)
Lane, Granville to Sarah J. Foster 1-25-1859 (1-31-1859)
Lane, John J. to Catherine Boyd 8-30-1853 (no return)
Lane, Joseph H. to Sarah J. Robinson 2-18-1863 (no return)
Lane, L. P. to Lucindy J. Fisher 10-14-1871 (10-16-1871)
Lane, Leroy A. to Frances Close 12-9-1862 (no return)
Lane, R. B. to R. Lane 5-16-1868 (no return)
Lane, Stith H. to Elizabeth Foster 11-1-1848 (11-2-1848)
Lane, Wm. A. to Roselinda Fisher 2-19-1855 (2-20-1855)
Lasater, John J. to Easter Price 9-12-1867 (9-13-1867)
Lasiter, Azariah to Rosajane? Cantrell 7-18-1866 (7-19-1866)
Lasitor, Daniel to Elizabeth Kelly 9-20-1850 (9-28-1850)
Lasitor, Daniel to Malisa J. Pike 8-11-1855 (8-12-1855)
Lasitor, David to Rebecca Ann Clouse 8-11-1854
Lassiter, E. J. to Catharine Cantrill 9-3-1874 (9-4-1874)
Laster, E. J. to R. J. Cantrell 9-25-1876
Latamore, Wm. B. to Elizabeth Nova 8-21-1856 (8-22-1856)
Lawrance, Jacob to Elizabeth Simes 11-2-1871 (no return) [B]
Lawrence, Alford to S. E. Cullard 2-18-1866
Lawrence, Harrey to Heny Edings 12-20-1876 (12-24-1876)
Lawrence, I. to C. Vantrease 10-29-1878

Lawrence, Isam to Sarah Gross 2-23-1879 (no return)
Lawrence, Jacob to Mary Lawrence 12-25-1872 (no return) [B]
Lawrence, James to Elizabeth Hellums 4-20-1870 (5-3-1870)
Lawrence, John R. to Nancy David 2-1-1862 (no return)
Lawrence, Joseph T. to Mary Ann Seay 8-28-1851 (9-2-1851)
Lawrence, Joseph T. to Mary T. Bridges 1-14-1868
Lawrence, Morgan to Narcissa C. Reynolds 11-3-1849 (11-8-1849)
Lawrence, R. A. to S. F. Alvis 10-2-1872 (10-10-1872)
Lawrence, Thomas W. to Mary Ann Page 11-8-1856 (11-13-1856)
Lawson, Eli to Margaret E. Herd 7-27-1864 (no return)
Lawson, Furstman to Cardelia Johnson 8-21-1875 (no return)
Laxiter, John to Nancy Pack 2-3-1863 (2-4-1863)
Laxitor, Levy to Mary Cantrell 11-5-1862 (11-9-1862)
Leage, James to Martha Foster 5-19-1877
League, Cain to Amanda Philips 10-6-1868 (10-?-1868)
League, Edmond to Caladonia Puckett 10-5-1857 (10-6-1857)
League, Edmond to Lucy Terry 1-8-1857
League, Frank to Violet Fazier 9-16-1867 (9-18-1867)
League, Joshua L. to Jane Pedigo 4-13-1853? (4-13-1854)
Ledford, J. B. to Victoria Jones 9-11-1877 (no return)
Lee, A. V. to Mary Terry 5-5-1859
Lee, A. W. to M. M. Perry 3-8-1876 (3-9-1876)
Lee, F. P. to V. F. Atwell 3-21-1869
Lee, James T. to Brunetta B. Ferrell 9-22-1871 (9-23-1871)
Lee, James to Louisa Hill 10-5-1857 (10-6-1858?)
Lee, Lason to Rutha Florida 12-5-1874 (12-6-1874)
Lee, P. J. to Bethena Tyson 10-17-1870 (10-19-1870)
Lee, Thomas J. M. to Sarah E. Garner 12-5-1868 (12-6-1868)
Leek, Thomas to Elizabeth Strong 6-20-1856 (6-29-1856)
Lefever, J. M. to Mary Baker 12-25-1878 (12-26-1878)
Lefever?, John W. to Louisa Love 12-30-1865 (no return)
Lever, George to Mary Ann Frazer 8-19-1850 (8-20-1850)
Lewis, G. W. to Lelia Coffee 9-1-1877 (9-3-1877)
Lewis, J. P. to Mary Smith 4-8-1863
Lewis, W. J. to Martha Clause 9-7-1853
Liden, Benjamin H. to Jane Stoner 10-22-1872
Liles, J. R. to M. Pack 2-5-1865
Liles, James H. to Ester Murphy 12-12-1861
Liles, James T. to M. B. Pack 9-21-1878 (9-23-1878)
Liles, Lewis to Mary Jane Edwards 12-1-1859 (1859?)
Liles, Samuel to Sarah A. Melton 3-16-1861 (3-17-1861)
Liles, Wm. to Nancy Brown 1-30-1859 (1-31-1859)
Limb, Yance to Malissa Sneed 4-27-1855 (ret.not exec.)
Linder, John M. to Elizabeth Cantrell 9-14-1859 (9-20-1859)
Linder, W. M. to Martha V. Thompson 1-20-1880 (no return)
Linder, Wm. to Julia Ann Cantrell 9-5-1859 (not endorsed)
Linney, J. B. to Nancy E. Hale 3-3-1874 (3-4-1874)
Lock, J. B. to Hannah Magness 4-12-1871 (no return)
Lock, Josiah L. to Sallie Potter 10-30-1873
Lockhart, Joseph to Lucy R. Hunter 3-18-1864
Lockheart, Andrew to Tassie Hall 1-17-1874 (1-18-1874)
Long, George to Cassander Adcock 1-5-1860 (not endorsed)
Looney, John C. to Nancy V. Turner 1-24-1868 (1-26-1868)
Looney, P. G. to Mary Cantrell 9-15-1869 (9-16-1869)
Looney, Samuel T. to Malissa Thurman 2-1-1872 (2-8-1872)
Louise, Solley to Helen Young 10-7-1878 (10-10-1878)
Love, F. F. to Parlee Francis Trusty 9-10-1874 (9-9-1874)
Love, F. H. to Sarah J. Robinson 1-22-1863 (no return)
Love, H. F. to Rebecca Page 10-12-1867 (10-13-1867)
Love, Hezekiah to Lucinda Johnson 10-22-1856 (10-23-1856)
Love, Hezekiah to Lucinda Johnson 10-22-1856 (no return)
Love, James to Amanda West 11-4-1856 (11-6-1856)
Love, John to Mary Mitchal 3-29-1873 (3-30-1873)
Love, Joseph H. to Elizabeth Moss 6-29-1861 (no return)
Love, Luther G. to Nancy Jane Allen 10-14-1858
Love, R. B. to Mary Rolax 3-29-1866 (3-30-1866)
Love, R. S. to Tennessee Winchester 4-27-1867 (4-28-1867)
Loving, J. M. to H. P. Martin 11-4-1876 (11-5-1876)
Lowerey, C. P. to M. A. Cantrell 1-27-1877 (1-29-1877)
Lowery, L. J. to Martha J. Love 11-1-1879 (11-2-1879)
Lowery, Philip N. to Frances R. Merett 10-2-1871 (10-8-1871)
Luble, John B. to Harriette J. Richardson 3-18-1851
Luck, Abner to Martha Jane Stanford 7-28-1854 (7-30-1854)
Luckey, Samuel to Parila Bridges 9-16-1859
Lucus, Lemuel? to Jennie Lucky 12-25-1871 (12-28-1871)

Luna?, Elisha to Rebecca J. Vaughn 8-25-1874
Luney, David W. to Martha Ann Vaughn 9-2-1852
Luny, Elisha to Ziggy Rigsby 12-10-1851 (12-11-1851)
Luny, J. M. to Loucinda Young 5-24-1877
Lynam, ----- to Alice Measles 8-21-1878 (no return)
Maddux, N. G. to M. C. Wine 2-14-1865 (no return)
Madget, D. B. to July E. Oliver 7-18-1860
Madin, John to Jain Blackburn no date (exec.9-6-1866)
Magan, Thomas to Marth Johnson 1-5-1880 (no return)
Magee, James to Mary A. Smitson 7-26-1864 (no return)
Magee, Josiah to Emaly J. Smitson 7-26-1864 (no return)
Magerson, Wm. to Nancy J. Love 5-30-1857 (5-31-1857)
Mahattin, J. H. to M. E. Pack 2-4-1865 (2-5-1865)
Mainor, John H. to Elizabeth C. Pedigo 12-21-1864 (12-25-1864)
Maloane, Yancy to M. E. Parker 12-27-1877 (12-30-1877)
Malone, Abram S. to Martha E. Williams 9-13-1873 (9-21-1873)
Malone, Dallas to Locky J. Bates 2-1-1867 (no return)
Malone, George to Malinda Maler 5-7-1866 (no return)
Malone, Hardy to Caroline Eddings 8-29-1877 (8-30-1877)
Malone, Harvey to Elizabeth Park 10-21-1875 (10-24-1875)
Malone, Henry to Caroline Jones 3-22-1849
Malone, J. to Martha Hany 1-5-1864 (1-6-1864)
Malone, Jackson to Harriet E. Christian 3-24-1858 (3-25-1858)
Malone, Jackson to Marildy J. Malone 3-17-1866 (sol. no date)
Malone, James M. to Mary Lawrence 5-3-1853
Malone, James M. to Sarah J. Hunt 9-18-1873
Malone, James to Kanzada Mires 11-15-1849 (11-18-1849)
Malone, John M. to Sarah E. Crook 8-15-1877 (8-16-1877)
Malone, John to Emaline Vantrease 1-5-1872
Malone, Mark A. to Amanda Driver 9-16-1873 (9-18-1873)
Malone, Samuel H. to Martha E. Lafever 3-15-1871 (3-16-1871)
Malone, Samuel H. to Sarah A. Johnson 10-3-1878
Malone, Samuel to Allis Goggin 10-4-1855 (no return)
Malone, Samuel to Arbell Kyle 8-9-1879 (8-17-1879)
Malone, Shane L. to Mary J. Braswell 10-4-1870 (10-9-1870)
Malone, Thomas J. to Malinda J. Chapman 10-9-1872 (no return)
Malone, Thomas to Norah Cooper 1-25-1879 (1-26-1879)
Malone, W. F. to Elizabeth White 8-22-1867 (8-25-1867)
Malone, Wm. C. to Emeline Sims 3-6-1849 (3-8-1849)
Malone, Wm. L. to Mary J. Jones 10-1-1873 (no return)
Malone, Wm. to Elizabeth Livertak? 7-14-1879 (7-20-1879)
Malone, Wm. to Elizabeth Tillmen 1-25-1867 (1-26-1867)
Malone, Y. to Permetia Crook 4-15-1879 (4-16-1879)
Malvane, T. J. to Tennessee Jacobes 7-15-1876 (7-16-1876)
Mandlebame, Hanry to Eliza F. Hayse 11-3-1858
Mandlebaum, Henry to Susan E. Tyree 10-4-1854 (10-5-1854)
Mands, Alexander to Hannah Hicks 11-3-1848 (11-5-1848)
Maner, Alexandria to Mandy Axem 3-17-1868 (3-22-1868)
Mangrum, Berry to Ruth Adkins 6-21-1860 (exec. no date)
Mangum, P. J. to Dora Pistole 2-10-1873
Manier, J. T. to Adaline Atnip 7-21-1860 (7-28-1860)
Maning, John to Tildy Ray 9-1-1869 (exec. no date)
Maning, Robert to Adelia Ledford 4-11-1868 (4-19-1868)
Maning, Wm. to Darthula Jones 2-12-1874
Manning, J. L. to Susan Rankhorn 10-4-1876 (10-5-1876)
Manning, Jasper to Parilee Biss 1-8-1870 (1-9-1870)
Manning, Thomas C. to Susan Turner 9-15-1864 (9-18-1864)
Manning, Wm. to Sarah Ann Taylor 10-9-1864 (no return)
Mansel, Buel to Elizabeth Ami Lefer no date (exec. 8-12-184
Manson, James to Betsy Ashworth 11-7-1874 (11-9-1874)
Marcrum, Wm. H. to Nancy Brewington 1-9-1852
Marcum, John to Nancy Brimm 4-20-1866 (no return)
Marimon, James to Susan Pitts 7-15-1868 (7-16-1868)
Marks, Alford to Adline Parker 8-2-1871 (8-8-1871) [B]
Marks, George to Elisabeth M. Bonds 6-17-1868 (6-18-1868)
Marks, George to Josephine D. Buckly 12-29-1870
Marks, James A. to Adah Allen 3-30-1870 (3-31-1870)
Markum, L. M. to Callie Stokes 10-23-1876 (10-26-1876)
Marler, A. J. C. to Juley A. Rowland 1-13-1873 (1-14-1873)
Marler, C. F. to Allis West 12-19-1877 (exec. no date)
Marshall, J. K. to Sarah Farrell 9-10-1872 (9-15-1872)
Marshell, James to Rebecca Goodson 6?-29-1849
Martain, Mat to Susan Auston 12-21-1878 (12-22-1878)
Martan, Rubin to Liza A. Herndon 11-18-1876
Martin, Abner to Mary C. Parker 11-27-1850 (11-28-1850)

Martin, B. A. to Martha J. Burton 4-21-1880
Martin, B. P. to R. J. Stuart 3-26-1872 (3-28-1872)
Martin, Benson? to Betty Hays 2-1-1878 (no return)
Martin, E. C. to M. R. Coggin 10-9-1879 (10-12-1879)
Martin, Friley to Martha A. Lack 1-7-1851 (1-9-1851)
Martin, George W. to Martha Talley 11-22-1873
Martin, George to Matildy E. Parker 9-22-1870 (1-3-1871)
Martin, J. P. to E. J. Reivs 5-22-1858 (5-26-1858)
Martin, James J. to Louisa Kersey 1-4-1854
Martin, James to Adeline Peples 7-25-1877
Martin, James to Nancy V. Witt 11-5-1873 (11-6-1873)
Martin, John B. to Elenor G. Pistole 3-29-1849 (4-1-1849)
Martin, John to Elizabeth Goodner 12-22-1865 (12-24-1865)
Martin, M. T. to Nancy Tree 1-20-1857 (1-28-1857)
Martin, S. B. to Florence Adcock 3-2-1874 (3-24-1874)
Martin, Sampson to Elizabeth Judkin 12-11-1873
Martin, Thomas J. to Martha Parker 1-9-1866 (1-10-1866)
Martin, Thomas to Ann Hicks 3-10-1855
Martin, Thomas to Emalin Martin 11-29-1865 (12-30-1865)
Martin, W. H. to Alice Redmon 11-19-1879 (no return)
Martin, Watson to Louisa Meggerson 2-11-1880 (2-13-1880)
Martin, Wiley to Elenor Parker 12-26-1855
Marton, H. C. to Lucy Shields 9-22-1877 (no return)
Mash, Wesly to Rachel Bracken 9-18-1851
Mason, J. F. to Sallie J. Thomkins 10-3-1870 (10-8-1870)
Mason, Levi to Sarah Joins 5-31-1869 (no return)
Mason, R. W. to Mary H. Wilson 10-24-1878
Mass, Wm. to Salley McMillin 8-2-1876 (exec. no date)
Massey, B. L. to L. E. Pickett 4-28-1871 (no return)
Mathes, John to Mary A. Turner 10-18-1878 (solmzd no date [B]
Mathes, Richard N. to Nancey Ann Vistal? 7-4-1866 (no return)
Mathis, Bluford to Kalhael Pistole 1-10-1861 (1-13-1861)
Mathis, Bluford to Mary Dirting 12-9-1870 (12-12-1870)
Mathis, Daniel to Frankey Pistol 12-10-1867
Mathis, Daniel to Mary E. Bullard 7-23-1864 (7-24-1864)
Mathis, H? N. to Annie Pistol 7-4-1866 (7-5-1866)
Maxwell, G. W. to Canzada Johnson 1-12-1876
Maxwell, James to E. J. Robinson 11-17-1864 (no return)
Maxwell, Joseph G. to Neoma E. C. Prichard 11-19-1872 (11-20-1872)
Maxwell, W. W. to N. A. Prestley 2-15-1866 (2-18-1866)
Maylone, Yance to Dorainis Washer 8-27-1866 (8-29-1866)
Maynard, George W. to Lousa Johnson 10-12-1860 (10-16-1860)
Maynard, Lewis to Sarah Herren 5-12-1856
Maynard, Micager to Martha Henley 11-15-1856
Maynard, Monroe to Sarah Smith 12-13-1871
Maynard, Noah W. to Martha Kerklin 12-4-1856
Maynard, Teral to Eliza Stover 3-6-1850 (no return)
Maynard, Thomas to Susan Johnson 9-4-1879
Maynard, Wm. to Sarah Crips 1-22-1880
Maynor, Ezekial to Angaline Burton 2-5-1865
Maynord, Gibson to Elizabeth Lockhart 12-4-1876 (11?-7-1876)
Maynord, Gibson to Elizabeth McGinis 10-11-1865
Mazab, Thomas to Bettie W. Smith 11-8-1879 (11-11-1879)
Mc----, Thomas to Bettie ----- 12-22-1879 (no return)
McAfferty, C. H. to Lucy J. Fuson 11-23-1869 (11-24-1869)
McBrian, Jesse to Susie Carter 10-15-1859 (no return)
McBride, John to Ciynthia A. Tippit 11-30-1878 (12-1-1878)
McCaffrey, James to Matildy Clayborn 6-20-1878
McCheaver, Rily to Mandy Carder 8-19-1867 (8-20-1867)
McClaine, Jackson to Adah Foutch 12-25-1873 (no return) [B]
McClellen, W. H. to M. E. Geln? 4-30-1877 (no return)
McClellon, John L. to Elizabeth Trapp 8-19-1851
McClelon, Ness to Lizzie Oakly 6-25-1866 (6-30-1866)
McClenin, Governor to Mary Brow ? (no return) [B]
McClenon, Albert to Nancy Tramel 1-26-1854
McCool, John to Pheby Panther 12-11-1849 (no return)
McCorkle, Timothy to Elizabeth Hayes 1-7-1869
McCray, George to Babe Cozzin 12-30-1878 (6?-2-1878)
McCulley, G. W. to Sitha J. E. Maxwell 6-5-1879
McDaniel, Allen F. to Mary Ann McGinness 2-11-1851
McDaniel, Wm. to Eliza Plunkett 10-31-1862 (no return)
McDonald, Jessee W. to Josephine Oakley 5-30-1872 (6-2-1872)
McDonell, Wm. to Josephine Sandin 7-25-1864 (12?-26-1864)
McDowel, Wm. to M. J. Coilly 11-10-1877 (11-11-1877)
McDowell, Thomas to Jennett Fisher 10-16-1871

McElroy, George to Elizabeth Groomes 12-22-1875 (12-23-1875)
McGann, Wm. C. to Jane Griffin 8-14-1856
McGee, G. M. to Ann C. Storm 8-1-1871
McGee, Jesse M. to Mary Rody 11-16-1864 (11-17-1864)
McGiness, Jephthah to Artemeri Page 7-13-1850 (7-14-1850)
McGinis, P. J. to Nancy E. Read 7-8-1863 (no return)
McGinis, Richard to Mary Clark 12-4-1867 (12-5-1867)
McGinness, Andrew to Biddy M. Aldrige 9-4-1852 (9-5-1852)
McGinnis, E. L. to Matilda Monard 12-3-1860 (12-5-1860)
McGinnis, Elisha L. to Martha Ann Trapp 5-7-1856
McGinnis, Elisha to Sarah Ferril 3-16-1853 (no return)
McGinniss, L. H. to Elizabeth Read 8-6-1864? (no return)
McGinniss, Larkin? to Julan Sewell 9-3-1853
McGuffin, Levi to Carolina Parkerson 7-16-1850
McGuines, J. G. to Lou Judkins 8-22-1878 (8-24-1878)
McGuinness, M. H. to Lucy Pullem 2-3-1879 (2-6-1879)
McGuire, Haris to M. A. Smith 10-9-1869 (10-10-1869)
McHord, John F. to Louizey E. Coggin 1-13-1874 (1-20-1874)
McInteer, G. C. to Elizabeth Snow 11-3-1849 (11-4-1849)
McIntire, James G. to Rebecca Williams 9-21-1862
McIntire, James T. to Carline A. Hill 2-10-1864 (2-11-1864)
McLellin, Nep to Jane Garner 3-8-1875 (3-11-1875)
McMillan, James to Lettie B. Davise 12-21-1878 (12-22-1878)
McMillon, James to Harriet Measles 12-10-1851
McNamer, M. H. to Martha Fite 3-31-1870
McNelly, George D. to Sallie Stokes 12-23-1872 (12-24-1872)
Meadly, Owen to Illinois Austin 12-17-1872 (12-18-1872)
Meador, John W. to Harriette Rigsby 7-15-1878 (7-18-1878)
Meaks, Richard? to Martha A. Mason 8-15-1860
Mears, G. M. to S. M. Banks 8-29-1877 (no return)
Measle, J. S. to Angie Giveon 11-6-1878 (no return)
Measles, George to Elizabeth Grindstaff 11-27-1865 (11-29-1865)
Measles, Wm. to Nancy Truette 10-2-1858 (exec. no date)
Medley, W. R. to Mary E. Petigo 3-3-1879 (solmzd no date)
Medley, Wm. to Mary Clemmons 10-19-1876 (10-20-1876)
Medlin, Almon R. to Elizabeth Childers 1-2-1851 (1-7-1851)
Medlin, Wm. to S. L. Bozarth 10-25-1875 (11-3-1875)
Meggerson, John S. to Oma Leaguel 1-12-1876 (1-17-1876)
Megginson, John to Elizabeth Looney 3-31-1854 (4-2-1854)
Mellin, Samuel M. to Rebeca Francis 5-16-1861 (no return)
Melton, James W. to Martha Ann Cantrell 3-20-1851
Melton, Robert W. to Sarah E. Ferrel 10-3-1853 (10-6-1853)
Merett, Wm. to Manda Taylor 3-13-1867
Merfey, James to Parilee Thompson 11-26-1865 (no return)
Meritt, Albert V. to Helan C. Smith 6-22-1863 (no return)
Meritt, Benjamin M. to Elizabeth Foster 12-17-1868 (no return)
Merrett, B. M. to Margaret O. Terry 4-18-1870 (4-21-1870)
Merrett, Benjamin to Margaret Fuson 7-13-1854
Merrette, James R. to Frances R. Wood 3-6-1850
Merrit, Hansford to Mariah Clarke 1-3-1857 (1-4-1857)
Merrit, Wm. to Sarah F. Johnson 10-6-1860 (10-11-1860)
Midget, Daniel to E. J. Denny 11-25-1867 (11-27-1867)
Miget, Bence to Zade Yergan 1-15-1880
Migginson, Wade H. to Mary Ann League 4-7-1849 (4-12-1849)
Millar, George to Julia Phillips 11-10-1877 (no return)
Miller, Alexander to Reney Page 8-5-1879
Miller, Dennis to Ann Stokes 7-15-1868 (no return) [B]
Miller, John W. to Malinda H. Foster 12-31-1858 (1-2-1859)
Miller, John to C. E. Johnson 10-9-1869 (10-12-1869)
Miller, Robert to Fannie Wooldrage 9-6-1859 (?-7-1859)
Miller, Thomas P. A. to Matildy A. Johnson 1-23-1872 (1-24-1872)
Milligan, Alexander to Parilla Braswell 8-2-1860
Mills, J. L. to Susan Anna Mills 9-16-1875
Millstead, John to Jane Rich 4-18-1871
Mingle, Mikael to Sarena Bratton 1-14-1860 (1-18-1860)
Minor, Jackson to Mary Jane Coble 12-17-1850 (12-18-1850)
Minton, John H. to Eliza A. McDaniel 12-25-1864 (no return)
Mitchel, J. B. to M. A. Caleps 9-11-1877 (9-13-1877)
Mitchel, Wesly to Jane Cooper 2-13-1879 (solmzd no date
Mitchell, Charles T. to Martha J. Moss 2-6-1861 (2-11-1861)
Mitchell, George to Liddy Stoner 10-21-1872 (10-22-1872)
Mitchell, T. J. to Frances M. Presley 9-28-1857 (9-29-1857)
Molone, David to Maggie Robinson 3-25-1873 (3-27-1873)
Montgomery, R. J. to Amanda Warren 12-5-1877 (no return)
Moon, James E. to Nancy Walker 12-22-1864

Moon, Wm. to Elizabeth Staly 1-21-1874 (1-22-1874) [B]
Moore, Archibald to Hixa Grayham no date (exec. 5-22-186
Moore, Frank S. to Dave C. Sellars 7-4-1874 (7-5-1874) [B]
Moore, Frank to Hester Wilson 1-11-1876 (1-13-1876)
Moore, H. L. C. to Nancy Cantrell 3-30-1867 (3-31-1867)
Moore, Henry to Ader Hariss 2-27-1878 (2-28-1878)
Moore, J. D. to Susan Farmer 4-21-1876 (4-23-1876)
Moore, James M. to Barby Cantrell 10-16-1856 (no return)
Moore, James T. to Mary E. Pertle 12-11-1858 (12-12-1858)
Moore, John to Mary J. Allen 9-18-1866 (9-12?-1866)
Moore, L. D. to Adline Dodd 10-26-1870 (10-27-1870)
Moore, L. F. to Thursey Wilson 1-4-1864 (no return)
Moore, L. T. to Elisabeth Norton 7-10-1868 (7-12-1868)
Moore, Thomas to Sarah Cantrell 7-10-1879 (no return)
Moore, Walker to Mary Cantrell 1-21-1871 (1-22-1871)
Moore, Washington to Volka? Staley 9-18-1870
Moore, Wm. L. to Mary P. Close 10-12-1878 (10-14-1878)
Moores, E. N. to Milley Lowery 11-29-1871 (11-30-1871)
Moores, J. E. to Sarah Venon 3-8-1873 (3-9-1873)
Moores, James A. to Amanda Parsley 1-1-1867
Moores, Wm. T. to July E. Woods 10-21-1871 (10-24-1871)
Morgan, Milton to Eliza Gilbert 3-19-1867
Morgan, Wm. to Mary Driver 5-13-1875
Moris, George T. to Edney Tittle 3-26-1869 (3-28-1869)
Moris, James H. to Tennessee Hap? 9-12-1865 (no return)
Moris, W. A. to Margret Tramell 7-21-1871 (7-22-1871)
Morris, James to Malejing? Parsons 9-26-1870
Mosier, D. P. to L. E. Snow 2-14-1880 (2-15-1880)
Mosier, H. S. to R. J. Vickars 1-7-1878 (1-10-1878)
Moss, G. W. to Josie Griffith 10-22-1879
Moss, H. A. to S. J. Ferrill 3-28-1873 (3-30-1873)
Moss, J. B. to Sarah F. Mitchel 1-3-1879 (1-5-1879)
Moss, John to Jane Massie 6-11-1851 (no return)
Moss, John to R. J. Close 12-31-1868
Moss, Joseph to Luella Exum 1-5-1872 (1-7-1872)
Moss, Wm. A. to N. C. Pressley 9-3-1872 (9-10-1872)
Moss, Wm. B. to Mary J. McCray 8-1-1870 (8-15-1870)
Mulican, A. C. to M. E. Cantrell 12-15-1877 (12-16-1877)
Mullica, James L. to S. Allen 4-28-1858 (4-29-1858)
Mullican, Greenberry to Amanda C. Ferrell 10-5-1869 (10-7-1869)
Mullican, J. J. to Rebecca F. Allen 2-18-1875 (no return)
Mullican, James L. to Sarah C. Taylor 10-7-1857 (no return)
Mullican, James to Katy Forester 4-27-1865 (5-3-1865)
Mullican, N. to Mary Wats 4-12-1856 (4-13-1856)
Mullican, Ninavey to Cindy Atnip 7-6-1854
Mullican, Wm. J. to Elizabeth Roberts 9-2-1862 (9-11-1862)
Mullicen, Wm. C. to Margrett N. Stiles 3-12-1872 (3-14-1872)
Mullinax, Benjamin to Malissa Goodner 3-5-1873 (3-6-1873)
Mullins, James to Allis Wright 12-31-1855 (1-2-1856)
Mullins, John to Nancy Sheahon 9-23-1853 (9-25-1853)
Murdock, D. P. to Mary Keerald 1-30-1880 (2-1-1880)
Murdock, G. H. to Elisa Harvel 3-10-1870
Murdock, George H. to Silvey J. Pressley 9-12-1872
Murfey, Wm. C. to Parilee Viers 11-1-1864 (11-2-1864)
Murphey, John to Martha McIntire 1-4-1873 (1-5-1873)
Murphy, Isaac N. to Elizabeth Scurlock 9-11-1857 (9-12-1857)
Murphy, James to Lucy¹ Hathaway 9-13-1875
Murphy, John M. to Elizabeth Harnould 10-29-1873 (10-30-1873)
Murry, Isaac to Martha Joines 5-13-1869 (5-15-1869)
Myers, A. R. to Mary Williams 5-1-1880 (5-2-1880)
Naill?, J. W. to N. E. Williams 8-10-1876
Neal, Elijah to Lucinda T. Chapman 9-16-1870 (9-18-1870)
Neal, George to Mary Braswell 6-28-1861 (6-31-1861)
Neal, James to Mary T. Hale 1-9-1879
Neal, Layfayette to Nancy Young 2-24-1876
Neal, Levi to Rody Frances Chapman 8-28-1867
Neal, Luke W. to Parile Bennett 4-3-1861 (exec. no date)
Neal, Samuel to Manervy Jackson 4-11-1866 (no return)
Neal, U. M. to Martha West 12-17-1879 (no return)
Neal, W. H. to Mary A. Foutch 6-15-1877 (6-17-1877)
Neale, David to Susan F. Arnold 4-12-1873 (4-13-1873)
Neale, Henry to May Pack 11-26-1872 (11-28-1872)
Neale, Hyram to Elizabeth Whaley 2-5-1866 (2-15-1866)
Neale, Jacob to Callie Baker 2-21-1874 (2-22-1874) [B]
Neale, James to Lectes Vantreace 2-21-1875 (2-22-1875)

Neale, Joshua G. to Mariah E. Johnson 2-9-1874 (2-12-1874)
Neale, Luke to Mary J. Hicks 6-24-1871 (6-25-1871)
Neale, W. to M. J. Vantreace 8-3-1871 (8-6-1871)
Neasmith, James A. to Elizabeth J. Miller 1-8-1868
Neel, Amous to Susan Allen 6-2-1858 (6-3-1858)
Neel, C. M. to P. E. Waller 7-24-1878 (no return)
Neel, Charles to Etily Simeril 2-10-1857 (2-12-1857)
Neel, John to Elizabeth Adkins 6-19-1879
Neel, Joshua to Rachel Printes 10-12-1854 (10-13-1854)
Neel, Luke to Matilda Moore 2-23-1859 (2-24-1859)
Neel, Monro to Madcid Kiel 2-15-1878 (2-20-1878)
Neel, Samuel to Margart Frazor 10-11-1850 (10-12-1850)
Neel, Wm. to Matilda Chapman 10-29-1858 (10-31-1858)
Neele, Alexander to Mary Taylor 9-28-1848 (10-8-1848)
Neele, Joshaway to Sarah Taylor 8-6-1877 (no return)
Neell, George W. to Tulina O. Mitchel 5-29-1858 (no return)
Neely, E. to Haseltine Fisher 11-10-1879 (11-20-1879)
Neet, Francis to Elicetta Johnson 4-2-1875 (4-4-1875)
Nelson, Ira to Mary Watson 8-28-1854
Nelson, John A. J. to Ann C. Adamson 12-24-1854 (endrsd.no prop)
Nelson, John A. J. to Sarah Kisey 8-5-1857 (8-6-1857)
Nesmeth, James A. to H. A. McLellan 11-9-1858 (12-23-1858)
Nesmith, R. W. to Thena Foutch 12-18-1869 (12-26-1869)
Nesmith, Wm. to Nancy C. Self 1-7-1865 (1-8-1865)
New, John to Emenley Cogins 6-3-1866 (no return)
Newbey, W. B. to Charlotty Stokes? 12-21-1866
Newby, Robert to Margaret Allen 5-24-1879 (5-25-1879)
Newman, J. R. to R? Neele 1-27-1863 (1-29-1863)
Newsom, H. R. H. to Candis Sandlin 8-23-1862 (no return)
Newsom, James R. to Mary A. Bailiff no date (exec.2-16-1854
Nichouls, B. B. to Margaret Allen 8-25-1866
Nickson, James to Lowezia Johnson 4-9-1877 (4-19-1877)
Nickson, Levy to Anerilas Self 4-19-1875 (4-22-1875)
Nix, S. T. to Lavina Dodson 7-17-1860
Nixon, J. A. to Sarah E. Pitman 3-17-1876 (3-19-1876)
Nixon, John J. to Mary Starnes 5-15-1879 (5-16-1879)
Nixon, Levy to Elizabeth League 3-21-1878 (3-24-1878)
Nixon, Thomas to Anna E. Malone 1-12-1875 (1-14-1875)
Nixon, Wm. to Achsah Winfree 11-3-1851 (11-6-1851)
Noaks, Wm. H. to Charlotte J. Adamson 8-26-1861 (8-27-1861)
Nolner, F. B. to Martha Doak 9-22-1875 (9-23-1875)
Nolner, F. B. to Mary E. Prichard 2-23-1859 (2-24-1859)
Norice, John G. to Sarah Wallen 1-2-1850
Noris, Bethel to Sarah Fuson 10-19-1852
Norman, Ed to Alice Whitlock 3-29-1879
Norten, Alexander to Mary E. Parkerson 4-25-1874 (no return)
Northcut, E. R. to Sarrah Sepha Evans 2-18-1867 (no return)
Northcut, Milus to Betty Smith 6-27-1878
Northrell, G. N. to L. M. Adcock 6-28-1865 (no return)
Norton, George W. to Sarah Braswell 8-12-1869
Null, George W. to Mary Anis Winchester 10-1-1862 (10-2-1862)
Nunley, Joseph to Martha Angleman 3-18-1872 (3-19-1872)
Nunley, Wm. to Hattie Gilbey? 1-19-1878
Nunnelly, Leroy to Harriett M. Fultz 4-24-1876
O'Conner, Torrence to Jane Adamson 8-2-1873 (8-3-1873)
Oakes, James to Jane Cantrell 3-23-1850 (3-24-1850)
Oakley, Dawson to Laura Lawrence 12-8-1872 (12-6?-1872)
Oakley, Eligiah to Matildy Plumlee 12-11-1872 [B]
Oakley, John to Martha J. Baits 9-7-1867 (no return)
Oakley, Joseph to Mary J. Pain 9-13-1865 (9-16-1865)
Oakley, Thomas D. to Eady Jones 1-4-1866
Oakley, W. C. to A. P. Wright 10-9-1875 (10-12-1875)
Oakley, Wm. to Jane Migget 12-2-1869 (12-3-1869)
Odem, Wm. to Charlott B. Magness 10-3-1854
Officer, George to Em Johnson 3-19-1866 (7-14-1866) [B]
Officer, Martin to Martha Bess 8-13-1870 (no return) [B]
Officer, Richard to Clarsey Turner 2-1-1870 (2-3-1870)
Olovers, Matthew S. to Martha M. Batton 8-17-1849 (exec. no date)
Oneal, Wm. to Sarah Claborn 7-2-1867 (7-3-1867)
Orsben, Benjamin to Kiah Worley 5-25-1852 (5-27-1852)
Orton, Richard to Mary Hughes 6-11-1880 (6-13-1880)
Osburn, S. A. to Susan J. Thompson 3-12-1879 (3-13-1879)
Oston, John to Eliza Medley 2-1-1875 (2-4-1875)
Overall, H. A. to Bellsora Hobbs 10-7-1878 (10-8-1878)
Overall, J. H. to Kenie Turner 2-15-1870 (2-16-1870)

Overall, John C. to Nancy T. Adams 1-11-1868 (1-23-1868)
Overall, Mitchael to Mandy Williams 3-17-1866 (3-18-1866)
Overall, Wm. P. to Elizabeth C. White 7-31-1856
Owen, James D. to S. C. Adams 1-14-1880 (2-15-1880)
Owen, Jasper to Nancy E. Goggin 11-1-1864 (11-3-1864)
Owen, Joseph S. to E. C. Anderson 9-10-1870 (9-11-1870)
Owen, Judy to Evaline Plenner 6-20-1874 (6-21-1874) [B]
Owens, David to Jennie Britton 11-28-1879 (no return)
Owens, Jackson to Vina Smith 12-26-1877 (12-28-1877)
Owens, John to Ann Sims 4-11-1870 (4-14-1870)
Ownes, James to Parlee Anderson 8-26-1873
Ownes, James to Tennessee Overall 12-28-1875 (12-30-1875)
Pace, William to Nancy Norton 7-21-1865 (no return)
Pack, Archibald to Elizabeth Colwell 9-5-1860
Pack, Bartemius to Elizabeth Pack 10-27-1871
Pack, Bartemus to Charity Colwell 9-24-1859 (9-25-1859)
Pack, Bartimas Hays to Melvina Mulican 3-30-1867 (3-31-1867)
Pack, Esau to Elizabeth Johnson 6-23-1855 (6-25-1855)
Pack, Jacob to Elizabeth Laseter 11-5-1862
Pack, Jacob to Rosannah Bowers 1-27-1850
Pack, James C. to Tennessee Worley 5-11-1876 (5-16-1876)
Pack, James Munroe to Mary J. Liles 11-4-1867
Pack, John S. to Margaret Pack 2-14-1859
Pack, John to Elizabeth Pack 12-31-1858 (1-3-1859)
Pack, John to Emaline Pack 11-14-1867
Pack, John to Norcissa Bane 1-29-1853 (1-30-1853)
Pack, Joseph M. to Amanda Smith 6-27-1868 (6-28-1868)
Pack, Joseph to Ana Rush 11-30-1865 (no return)
Pack, Joseph to Margrett Johnson 1-11-1871
Pack, Joseph to Nancy Henly 8-7-1874 (8-9-1874)
Pack, Joseph to Uphema Edwards 11-21-1855 (11-22-1855)
Pack, M.H. to Martha Frazier 4-6-1871
Pack, Moses to Nancy Ann Bane 1-25-1860 (1-29-1860)
Pack, P. C. to Parthena F. Pack 3-7-1877 (3-8-1877)
Pack, Partemas to Elvira P. Melton 3-19-1860
Pack, Thos. to Martha C. Patterson 10-23-1862 (10-25-1862)
Pack, William C. to Mary E. Hickison 2-20-1875
Pack, William M. to Sarah Cantrell 12-9-1867
Pack, Wm. to Elizabeth Ingram 1-3-1865
Pack, Wm. to Parelee Frazier 7-7-1875 (7-11-1875)
Page, Allen to Lucinda C. Hayse 3-27-1850 (3-28-1850)
Page, Arwine to Amanda A. Trapp 2-23-1857 (2-3?-1857)
Page, B. B. to Hanah Walker 7-5-1879 (7-8-1879)
Page, Barnabas R. to Eliza J. Walls 3-11-1870 (3-12-1870)
Page, Barney to S. A. H. Page 5-19-1868 (5-20-1868)
Page, Hugh to Gemima Atnip 2-3-1863
Page, J. J. to S. E. Lee 10-4-1876
Page, James M. to Harriett Drurey 1-28-1873 (2-6-1873)
Page, James M. to Malinda Arnell 5-19-1880 (5-20-1880)
Page, John J. to Malindy Hornel 1-27-1872 (1-28-1872)
Page, Nelson to Amandy E. Allen 12-16-1873 (12-18-1873) [B]
Page, R. L. to M. L. Mulican 7-24-1876 (7-26-1876)
Page, Seburn to Louisa Trammell 5-11-1850 (5-12-1850)
Page, T. J. to Tennie Drewry 7-17-1879
Page, Thomas to Emaline Rankhorn 8-20-1873 (8-29-1873)
Pain, David to Elizabeth Pitmon 7-14-1875 (7-18-1875)
Pain, Mason to Samantha Tayson? 8-11-1875 (8-12-1875)
Pain, Rufus to Jane Baty 10-3-1874
Pain, Wm. to Betsey Putman 5-8-1877
Paisley, Owen to Darcas William 3-7-1861
Paity, J. M. to Vina Braswell 9-25-1875
Palinor, John to Elizabeth Leay 11-2-1853 (11-4-1853)
Palmer, George to Angeline Heren 6-8-1870 (6-9-1870)
Palmer, James S. to Manerva E. Dyer 9-5-1859 (9-15-1859)
Palmer, William S. to Martha E. Jones 1-10-1859 (no return)
Parcly, Thomas to Calley Foster 6-24-1876 (no return)
Parcly, W. J. to M. F. Pedago 9-28-1876 (9-1?-1876)
Parker, A. C. to Sarah J. Rich 10-24-1879 (10-26-1879)
Parker, A. M. to M. J. Hayse 10-3-1874 (10-31-1874)
Parker, C. N. to Emmis Ceton 2-28-1878
Parker, D. A. to Elizabeth Been 11-30-1871 (12-1-1871)
Parker, D. A. to Ollivia Dukes 7-29-1874 (7-31-1874)
Parker, Freling W. to Martha Dabbs 12-18-1855 (12-20-1855)
Parker, Isaac to Martha J. Taylor 9-18-1878 (9-19-1878)
Parker, James to Catharine Burton 1-2-1852 (1-4-1852)

Parker, James to Catherine Grindstaff 7-7-1877
Parker, John B. to Elizabeth Driver 9-22-1857 (9-30-1857)
Parker, John M. to Susan F. Chapman? 8-8-1872
Parker, John to Caroline Dodd 4-6-1863
Parker, John to Mesane Scott 3-17-1875 (3-18-1875)
Parker, Napoleon to Anny Adcock 11-17-1856 (no return)
Parker, Napoleon to Mary Kerby 1-6-1849 (1-7-1849)
Parker, Nathaniel to Hellen Smith 7-2-1873 (7-5-1873)
Parker, S. B. to C. E. Dodd 2-14-1870 (2-16-1870)
Parker, Thomas to Mathe Hall 8-13-1879 (8-15-1879)
Parker, Thomas to Mattie Hall 8-13-1879 (8-15-1879)
Parker, William to Mary J. Cantrell 4-4-1874 (4-5-1874)
Parker, Wm. J. to M. L. Vandegriff 3-21-1876 (3-23-1876)
Parker, Wm. to Milley Hayes 11-3-1871 (11-5-1871)
Parker, Zackariah to Martha J. Vantrease 3-7-1870 (3-10-1870)
Parkerson, Francis M. to Elizabeth Stanford 7-19-1852 (no return)
Parkerson, J. H. P. to Lucinda T. Bennett 11-2-1872 (11-3-1872)
Parkerson, John to Nancy Bennett 9-7-1857 (9-8-1857)
Parkerson, Levi to Mary Griffith 6-29-1872 (6-30-1872)
Parrish, Calvin to Elizabeth Potter 7-14-1860 (7-16-1860)
Parrish, F. P. to Callidonia Rigsby 7-10-1874 (7-15-1874)
Parrish, W. R. to Smith Readman 8-27-1864 (8-31-1864)
Parsley, Alexander to Betty Fucell 9-29-1871 (10-1-1871)
Parsley, Ammon to Mary Jane Spurlock 9-7-1854
Parsley, B. J. to Mary Ann Lefever 11-16-1854
Parsley, George to Martha Vickers 1-4-1879 (1-5-1879)
Parsley, John to Samantha T. Mullican 4-9-1872 (4-11-1872)
Parsley, Jud S. to Talitha Lefever 4-18-1854 (4-19-1854)
Parsley, Richard to Elender C. Nicholas 10-23-1854
Parsley, W. J. to Sarah Davis 2-27-1860
Parsly, J. A. to Mary McClenen 1-23-1879
Parsly, J. W. to M. A. James 8-16-1879 (8-21-1879)
Parson, S. J. to Mary Jones 7-5-1875 (7-8-1875)
Parsons, James to Matilda Pack 12-21-1855
Patten, Johnathan to Serah E. Griffith 10-27-1866 (11-1-1866)
Patterson, A. W. to Priscilla Braswell 2-2-1864 (no return)
Patterson, E. W. to C. A. Laster 10-20-1876 (10-22-1876)
Patterson, F. N. to M. A. Lee 5-10-1866 (no return)
Patterson, Harvey to America Hicks 12-21-1853 (12-22-1853)
Patterson, Mathew to Molly Pattager? 2-3-1873 (2-6-1873)
Patton, John A. to Amanda Davis 12-24-1856 (12-?-1856)
Patton, Joseph L. to Nancy T. B. Foster 9-29-1865 (no return)
Patty, N. J. to Martha J. Arnold 12-12-1862 (no return)
Patty, William Smith to Eliza Ann Sneed 11-26-1850 (11-28-1850)
Paul, Richard to Mary Turner 4-26-1873 (4-27-1873) [B]
Payne, James to Elizabeth Hunt 1-28-1851 (1-29-1851)
Payne, Manson to Mary Parkerson 8-20-1879 (8-21-1879)
Payne, W. J. to Felby Williams 5-10-1873 (5-11-1873)
Peak, Porter to Perelee Trammell 7-17-1878 (7-18-1878)
Peckette, Joshua W. to Masey Yeargan 3-7-1849
Pedigo, Alexander to Sarah Lafever 4-14-1869 (4-15-1869)
Pedigo, G. B. to Virginia Foster 12-9-1868
Pedigo, Green B. to Ann Maginis 1-14-1858
Pedigo, J. J. (G?) to Susan Trpp? 8-25-1859
Pedigo, Richard to Eliza Buckner 11-3-1869 (12-4-1869)
Pedigoe, Robert to Jane Lefever 3-26-1857
Pedigoe, W. H. to Amanda Lefever 10-30-1867 (10-31-1867)
Pendleton, James to Elizabeth Johnson 2-7-1880 (4-21-1880)
Penegar, Davis to Oma C. Adcock 10-21-1866
Pepkin, Joseph J. to Nancy C. Hayse 3-14-1849 (3-15-1849)
Perkey, Oval to Maggie E. Williams 11-1-1859 (11-3-1859)
Perryman, James S. to Nancy E. Starke 3-1-1870
Person, Robert to Elizabeth Pack 5-25-1855
Pertle, Edward to Rachel Young 4-2-1851
Petress, Rufus to Sarah J. Petress 6-17-1874 (6-18-1874)
Pettey, John P. to Easter H. Cutler 11-20-1872 (11-21-1872)
Pettey, Samuel to Jane Young 7-19-1879 (7-20-1879)
Pettigo, Harvey to Helen Megerson 11-9-1878 (11-10-1878)
Pettigo, Jack to Sarah Hooper 3-22-1879 (3-23-1879)
Petty, Winship to Charloty Green 2-12-1863
Petty, Woodson to Sarah Wouldridge 11-4-1870 (11-7-1870)
Pew, Jackson to Nancy C. Dood 1-8-1865
Pew, William J. to Elizabeth Dale 11-12-1866 (11-13-1866)
Pharmer, John H. to Louisa Agee 3-5-1856 (4-15-1856)
Pheahane?, J. T. to N. B. Paddy 9-11-1878 (9-12-1878)

Philips, Andrew to Harait Stokes 12-7-1870 (no return) [B]
Philips, Elick to Jenny Doss 1-5-1872 (no return) [B]
Philips, J. D. to M. E. Johnson 11-25-1868 (11-26-1868)
Philips, J. D. to M. F. Hooper 10-14-1865 (10-22-1865)
Philips, Wm. R. to Rebecca Lockhart 2-8-1852
Philips, Wm. to Elizabeth Bass 11-9-1862
Phillipes, Wm. to Salley Kagle 5-7-1878
Phillips, A. T. to Emma V. Allen 12-4-1866
Phillips, Rubin to Fannie Sneed 11-20-1878 (11-21-1878)
Phillips, Wm. B. to Martha J. Loona 10-29-1872
Picket, James to Mary P. Wright 8-18-1853 (exec. no date)
Picket, Joshua W. to Jenymae? Allen 4-6-1858
Pickett, G. W. to Mary A. Benton 8-12-1873 (8-14-1873)
Pickett, Hezakiah to Mary Lochart 10-6-1874 (10-11-1874)
Pickett, Wm. P. to Ele Goodin 10-19-1866 (no return)
Pillips?, M. M. to S. F. Magnes 11-18-1876 (11-21-1876)
Pinager, Wm. to Mary S. Neal 6-25-1869
Pinegar, Isaac to Sarah Pinegar 7-3-1879
Pinegar, John to C. L. Turner 9-6-1879 (no return)
Pinegar, John to Mary Jane Turner 9-19-1864 (9-22-1864)
Pinegar, Levi to Mary E. Turner 1-9-1871 (1-10-1871)
Pinegar, Levy to Mary J. Turner 8-19-1873
Pinegar, Mathias T. to Mary T. Dunham 2-11-1873 (2-16-1873)
Pineger, C. G. to Martha Petty 9-4-1876 (9-6-1876)
Pipkin, Henry to Matilda Ann Bains 9-10-1851 (no return)
Pipkin, Joseph to Melvina Keaton 7-5-1877
Pipkins, Thomas to Mary Bennett 4-3-1876 (4-5-1876)
Pirtle, J. M. to Asenith Driver 4-11-1873 (4-13-1873)
Pirtle, John L. to Susan Jane Young 3-8-1860 (not endorsed)
Pistole, H. H. to Mahala Lee 8-31-1861
Pistole, J. P. to Mary Rhody 1-18-1870 (1-19-1870)
Pistole, James M. to Mary P. Strong 10-30-1850
Pistole, John to Jane Keath 3-19-1851
Pistole, Joseph to Elisa Adamson 8-7-1868 (no return)
Pitly, Alexander to Charlotta Gothard 8-23-1861 (8-24-1861)
Pitman, James to Rutha Turner 10-12-1869 (10-13-1869)
Pitman, John H. to Sarah F. Webster 8-5-1872
Pitman, Wm. B. to Elizabeth Lawrance 5-17-1873 (exec. no date)
Pittman, David to Mary D. T. Adcock 12-21-1859 (12-22-1859)
Pitts, James to Sariah An Hall 1-20-1859
Pitts, John W. to Cynthia A. Sneed 8-14-1850
Pitts, John to Sarah Hicks 1-6-1878
Pleantice, A. to L. V. Elkins 11-26-1864 (no return)
Pledger, Philip to Mandy Floyed 2-25-1868 (3-1-1868)
Pledger, Phillip J. to Rinda Neasret? 12-27-1876
Pledger, Stephen to S. A. Dinwiddy ?-30-1866 (8-2-1866)
Pollard, Edward to America Titsworth 11-2-1868
Pollard, Wm. to Nancy Cantrell 8-25-1849 (no return)
Poller, Wm. A. to Nancy Cantrell 7-24-1852 (7-27-1852)
Ponder, R. H. to Nancy Young 8-21-1867 (8-22-1867)
Ponder, W. J. to Tennessee Sandlin 4-29-1876
Pope, James K. to Lusinda Hathaway 9-1-1855 (9-2-1855)
Pope, Wm. to A. P. Page 9-13-1877 (no return)
Porter, Albert to Julia Crepps 5-12-1866 (5-17-1866) [B]
Potter, A. J. to A. A. Youngblood 1-16-1860 (1-17-1860)
Potter, D. W. to Haraett Parsley 4-5-1869
Potter, E. W. to Molly Fisher 2-13-1869 (2-16-1869)
Potter, F. P. to Fimantis? T. West 12-6-1865
Potter, L. J. to M. E. Whaley 1-4-1877
Potter, L. W. to Mattie Potter 9-29-1870 (9-30-1870)
Potter, O. D. to S. Cantrell 1-7-1860 (1-9-1860)
Potter, W. C. to M. H. Avant 11-10-1869
Powel, James to Batheana Camden no date (exec. 4-22-182
Powel, P. L. to Martha Jane Stokes 6-22-1859 (no return)
Powel, Thomas to Elisabeth Jones 8-16-1867 (8-18-1867)
Pratt, Z. B. to Elizabeth Cheatham 10-11-1860
Presley, B. H. to E. J. Prichard 8-30-1866 (no return)
Presley, John to Nancey Roberts 10-10-1866 (no return)
Presley, R. V. to Louisa Petty 10-4-1876 (exec. no date)
Presley, W. C. to Eliza Rich 12-4-1879
Presly, J. J. to N. M. Robert 7-5-1867 (no return)
Pressly, A. M. to Mary L. Ferrell 10-4-1869 (10-6-1869)
Pressly, B. H. to E. H. Waldon 2-11-1867 (no return)
Preston, A. M. to Mary Ann Brady 9-19-1869 (no return)
Preston, Charles to Elizia Green 9-4-1870 (no return) [B]

Preston, Lucian to Polley Gowans 2-17-1869 (2-19-1869) [B]
Preston, S. to M. Burk Cotton 12-25-1866 (no return)
Preston, Simo to Adline Moore 11-10-1870 (no return) [B]
Preston, Wm. B. to Tennessee Givin 11-9-1861 (12-1-1861)
Preston, Wm. to Jane Neel 11-15-1854 (11-14?-1854)
Price, Spencer to Torry A. Malone 4-19-1879 [B]
Prichard, Alex to Rachel Marshel 12-25-1868 (12-27-1868)
Prichard, Benjamin to Jane F. Robinson 4-21-1856 (4-22-1856)
Prichard, Christopher C. to Mary A. Hunt 9-12-1872
Prichard, Sidney to Martha Robinson 11-7-1870 (11-10-1870)
Prichard, W. D. to Manervy A. Robinson 12-23-1867 (1-9-1868)
Prichard, Zachariah to M. J. Guarner 11-9-1870 (11-10-1870)
Prichird, James to Martha Wallace 9-21-1870 (9-22-1870)
Pridy, Thomas to Talitha Davis 12-25-1848 (no return)
Prim, Gorge H. to Sarah Johnson 12-26-1850 (12-26-1850)
Pritchet, George to Saphronia Fite 1-23-1861 (exec. no return)
Puck, J. M. to C. C. Edwards 2-29-1872
Puckett, Henry L. to Sarah A. Brown 3-9-1874 (3-12-1874)
Puckett, J. Sylvanus to Susan E. Carter 5-10-1861 (5-16-1861)
Puckett, Sylvanus to Mary F. Carter 2-14-1874 (2-16-1874)
Puckette, Wm. to Elizabeth Shaw 10-14-1876 (10-15-1876)
Pullen, Charles to Louisa Ann Coggin 12-13-1858
Purser, George to Mary Ferrel 8-7-1866 (no return)
Pursley, Travis to Martha Pedigo 11-24-1857 (12-5-1857)
Purtle, Washington to Susan Baker 9-17-1856
Quarles, J. T. to C. D. Doss 8-14-1857 (no return)
Quarles, James T. to Darthuly F. Doss 10-2-1860 (not endorsed)
Quillin, Danial to Palmetia Lack 11-30-1872 (12-8-1872)
Rackley, Ruffin to Elizabeth Farel 2-28-1862 (no return)
Rackly, Rufus to Empy Whitly 2-24-1850 (2-25-1850)
Rackly, Washington to Manervy Ann Fite 11-15-1850
Raliff, C. A. to Mary F. Driver 2-20-1874 (no return)
Ramy, Wm. to Kiziah Wilson 2-11-1849
Raney, J. W. to Polly Ann James 10-14-1868 (10-18-1868)
Raney, John to Charity Medley 7-13-1870 (7-15-1870)
Rankhorn, G. B. to Mary Atnip 12-29-1857
Rankhorn, James to Elizabeth Lewis 9-5-1860
Rankhorn, Joseph to Matilda Rankhorn 11-24-1879 (no return)
Rankhorn, Wm. J. to Elizabeth Mullins 2-6-1879 (no return)
Rankhorn, Wm. to Mary Capshaw 4-23-1859 (4-27-1859)
Ratleph, George W. to M. S. Underhill 7-10-1868 (7-12-1868)
Ratliff, George W. to Martha T. Smithson 9-4-1872
Ravelin, Benjamin to Aseneth Bulington 12-21-1867 (no return)
Ray, Denis to Tennessee Goodner 7-11-1867 (no return) [B]
Ray, James to Cathrine Boyd 3-9-1854
Ray, Joseph to Martha A. P. Dunham 3-27-1863 (no return)
Ray, Joseph to Mary C. Robinson 8-19-1875 (8-22-1875)
Raymond, F. W. to Elen Gilbert 7-22-1869
Reasonover, Allen to Betty Smith 6-26-1878
Reasonover, Allen to Eliza Odins 3-4-1868 (3-22-1868) [B]
Reasonover, Jeremiah to N. P. Warford 8-10-1865 (no return)
Reasonover, Wm. to Mary Eaton 9-14-1869 (no return)
Reaton, F. W. to L. L. Overall 8-12-1867 (8-13-1867)
Redman, J. M. to Martha J. Cantrell 8-18-1864
Redman, James to Nancy Jane Keel 4-15-1873
Redman, Jessee to Julia Ann Driver 3-4-1858 (3-5-1858)
Redman, Wm. to Martha Mason 4-22-1865 (4-23-1865)
Redmon, Archabald to Elisa Cantrell 11-15-1852
Redmon, Banjamin to Nancy G. Purtle 1-19-1852
Redmon, Benjamin to Elenor Fowler 11-8-1852
Redmon, Dr. A. S. to Mary J. Robinson 3-1-1859
Redmon, J. W. to M. J. Manford 6-1-1878 (6-2-1878)
Redmon, W. C. to Frances Robinson 11-9-1878 (11-10-1878)
Reed, Wm. to Martha Phillips 10-11-1879 (10-13-1879)
Reeder, Edmon P. to Nellie Davis 2-25-1861 (2-28-1861)
Reeder, J. R. to Eliza E. Cantrell 12-11-1875 (12-16-1875)
Reeves, Hammelton to Mary Ann Julin 10-6-1848 (10-8-1848)
Reives, John to Kizanie Woodrell 7-24-1858 (7-25-1858)
Reynolds, A. L. to Josephine Smith 7-31-1872 (8-4-1872)
Reynolds, Alonzo to Emiline Lamberson 6-1-1867 (6-7-1867)
Reynolds, Andrew to Nancy Calicot 5-7-1866 (5-9-1866)
Reynolds, Andy to Nancy Calicut no dates (w/ '66 entries) [B]
Reynolds, H. B. to Sarah J. Thomas 9-17-1878 (9-19-1878)
Reynolds, H. to Jane Wouldred 11-25-1876 (11-26-1876)
Reynolds, Henry to Delia Wooden 4-29-1874 (5-3-1874)

Reynolds, J. W. to Elizabeth Oakley 12-6-1867 (12-8-1867)
Reynolds, James to Mary J. Robinson 12-9-1854 (12-10-1855?)
Reynolds, Jessey to Elizabeth Hall 8-4-1866 (8-5-1866)
Reynolds, John A. to Mary A. S. Davis 8-24-1876 (8-26-1876)
Reynolds, John G. to M. J. Tanbersan 3-10-1866 (3-11-1866)
Reynolds, John to Elizabeth Lawrence 10-3-1858 (10-5-1858)
Reynolds, John to Jennie Ford 10-24-1870
Reynolds, John to Polly Herington 10-30-1869 (10-31-1869)
Reynolds, Landon to M. L. Vantrease 8-24-1877 (8-26-1877)
Reynolds, Mariun to Louisa Robinson 9-26-1854
Reynolds, Newton to Mary Williams 7-28-1869 (8-15-1869)
Reynolds, T. M. to M. J. Titsworth 3-30-1872 (3-31-1872)
Rhea, Wm. T. to Sarah M. Leek 9-10-1850
Rhody, John to M. A. Adamson 10-23-1877 (10-29-1877)
Rhody, Wm. H. to Eliza J. Pack 3-30-1880 (4-4-1880)
Rice, Marion to Mary A. Mires 6-18-1870 (6-16?-1870)
Rich, Alaxander to Elizia Narros? 9-26-1873
Rich, Book to Caroline Anderson 9-28-1875
Rich, Epps M. to Sarena A. Roady 8-14-1851 (9-10-1851)
Rich, James to Hannah Rich 9-8-1874 (9-9-1874) [B]
Rich, S. R. to Parilee Snow 11-27-1875 (11-28-1875)
Rich, W. E. to Liza Dinwittie 11-27-1879
Rich, W. E. to N. E. West 11-19-1867 (no return)
Rich, Wm. B. to Parale Craddock 10-18-1871 (10-19-1871)
Richardson, Isaac to Rosy Clark 4-2-1866 (4-6-1866) [B]
Richardson, John to E. J. Williams 8-25-1866 (no return)
Richardson, L. B. to Martha Ann Turner 4-17-1858 (4-18-1858)
Richardson, Richard to Mary Eathaly 10-1-1864 (10-2-1864)
Ricketts, Isaac W. to Louisa Famer 3-13-1860 (3-25-1860)
Right, David W. to Matilda Fuson 10-7-1850 (10-13-1850)
Right, Wm. to Mary Ann Ford 9-19-1852 (9-23-1853)
Righte, W. T. to Manda Allen 2-28-1878 (3-3-1878)
Rigsby, A. P. to Callidony Dilldine 7-13-1878 (7-14-1878)
Rigsby, Andrew to Mary J. Henly 6-25-1869
Rigsby, Charles to Susan Young 9-4-1876 (no return)
Rigsby, David to Louisey Pinegar 12-2-1870 (12-4-1870)
Rigsby, Foster F. to Catharine Penegar 2-26-1875
Rigsby, James A. to Permelia Cantrell 7-27-1852 (no return)
Rigsby, John to Mary Ann Tippet 9-19-1850 (no return)
Rigsby, Moses to Rebeca Olburd 9-4-1868 (9-6-1868)
Rigsby, Samuel T. to Delila Lewis 8-31-1853 (9-3-1853)
Rigsby, Wm. J. to Elizabeth Ann Crips 8-28-1856 (8-29-1856)
Rigsby, Wm. to Elizabeth Hunt 4-17-1852
Rigsby, Wm. to Martha Jane Adcock 9-27-1869 (10-3-1869)
Roady, L. W. to Ann Frazor 7-14-1853
Roady, Wm. L. to Margaret Smithson 1-30-1864 (no return)
Roady, Wm. to Nancy Frazier 8-1-1861
Roberson, Thomas to Harret Heflin 5-2-1867 (5-4-1867)
Roberts, J. H. to Isibell Self 1-17-1867 (1-20-1867)
Roberts, J. W. to Jane Meggerson 8-9-1863 (no return)
Roberts, James H. to Malvina M. S. W. Wanford 7-21-1873 (no return)
Roberts, James to Keziah Cantrell 11-10-1863
Roberts, John F. to Elizabeth Murfrey 11-27-1862 (no return)
Roberts, John H. to Hannah Cantrell 8-26-1871 (8-27-1871)
Roberts, John S. to Martha Nixon 5-30-1855
Roberts, John S. to Nancy E. Malone 12-26-1871 (12-27-1871)
Roberts, Mallocki to Alunda Parker 8-11-1866 (8-12-1866)
Roberts, O. W. to Lucy A. Whitley 4-20?-1860 (exec. no date)
Roberts, Thomas to Jennie Jenkins 10-29-1874 (no return)
Roberts, Washington to Mary Ann Parker 1-27-1858 (1-28-1858)
Robertson, J. D. to N. P. Hays 9-1-1865 (9-3-1865)
Robertson, Wm. to Katherine C. Smith 9-7-1859 (9-8-1859)
Robins, Andrew J. to Rachel Love 2-17-1880 (2-19-1880)
Robinson, A. H. to Rebecca L. Williams 1-6-1869 (1-10-1869)
Robinson, A. M. C. to Thena Malone 9-14-1858 (9-16-1858)
Robinson, Ambrose to Zenora Dooling 6-21-1859
Robinson, Andy to Isabell Davis 4-20-1880 (no return)
Robinson, Banjamin S. to Mary J. Edge 5-15-1855 (5-10-1855)
Robinson, C. to S. E. Fissen 8-24-1870 (8-25-1870)
Robinson, C. to Sarah Martin 12-25-1864 (no return)
Robinson, Carls to Amanda Medley 1-8-1870 (1-9-1870)
Robinson, Charles to Elizabeth Johnson 9-25-1878 (9-29-1878)
Robinson, Charley to L. J. Clouse 3-25-1876 (no return)
Robinson, David to Rhacal Taylor 11-27-1878 (11-28-1878)

Robinson, Eliga to Mary E. Givines 9-19-1865 (9-21-1865)
Robinson, F. M. to Sallie Richman 11-15-1870 (11-20-1870)
Robinson, G. L. to Emily D. Anderson 9-6-1851
Robinson, G. W. to M. S. Stanly 10-2-1876 (10-5-1876)
Robinson, George to A. B. Taylor 3-2-1876
Robinson, George to Mary Derham 8-29-1879
Robinson, Hiram to Susan Childress 4-2-1870 (no return)
Robinson, James G. to Narcissa Newson 1-20-1852 (1-21-1852)
Robinson, James L. to Mary Carder 12-6-1854 (no return)
Robinson, James S. to Samantha Odom 4-29-1871 (4-30-1871)
Robinson, James to Frances Maxwell 5-13-1858
Robinson, Jesse to Susan Robinson 2-12-1880
Robinson, John A. to Martha E. Hunt 1-13-1875
Robinson, John E. to Margaret Smith 12-13-1854 (12-14-1854)
Robinson, John T. to Supprona J. Baughan 11-16-1853
Robinson, Levey to Anna Baine 1-13-1873
Robinson, Levi to Sarah Taylor 4-14-1850 (4-18-1850)
Robinson, Line to Elizabeth Sweet 4-7-1849 (not exec.)
Robinson, Moses to Margaret Alexander 2-28-1855 (3-1-1855)
Robinson, Ozious D. to Martha Certain 12-19-1867
Robinson, Peter to Q. V. Stokes 1-7-1874 (1-10-1874)
Robinson, Pleasant to Martha Taylor 10-13-1852 (10-14-1852)
Robinson, W. H. to Alice B. Stark 1-8-1878
Robinson, Winket to Lucy Jane Callicut 9-20-1854 (9-21-1854)
Robinson, Wm. B. to Elizabeth P. Reynolds 2-6-1856 (2-8-1856)
Robinson, Wm. F. to Martha F. Robinson 9-8-1855 (9-9-1855)
Robinson, Wm. R. to Armelda Vantrease 7-20-1851 (7-22-1851)
Rodey, Hanry to Mary E. English 12-24-1872 (12-25-1872)
Rogers, J. T. to Nancy E. Hollinsworth 10-29-1864 (10-31-1864)
Rogers, Jackson to Elizabeth Mortain 5-14-1880 (5-15-1880)
Rogers, Washington to Sinthey A. Evans 10-30-1879
Roggers, John to Partheny Allen 1-9-1851 (1-1?-1851)
Roland, B. C. to Irenia A. R. Beal 8-18-1860 (8-19-1860)
Rolland, L. S. to Sarah J. Martin 9-29-1872
Rollins, Jo to Josy Doss 7-4-1873 (7-13-1873) [B]
Rollins, Wiat to Rody Doss 1-22-1869 (1-24-1869) [B]
Romines, James to Nancy Adamson 4-5-1872 (4-7-1872)
Rosa, Trandus? to Rachal Barret 6-27-1865 (no return)
Rose, Ezekiel T. to Hester Ann Neill 9-16-1856 (9-18-1856)
Rose, Wm. N. to Helen A. Frazier 10-22-1879 (10-23-1879)
Ross, David to Lucy Ross 3-17-1866 (3-28-1866)
Ross, John to Carolina Hickman 8-20-1856
Roveland, Benjamin to Asanith Butington 12-21-1867 (12-22-1867)
Rowland, David to Mavinia Sexton 3-16-1871
Rowland, Eli to Elizabeth Bethells 1-27-1849 (1-31-1849)
Rowland, F. P. to Mary Carter 9-4-1879
Rowland, James to Catharine Christian 2-21-1871 (2-23-1871)
Rowland, James to Mary Ann Evans 12-14-1875
Rowland, Marcus C. to C. Victory Ford 11-15-1875 (no return)
Rowland, W. G. to Liza Vick 1?-16-1878 (no return)
Roy, H. G. to N. A. Vick 11-25-1867 (11-26-1867)
Roy, J. F. to Helan F. Yeargan 2-21-1870 (2-24-1870)
Roy, Stephen to Luisa Groom 4-4-1870 (4-8-1870)
Rucker, James to Matilda Horton 10-16-1854
Rugle, Thomas to Elizabeth Blair 5-10-1871 (5-14-1871)
Rule, Jasper to Matilda Wright 8-13-1868
Rutledge, George B. to Siller Stoner 8-24-1859
Saddler, Henry T. to Mary D. Keeton 8-8-1879 (8-10-1879)
Sadler, Wm. to Rachel Strong 10-26-1848
Sailers, Winfield S. to Luizee J. Rigsby 7-31-1874 (8-2-1874)
Sams, James to Allis Mulican 4-25-1878 (5-7-1878)
Sanders, Erwin to Mary (Hooker) Jones 12-6-1848 (12-7-1848)
Sanders, F. P. to Fanna Titsworth 3-2-1878 (3-3-1878)
Sanders, John W. to Ann Taylor 6-26-1859 (6-27-1859)
Sanders, John to Ellen Parker 5-9-1859 (no return)
Sanders, Wesley to Samanth Cantrell 12-27-1865 (12-28-1865)
Sanders, Wesley to Talitha Cantrell 11-23-1848
Sandlin, Fuller to Eliza Cader 10-26-1876
Sandlin, Isaac M. to Mary J. Foutch 3-31-1860
Sandlin, Jake to Marinda Ponder 4-29-1876
Sandlin, James to Bitha Chapman 12-18-1868 (12-20-1868)
Sandlin, James to Permelia E. Bennett 1-15-1866
Sandlin, John W. to Martha Griffith 7-4-1855 (7-14-1855)
Sandlin, John to Lutisia Pack 10-9-1861 (no return)
Sandlin, McAdo to Eliza Bennett 5-11-1867

Sartean, Christofer P. to Mary Whitley 3-6-1854 (3-7-1854)
Satterfield, Anthoney to Polly Cantrell 9-27-1873 (9-29-1873)
Scale, Lewis to Rosa A. Lisk 12-22-1873 (no return) [B]
Schurer, J. H. to Mattie Myers 1-20-1872 (1-23-1872)
Scott, C. to Mary Adge 1-10-1878 (1-14-1878)
Scott, Eligah to Mary Hill 9-24-1875 (9-26-1875)
Scott, Elijah to Dovy Davis 8-30-1849 (9-2-1849)
Scott, James to Barthena Carter 2-29-1852 (3-1-1852)
Scott, James to Nancy Jane Pratt 6-6-1852 (6-15-1852)
Scott, James to Sarah B. Chapman 3-29-1879 (3-30-1879)
Scott, Jasper B. to Catharine Cleyborn 12-24-1851
Scott, John to Lucity Bennett 1-13-1849 (1-14-1849)
Scott, Joseph to E. F. Griffith 12-14-1876 (exec. no date)
Scott, Joshua B. to Marth Griffith 9-8-1855 (9-20-1855)
Scott, Leonard to Melissa Sandlin 12-29-1853
Scott, Manson B. to Jan? Sandlin 11-10-1851 (no return)
Scott, Newton to Pheby Ann Fields 2-6-1850 (2-13-1850)
Scott, Wm. to Melissa Ann Bennett 10-14-1850 (10-20-1850)
Scott, Wm. to Nancy J. Scott 2-10-1853 (2-13-1853)
Scott, Wm. to Polly Ann Bennett 2-26-1862 (3-2-1862)
Scrivner, A. T. to Juda Trane? 11-20-1872 (11-21-1872)
Scruggs, Robert L. to Delia Avant 6-1-1874 (6-3-1874)
Scuders, B. F. to E. J. Prichard 10-11-1868 (10-14-1868)
Seawell, J. H. to Amanda Cannady 7-30-1876
Seawell, J. Q. to Alice Mandlebaum 10-7-1875 (10-8-1875)
Seay, James L. to Mallissia A. Holand 9-2-1870
Segraves, Henry to F. Seay 5-24-1862 (5-25-1862)
Self, Abner to Isabeler Allen 4-16-1855 (4-17-1855)
Self, Abner to Jane Taylor 12-2-1851
Self, Eliga C. to Susan E. Melton 11-8-1873 (11-9-1873)
Self, Elijah to Jane Close 12-28-1861 (12-31-1861)
Self, George W. to Carlain Green 8-20-1853 (8-21-1853)
Self, John B. to Mary A. White 5-19-1858 (5-20-1858)
Self, Thomas to Catharine Green 10-17-1855 (10-18-1855)
Self, Wm. C. to Charity Ann Hoss 10-29-1869
Sellars, J. B. to Amanda Ferrel 2-27-1866 (no return)
Sellars, W. H. to Mattie Turner 9-22-1878
Sellers, Henry to Mary Dale 3-21-1853 (3-23-1853)
Sellers, Wm. to Sarah A. Smith 8-4-1858 (8-5-1858)
Selvedge, Thomas to Mary Bates 8-13-1863 (no return)
Sertain, Wm. to Ella Brock 10-17-1874 (10-18-1874)
Sewel?, Henry to Nancy Dandlee 5-24-1855
Sewell, D. W. to Amanda J. Martin 10-18-1860 (no return)
Sewell, Wm. to Caroline Aken 1-31-1863 (2-1-1863)
Sewell, Wm. to Caroline Askew 1-31-1863
Shane, J. A. to Mary A. Wilson 8-21-1867
Shares, P. T. to Bettie B. Whaley 3-20-1872
Shaw, Arrison to Inda Frazier 12-19-1878
Shaw, John W. to Sarah Billings 7-2-1873 (7-8-1873)
Shaw, Samuel to Alice Flowers 2-10-1876
Sheals, E. E. to Cora Allen 12-23-1876 (12-24-1876)
Sheham, Josiah to Charity Cubbins 6-6-1864 (no return)
Shehan, Josiah to Mary Scott 9-8-1868 (no return)
Shehane, Wm. B. to Elizabeth Braswell 1-13-1875 (1-14-1875)
Shehun, Isaac to Harret Braswell 2-12-1866 (2-13-1866)
Shields, T. W. to Sue E. Kidwell 12-2-1875
Shields, Thomas to Frances Atnip 5-11-1876
Shores, P. T. to Maggie Oames 4-18-1877
Show, Henry to Callie Cantrell 1-23-1879
Simens, James to Vira Hancock 2-3-1870 (2-5-1870) [B]
Simmons, J. A. to S. J. Hicks 2-1-1879 (2-2-1879)
Simmons, John D. to Mary Bevert 3-9-1863 (no return)
Simpson, Eliol to P. Turner 1-11-1875
Simpson, John S. to Elizabeth Woodson 6-1-1850 (6-2-1850)
Simpson, John to Martha Harben 3-19-1851
Simpson, Moses to Sarah Robinson 7-10-1854
Simpson, R. E. to Fally Williams 10-10-1878 (10-15-1878)
Simpson, Samuel to Artemisa Lawrence 7-30-1867
Simpson, Samuel to Susan Lawrence 2-6-1850 (2-7-1850)
Simpson, Wm. to M. E. Adcock 3-12-1871
Sims, Franklin to Elizabeth Thornberry 8-10-1852 (no return)
Sims, James to May Allen 8-2-1855
Sims, Jeff to Leona Pistole 6-20-1874 (6-21-1874) [B]
Sims, N. W. J. to Elizabeth J. Kennedy 8-16-1853 (no return)
Sisk, Henry to Mary A. Whitley 5-23-1867

Skerlock, James to Adlin Rich 12-29-1866 (12-31-1866)
Slaton, Gabrel to Polly Adcock 10-19-1853
Smallman, M. D. to C. A. Magness 5-26-1868
Smart, Fern. to Conny Tubb 7-21-1879 (7-24-1879) [B]
Smart, Randolph to Carolina Ruttan 3-17-1856 (3-19-1856)
Smith, A. P. to Alis Hoskins 4-5-1875 (4-8-1875)
Smith, A. S. to Hulda Ann Bratton 1-13-1857 (1-15-1857)
Smith, Alexander A. to Mary Ann Kelly 3-21-1853
Smith, Andrew to Mary J. Cubbins 3-8-1879 (solmnzd no date)
Smith, C. C. to Helen Bozorth 9-12-1860 (no return)
Smith, Charles to Pasly Fisher 12-19-1874 (no return)
Smith, David to Hannah Bates 10-12-1870 (no return) [B]
Smith, E. to M. E. Harper 7-19-1876 (7-26-1876)
Smith, Eurasta to Bell Windham 9-9-1872 [B]
Smith, F. H. to Sarah Terry 3-26-1860 (3-29-1860)
Smith, G. A. to M. A. Lamberson 2-27-1876
Smith, G. W. to M. J. Parker 12-16-1869
Smith, George R. to Rebecca Davis 5-1-1857 (5-3-1857)
Smith, George to Mary Bozart 11-26-1856 (12-27-1856)
Smith, Guy Taylor to Mandy C. Dewease 12-10-1867 (12-12-1867)
Smith, Henry to Tennessee Trewet 1-18-1867
Smith, I. S. to ElizabethWilliams Mooneham 3-18-1879 (solmnzd? no date)
Smith, Isaac M. to Jane Sellers 12-21-1857 (12-24-1857)
Smith, Isaac to Tresa Taylor 10-13-1855 (10-14-1855)
Smith, J. L. to Sarah E. Ward 3-3-1875 (3-4-1875)
Smith, J. to Mary Estis 8-24-1862 (no return)
Smith, Jackson to Sarah E. Vickers 11-14-1871
Smith, James to Sarah E. Fite 7-7-1857 (exec. no date)
Smith, Marsillis to Adline Parsley 1-19-1869
Smith, R. V. to Nancy Braswell 1-29-1857
Smith, Robert T. to Amanda T. Doss 12-12-1854 (no return)
Smith, Robert to Huldy Ann Smith 1-15-1864 (1-17-1864)
Smith, T. N. to Nancy Taylor 4-15-1878 (4-19-1878)
Smith, Thomas N. to Sallie Adkins 5-24-1866 (5-27-1866)
Smith, Thomas N? to Parilee Jane Ethrage 12-8-1859
Smith, Thomas to A. B. Taylor 12-23-1868
Smith, Timothy to Elizabeth Parsley 11-20-1850 (11-21-1850)
Smith, W. H. to Mary Ann Allen 2-19-1861 (2-20-1861)
Smith, W. P. to Mary Guinn 2-8-1854 (2-9-1854)
Smith, Wm. Ned to Malinda Lawrence 6-28-1855
Smith, Wm. S. to Parthena Vine 8-30-1862 (no return)
Smith, Wm. to Frances Greene 11-11-1870 (11-13-1870)
Smith, Wm. to Tempy Hall 1-22-1859 (1-23-1859)
Smith, Zacheriah to Louiza Braswell 10-18-1861 (no return)
Smithson, Davis to Catharine Smith 9-16-1851 (9-17-1851)
Smithson, Wm. to Parmelia Mosier 2-2-1871
Smitson, James to Martha J. Skurlock 9-13-1865 (no return)
Smitson, James to Rena Vaughn 9-4-1869 (9-5-1869)
Smitson, John to Alzena Hildreth 12-27-1874
Smitson?, John T. to Nancy J. Mozier 12-19-1862 (no return)
Sneed, A. H. to Syntha Richardson 3-18-1857
Sneed, H. J. to S. C. Webb 12-29-1877 (12-30-1877)
Sneed, Nels to Fanney Robinson 11-15-1877 (no return)
Sneed, T. J. to Emma M. Everett 12-1-1868 (12-2-1868)
Sneed, Thomas J. to Ellen F. Johnson 6-22-1858 (7-1-1858)
Sniders, Wm. to Elizabeth A. Taylor 10-28-1861
Snood?, Francis M. to Sarah A. Keaton 5-20-1874 (5-24-1870)
Snotgrass, George to Mary Braswell 10-14-1876 (10-15-1876)
Snow, Ebaneser to Nancy C. Anderson 1-24-1866 (no return)
Snow, Henry to Elizabeth Scott 9-3-1850 (9-4-1850)
Snow, J. M. to G. A. Mason 1-2-1869 (1-3-1869)
Snow, Wiley to Catharine Scott 5-15-1850 (5-16-1850)
Snow, Wm. to Martha Ann Harper 6-23-1849 (6-25-1849)
Sonellin, Littleton B. to Mary A. Neale 1-22-1873 (no return)
Sorsey?, D. P. to Mary L. Robinson 9-11-1856
Southeran, James P. to Martha J. Partlo 12-19-1873 (12-29-1873)
Span, John to Frances Pistole 9-?-1877 (no return)
Spark, Martin to Jane Gayin? 5-3-1866 (no return)
Sparkman, Spencer to Bethuna Culwell 7-12-1867
Sparks, Joseph to Lucinda Williams 6-14-1864 (6-19-1864)
Spencer, G. W. to Lucy Taylor 1-9-1867 (1-12-1867)
Spencer, James R. to Rebecca Adkins 2-22-1865
Spencer, James to Harriette M. Bane 9-27-1849

Spencer, John to Louisa L. Fish 5-10-1875 (5-1?-1875)
Spencer, Marion to Sinrellia Turner 2-22-1866
Spencer, Marion to Sucilla? Turner? no dates (w/1864 entries
Spradly, Wm. B. to Melviny Keath 6-26-1860 (no return)
Springfield, George W. to Sintha Williams 7-29-1865 (no return)
Spurlock, Andrew to Parris Dodd 9-11-1878 (9-12-1878)
Spurlock, Francis M. to Rexey A. Bung? 12-4-1856
Spurlock, George W. to Kissey C. Hunt 7-26-1859? (8-8-1859)
Spurlock, George to Hellen Richardson 7-13-1870 (8-21-1870)
Spurlock, J. R. to S. C. Lowery 10-30-1879
Spurlock, Jon J. to Mary F. Thompson 2-8-1873 (2-9-1873)
Spurlock, L. to H. C. Waldridge 11-4-1876 (11-5-1876)
Spurlock, Woodson C. to Lucindy E. Title 1-27-1873
Squires, J. G. to Sarah C. Vick 5-8-1873
St. John, B. S. to Delila Williams 3-20-1857 (3-22-1857)
Staley, Henry E. to Cordelia T. Terrey 5-15-1873
Staley, Jim to Sarah Turney 5-24-1869 (5-27-1869) [B]
Staley, O. B. to Safronia Dedmon 1-2-1861
Stalks, Biral to P. Frist 3-19-1866 (no return)
Standley, Jessee to Jane Duham? 3-4-1850 (3-6-1850)
Stanford, Farney H. to Susanah McGee 12-9-1872 (12-12-1872) [B]
Stanley, J. C. to Nancy Goodson 7-18-1856 (7-20-1856)
Stanley, R. J. to Elizabeth Stanley 2-21-1857 (no return)
Staren, Wm. to Rebecca Braswell 6-12-1858 (6-13-1858)
Stark, J. P. to M. E. Whaley 9-25-1879
Stark, John B. to Nancy Given 1-17-1860 (1-19?-1860)
Stark, John L. to Mary T. Allen 9-12-1873 (9-14-1873)
Stark, Moses A. to Sarah E. Barger 11-16-1865
Stark, Thomas H. to Nancy A. Berry 9-11-1872 (9-12-1872)
Starks, Daniel to Aulina Owen 12-28-1875 (12-30-1875)
Starks, Martin to Jane Gogars 5-30-1866
Starn, Joseph to Sarah Allen 3-29-1863 (no return)
Starnes, A. D. to Linda J. Petty 8-4-1868 (8-8-1868)
Starnes, Amon to Susan Coleman 8-10-1869
Starnes, B. F. to M. H. Coggin 9-14-1869 (9-26-1869)
Starnes, Fred to Elmina Garner 5-17-1879 (5-18-1879)
Starnes, J. M. to Mary Ann Stalks 1-25-1866 (no return)
Starnes, Jacob to Mahala Roberts 6-25-1859 (no return)
Starnes, John K. to Amandy R. Holly 10-15-1859 (10-26-1859)
Starnes, Milus J. to Elizabeth A. Nollener 6-19-1872 (6-17?-1872)
Starnes, T. H. to Miscellaney Hales 12-18-1876 (12-19-1876)
Steavens, Mary J. to ----- 1-3-1867 (1-8-1867)
Steel, Allen to Nancy Elrod 4-1-1850
Steel, James to Mary Lewis 3-7-1872 (3-10-1872)
Steel, Levi B. to Susan R. Strong 12-30-1854 (12-31-1854)
Steel, Wm. to Mary Owens 8-9-1879 (8-12-1879)
Steel, Wm. to Sissy McDole 10-6-1848 (10-5?-1848)
Steele, John to Amanda A. Elrod 3-4-1880 (3-5-1880)
Stephens, Ausly to Elliott J. Kerby 11-6-1860 (11-7-1860)
Stephens, B. F. to Mary J. Bowers 5-5-1857 (5-6-1857)
Stephens, J. H. to M. T. Berry 8-23-1872 (9-8-1872)
Stephens, James to Lena Thurman 7-5-1875
Stephens, John S. to Mary M. J. Bains 7-30-1856 (no return)
Stephens, John to Elizabeth Bains 11-25-1862 (11-26-1862)
Stephens, Joseph P. to Carry I. Lee 5-9-1879 (5-11-1879)
Stephens, Yancey to Ellit Kerby 1-23-1856 (no return)
Stephenson, David S. to Emily J. Hedgecock 1-31-1849
Stephenson, J. D. to Eliz. A. Hedgecock 1-17-1849 (1-18-1849)
Stephenson, J. M. to Susannah James 3-2-1857 (3-5-1857)
Stewart, Andrew J. to Marry F. Parsley 12-25-1867 (12-26-1867)
Stewart, John C. to Mary H. Mallun 9-12-1861 (9-14-1861)
Stewart, Penal to Nancy Pack 5-19-1866 (no return)
Stewart, Wm. G. to Sarah J. Mitchel 9-5-1872
Stiles, George to Mary Smith 9-3-1868
Stiles, John to Sarah Mares 1-7-1861 (not filled in)
Stimerage, Thomas to Rutha Rigsby 10-14-1875 (10-17-1875)
Stinebridge, Silas to Elizabeth Moss 12-31-1868 (1-6-1869)
Stipes, A. R. to Sarah Martin 8-16-1877 (8-19-1877)
Stogin?, Sidney to Catharine Johnson 6-2-1877
Stokes, Elias to Nancy League 10-24-1878 [B]
Stokes, George to Jane Robinson 3-17-1866 (3-18-1866)
Stokes, Henry to Adline Trice 7-4-1874 (7-5-1874) [B]
Stokes, Henry to Clary Braswell 1-3-1870 (no return)
Stokes, John T. to Liny Aldrige 12-28-1868 (12-29-1868)
Stokes, John to M. A. Tubb 1-7-1874 (1-8-1874) [B]

Stokes, John to Mariah Stokes 3-17-1866 (3-18-1866)
Stokes, Manuel to Nola Roberson 6-15-1867
Stokes, Nace to Lucy Foutch 5-11-1876 (5-12-1876)
Stokes, Richman to Sarah Reynolds 3-17-1866 (3-18-1866)
Stokes, Sampson to Laura Robinson 7-28-1871 (7-29-1871) [B]
Stokes, Silvanus to Nancy J. Fisher 2-9-1870 (2-10-1870)
Stokes, Thornton to Silvey Stokes 3-17-1866 (3-18-1866)
Stokes, W. J. to A. J. Dowell 1-3-1870 (1-5-1870)
Stokes, Young to Fanney Ashworth 10-17-1873 (10-18-1873) [B]
Ston?, Wm. H. M. to Annie L. Ferrell 11-19-1872 (11-21-1872)
Stone, John H. to Anna Hodge 5-23-1877 (5-24-1877)
Stoner, James P. to Mary Thompson 12-14-1872 (12-18-1872)
Stoner, James P. to Susan Cantrell 9-27-1855
Stoner, W. J. to L. C. Smitson 9-26-1868 (no return)
Stones, H. E. to Semantha E. Jones 11-12-1874
Stout, Charley to Sarah Turner 4-3-1875 (4-4-1875)
Stout, Henry to Manervey Ford 12-2-1871 (12-3-1871)
Strang, James to Bettiniah Witt 7-24-1852
Stricklin, John to Sarah Bayne 2-8-1860
Striclin, Wm. to Frances Bain 2-19-1867
Stuckrath, Lewis to Carolin Ward 6-23-1860 (no return)
Stuk?, Fay M. to Martha Anderson 1-29-1867 (1-31-1867)
Styles, George to Elizabeth Snow 6-5-1873
Sulens, Jack to Louizah Braswell 4-29-1866 (no return) [B]
Sullins, Eli to Paralee Tubb 1-15-1856 (1-17-1856)
Sullivan, Harris to Mary J. Stephens 6-22-1867 (6-25-1867)
Sullivan, John D. to Martha Reynolds 7-6-1874 (7-12-1874)
Sumars, R. B. to Palmer Givens 1-25-1875 (1-28-1875)
Summers, Wm. M. to D. A. Robinson 1-21-1878 (1-23-1878)
Suthin, Thomas to I. J. Bullard 8-17-1870 (8-18-1870)
Suttles, Henry to Amandy Christian 5-17-1869 (5-23-1869)
Sutton, Robert S. to Ruthana Goad? 1-24-1861
Swihar?, J. G. to Julia Romine 9-24-1852 (9-27-1852)
Swinegane, James to Frances Jones 3-19-1858 (no return)
Swyscher, Taylor to Mary Johnson 9-28-1864
Tafley, Wm. to Nancy Bly 9-20-1876 (9-21-1876)
Tales, John to Elisabeth Fisher 2-13-1866 (2-15-1866)
Taley, Green to Elizabeth Patton 3-27-1871
Tarply, John to Elizabeth Wilson 7-9-1853 (7-10-1853)
Tarply, John to Mary D. Hodge 6-4-1874 (6-9-1874)
Tates, William to Mary J. Trusty 8-9-1860
Taylor, Albert to Fannie Fish 3-22-1876 (3-23-1876)
Taylor, Anderson to Dorinda Arnell 12-24-1878 (no return)
Taylor, Barnabas to Durera J. Fitts 2-24-1866 (no return)
Taylor, Barzel to Pissilla Fish 5-1-1852 (5-2-1852)
Taylor, Barzela to Annis M. Tamel 5-3-1861 (5-9-1861)
Taylor, Barzelia to Elizabeth Hayse 3-23-1858 (no return)
Taylor, Benjamin to Miley Stricklin 1-15-1859 (no return)
Taylor, Borzela to Frances M. Hendrix 12-13-1873 (12-14-1873)
Taylor, C. A. to F. E. Capshaw 12-24-1875 (12-26-1875)
Taylor, Carroll to Eliza Allen 7-10-1854 (7-12-1854)
Taylor, Chesley to Frances M. McClenon 1-5-1854 (5-14-1854)
Taylor, Chesly to Parilee Spence 7-11-1860 (7-12-1860)
Taylor, D. E. to Nancy Parkenson 3-12-1877 (3-13-1877)
Taylor, David J. to Elizebeth Hendrix 11-6-1867
Taylor, David P. to Sarah Love 5-6-1873
Taylor, David to Margrett Trusty 12-15-1871 (12-17-1871)
Taylor, Dempsey to Frances Taylor 12-23-1878 (12-24-1878)
Taylor, Dempsey to Sarah Allen 8-19-1871 (8-20-1871)
Taylor, E. W. to Mary Martin 11-29-1866 (11-30-1866)
Taylor, Elias to Sarah E. Green 1-31-1869
Taylor, Ezekial to Malinda Taylor 1-4-1865 (no return)
Taylor, Ezekial to Mary E. Smith 11-27-1860 (11-28-1860)
Taylor, Ezekiel to Malissa Ethridge 12-26-1855 (12-27-1855)
Taylor, Garrison to Elizabeth Atnip 7-15-1852
Taylor, H. C. to Callidone Marton 3-18-1878 (3-21-1878)
Taylor, H. to Nancy A. Tibbs 5-29-1879
Taylor, Henry to Mary A. Self 5-1-1872 (5-2-1872)
Taylor, Henry R. to Lucritia Taylor 12-1-1859
Taylor, Henry W. to Anny Walking 12-14-1858 (12-19-1858)
Taylor, Isaac to Elizabeth Felps 1-10-1879 (1-12-1879)
Taylor, Isaac to Lizie Taylor 9-9-1879 (9-7?-1879)
Taylor, J. A. to B. E. Cantrell 9-24-1873 (9-28-1873)
Taylor, J. R. to N. E. Martain 9-27-1876 (9-28-1876)
Taylor, J? B. to M. Drury 1-2-1867 (date obscure)

Taylor, James A. to S. E. Pack 8-12-1869
Taylor, James to Nancey Robinson 1-24-1857 (3-5-1857)
Taylor, Jdavid C. to Erlina? Taylor 3-22-1855
Taylor, Jno. to Dora Trapp 3-1-1876 (no return)
Taylor, John B. to Nancey Drurey 9-4-1865 (9-11-1865)
Taylor, John R. to Elizabeth F. McClellon 8-8-1874 (8-9-1874)
Taylor, John T. to Martha J. Allen 5-18-1872
Taylor, John to Amandy Hendrix 8-19-1874 (8-20-1874)
Taylor, John to Elizabeth Garriette 1-8-1850 (1-10-1850)
Taylor, John to Luncindy Wooden 3-6-1869 (no return)
Taylor, John to Mary C. T. Adcock 1-18-1872
Taylor, Josiah W. to Hannah Taylor 9-20-1871 (9-24-1871)
Taylor, L. R. to R. J. Prentis 2-12-1869
Taylor, Lewis J. to Rody G. Fish 5-14-1863 (no return)
Taylor, Peter to Nancy Pitts 8-14-1865 (no return)
Taylor, Richard to Mary Asilian Wailes 5-7-1869
Taylor, Thomas J. to Nancy J. Taylor 9-13-1872 (9-22-1872)
Taylor, W. D. to Mary Foutch 10-4-1875 (10-7-1875)
Taylor, Washington to Nancy Mullican 4-29-1857
Taylor, William to Lucinda Aldridge 7-1-1850 (7-21-1850)
Taylor, William to Sarah Taylor ?-26-1853 (7-27-1853)
Taylor, Wilson to Catharine Mason 4-9-1852 (4-11-1852)
Taylor, Wilson to Elizabeth Fish 9-6-1865 (no return)
Taylor, Wilson to Lucy Robinson 3-27-1858 (no return)
Taylor, Wm. E. to Malinda Fish 8-?-1867 (8-22-1867)
Taylor, Wm. Riley to L. E. Farler 3-3-1878
Teague, Charles to Nancy Phillips 2-23-1866 (no date) [B]
Teague, E. R. to Manerva Exan 12-30-1866
Tenney, Isaac G. to Nancy E. T. Johnson 11-4-1873 (11-6-1873)
Tenney, William to Becky Certain 8-21-1866 (8-22-1866)
Terney, James to Margret Neel 4-5-1879 (5-6-1879)
Terrey, Felix R. to Marthy J. Dozier 5-14-1873
Terril, Benjamin to Louisa J. Hamilton 1-7-1858
Terry, Andy to Silvy Shane 2-16-1867 (2-20-1867)
Terry, J. L. to Martha Burton 3-14-1876 (3-16-1876)
Terry, James P. to Sarah C. Lee 12-18-1858 (12-19-1858)
Terry, Rowland to Sarah A. Eller 3-1-1871 (no return)
Terry, Weldon to Emily A. Isabell 5-16-1849
Thomas, A. H. to Frances Berry 8-31-1875 (9-2-1875)
Thomas, Andrew to Liza Simson 3-16-1878 (3-19-1878)
Thomas, Benjamin to Martha Allen 5-21-1855 (5-22-1855)
Thomas, Horres to Rean Hendrix 11-11-1879 (11-10?-1879)
Thomas, Isaac to Fanny Lefeaver 3-5-1849 (3-11-1849)
Thomas, W. R. to M. J. Robinson 9-12-1876 (9-28-1876)
Thomason, A. J. to Martha Purtle 10-22-1856 (10-23-1856)
Thomason, Alvis to Sarah Ann Parker 2-12-1857
Thomison, George to Olive Davis 3-8-1861 (3-11-1861)
Thompson, Benj. to Elvira Smith 8-8-1862 (8-20-1862)
Thompson, M. B. to Mary Parck 8-6-1873
Thompson, S. D. to L. A. Cantrell 12-26-1876 (no return)
Thompson, William to Mary F. Johnson 2-3-1874 (2-5-1874)
Thompson, Wm. to Nancy Todd 9-13-1879 (9-14-1879)
Thriek, W. G. to Roannia Walls 5-13-1875 (no return)
Thrucote?, James to Rebecca J. Harwell 12-3-1848
Thweatt, Johnathan D. to Mary J. Lane 11-17-1859
Tibbs, W. T. to M. A. Edge 6-12-1875 (1?-12-1875)
Tichle?, James P. to Mary Ann Bass 4-22-1851 (4-23-1851)
Tinsley, M. J. to Jane E. Martin 7-17-1849 (no date)
Tinsly, John M. to Nancy Martin 12-20-1868
Tipett, William to E. H. Rankhorn 2-14-1857 (2-15-1857)
Tisdale, Joseph S. to Frances Jones 2-28-1872 (2-29-1872)
Tish, E. D. to Anna Braswell 10-1-1866 (no return)
Titsworth, B. M. to Mary E. Johnson 2-25-1861 (3-3-1861)
Titsworth, Elisha to Rachel Hallam 4-14-1858 (4-4?-1858)
Titsworth, Foderick J. to America A. Cantrell 7-18-1855 (7-19-1855)
Titsworth, Isaac D. to Tabitha C. Mangum 1-24-1871
Tittle, Bethal to M. J. Embry 6-29-1878 (6-30-1878)
Tolbert, William to Elizabeth Cochran 8-31-1871
Tomerson, John to Harrett Etherage 1-4-1872 (1-5-1879)
Tomlin, Smith to Loucinda Herndon 1-23-1878 (6-24-1878)
Tompson, J. W. to Bette Patterson 10-7-1869 (10-13-1869)
Tooney, Benjamin F. to Josephine Barnes 2-4-1873 (2-6-1873)
Torbit, H. R. to Elizabeth Savage 4-2-1861
Tracy, Thomas A. to Emeline J. Smithson 11-2-1870 (9?-2-1870)
Trail, E. N. to Jane R. Denham 7-5-1858 (7-8-1858)

Trail, E. N. to Sarah Laseter 2-20-1862 (2-27-1862)
Trail, R. B. to P. T. Griffith 12-20-1876 (no return)
Tramel, J. L. to Margrett M. Walls 6-25-1879 (6-26-1879)
Tramel, James to Ester Caskey 12-2-1857
Tramel, John T. to Mary E. Fish 3-30-1867 (no return)
Tramel, John to Luraney McJulin 5-19-1861 (no return)
Tramel, Johnson to Leuvea E. Lawrence 2-21-1855 (2-22-1855)
Tramel, W. H. to Luisa McIntier 9-30-1865 (no return)
Tramel, Wm. H. to Mary Jane Hullett 7-18-1856
Tramell, John to Elizabeth Durham 5-29-1852 (5-30-1852)
Trammel, John H. to Martha J. McClelen 10-13-1853 (10-18-1853)
Trammel, Joshua to Paralee Hayse 3-27-1851 (no return)
Trammel, T. J. to Malissa Tubb 2-9-1875 (2-10-1875)
Trammel, W. A. to M. C. Baliss 1-11-1876 (1-13-1876)
Trammell, D. H. to F. T. Page 2-1-1878 (2-3-1878)
Trammell, R. A. to Delila Baine 4-30-1875 (5-2-1875)
Trammell, S. R. to Elizabeth Jones 8-6-1878 (no return)
Trammell, W. M. to Mary B. Trammell 11-12-1878
Tramol, William B. to Sarah E. Taylor 3-3-1873 (3-6-1873)
Trapp, J. M. to Nancy B. Williams 1-2-1861 (1-3-1861)
Trapp, Jobe to Elizabeth Hill 11-9-1877
Trapp, John to Isabella Judkins 1-8-1869 (1-10-1869)
Trapp, Mc. to Betty Mullican 9-21-1872 (9-22-1872)
Trapp, Terry to Anny Ferrell 4-22-1850 (ret, filed)
Trapp, Wm. D. to Haxa? T. Williams 1-5-1857 (1-6-1857)
Trewett, William to Rebeca Turney 7-16-1867 (7-18-1867)
Tribble, John W. to Mary V. Fite 4-19-1873 (4-20-1873)
Truett, Hiram to Rebecca Swearingin 4-7-1866 (no return)
Truett, John to Babe Allen 12-28-1878 (no return) [B]
Truett, Wm. to Tennessee Rowland 3-20-1872 (no return)
Truitt, James to Juley M. Allen 11-13-1867
Trulove, B. J. to Amanda Steele 11-29-1866 (no return)
Trustey, John to Margrett Hendrix 5-5-1879 (5-6-1879)
Trusty, Allen to Kizamore Taylor 10-28-1871 (10-29-1871)
Trusty, Horrace to Rhoda E. Taylor 12-11-1873
Trusty, Wm. to Martha Davis 1-16-1865
Truxton, Nicholas to Martha Ann Neel 7-13-1849 (7-15-1849)
Tubb, Alex to Carline Stoks? 1-25-1869 (1-26-1869) [B]
Tubb, Elias to Fanney Stokes 1-26-1876
Tubb, Eliel to Martha A. Brien 7-11-1852 (7-15-1852)
Tubb, Isaac to Fancy Adcock 5-25-1876 (no return)
Tubb, Jacob to Mary Vantrease 5-23-1878 [B]
Tubb, James P. to Ronea Washer 10-20-1879 (10-23-1879)
Tubb, James to Minney Allen 3-17-1866 (3-18-1866)
Tubb, John B. to Emily J. Johnson 7-7-1873 (7-12-1873)
Tubb, Lou? to Nannie Givven? 12-15-1876 (12-17-1876)
Tubb, Nathan to Rachel Whaley 2-5-1866 (no return) [B]
Tubb, Wm. to Rosy _____ 1-8-1876 (1-9-1876)
Tubbs, Ned to Izibel Stokes 5-26-1877 (5-29-1877)
Tuck, J. W. to Mary Coalmon 11-17-1879
Tumblson?, Abner to Matilda Wammac omitted (3-14-1865)
Tumey, Isaac to Parilee Williams 10-22-1866 (10-23-1866)
Tunny, Caswell to Sallie Shaw 8-10-1871 [B]
Turentine, J. N. to Mary E. Robinson 1-1-1873 (1-2-1873)
Turentine, Wilson to Margarett A. McNaimer 6-5-1878 (6-6-1878)
Turner, Alexnder? to Nancy Davis 10-6-1851 (10-15-1851)
Turner, B. S. to Margarett A. Martin 4-13-1861 (no return)
Turner, Chester to May Taylor 9-3-1853 (10-31-1853)
Turner, Chestly to Arteby Adcock 2-8-1873 (2-9-1873)
Turner, Edward to Jessemine Everett 5-12-1870 (5-15-1870)
Turner, Filling to Lodemia Adcock 7-25-1865 (no return)
Turner, Francis to Mary Ashworth 1-18-1860 (1-19-1860)
Turner, Fred to Nancy Ford 1-5-1871 (no return) [B]
Turner, George to Mary Jane Edens 4-6-1853 (4-7-1853)
Turner, Henry to Sarah C. Looney 10-6-1869 (10-7-1869)
Turner, Horace to Ann Hays 10-18-1873 (10-20-1873) [B]
Turner, Isaac to Talitha C. Foraster 3-1-1849 (no return)
Turner, J. T. to Frona Hall 9-29-1877 (no return)
Turner, James to Mary E. Mason 9-12-1867 (9-15-1867)
Turner, Jas. F. to Mary Wamac 3-3-1880
Turner, Jerry to L. L. Burden 2-11-1869 (2-12-1869) [B]
Turner, John to Martha Atnip 8-23-1879 (8-24-1879)
Turner, John to Susan Hooton 5-24-1860 (5-25-1860)
Turner, John to Virgina A. Gosset 12-3-1856
Turner, Joseph to S. D. White 1-29-1874

Turner, Paton to Harriet Adcock 5-11-1866 (5-13-1866)
Turner, Swet to Frances Eavens 4-2-1866 (4-7-1866) [B]
Turner, William A. to Mary E. Given 11-8-1854
Turner, William to Lida Taylor 9-16-1858 (9-19-1858)
Turner, William to Rutha Cummins 6-9-1854
Turner, Wm. F. to Sarah Jones 1-2-1877 (no return)
Turney, E. to E. O. Neal 12-7-1876 (12-10-1876)
Turney, G. W. to Mattie E. Bratton 8-3-1870
Turney, George to Clary Robinson 11-25-1868 (11-26-1868)
Turney, J. B. to Nancy E. Hale 3-3-1874 (3-4-1874)
Turney, James to Tarvy Holinsworth 11-21-1868 (11-22-1868)
Turney, John A. to A. E. Fite 9-1-1874 (9-2-1874)
Tyler, Andrew to Mattie Fish 2-2-1878 (2-3-1878)
Tyree, Thos. W. to Martha Herenton 12-6-1878 (12-8-1878)
Underhill(Loranhill), John to Susan Watson 11-23-1859 (no return)
Underhill, E. O. to Stacy Miller 2-9-1869 (2-11-1869)
Underhill, Rufus B. to Sarah E. Cates 10-17-1848 (10-19-1848)
Underwood, James C to Matilda M. Himbrel 6-27-1850 (no return)
Upchurch, Haywood to Elizabeth Parish 12-16-1859
Vanatta, Danel to Elizabeth Griffith 8-21-1879 (no return)
Vanatta, McAdoo to Sarah Measles 3-13-1853 (3-15-1853)
Vanatta, Samuel to Cynthia M. Hickman 7-13-1860
Vanatta, Samuel to Elizabeth Meazels 2-20-1878 (no return)
Vandagriff, Criss to M. J. Hendrix 7-14-1877 (no return)
Vandagriff, John to Ann Adamson 4-15-1855
Vandegrift, Isaac to Mary Watson 9-2-1870 (9-22-1870)
Vandegrifth, John C. to Marigath P. Penia? 1-6-1866 (1-7-1866)
Vandeigrift, Wm. to Malindy Parker 8-6-1873 (8-7-1873)
Vandergrift, H. C. to Parlee Hollen 11-15-1879 (11-17-1879)
Vandergrift, Isaac T. to Mary B. Smith 12-31-1879 (no return)
Vandigreft, Allen C. to Nancy E. Bratten 7-29-1874 (7-3-1874)
Vandigrift, Henry C. to Mary E. Hollinsworth 12-9-1868 (no return)
Vandigrift, Thomas W. to S. Jane Hathaway 12-6-1871 (12-7-1871)
Vandygrif, J. W. to Mary J. Craddock 4-18-1865 (no return)
Vanhooser, Isaac N. to Susan E. Tramel 7-12-1855
Vanhooser, Joseph M. to Eliza J. Gipson 9-15-1874 (9-16-1874)
Vanover, James to Jane N. Smith 7-31-1855 (8-2-1855)
Vansur, Henry to Nancy M. Amery 7-23-1851 (8-9-1851)
Vantreas, Tomas H. to Sarah McMillan 10-5-1874 (no return)
Vantrease, James to Sarah Jane Reynolds 9-30-1851 (10-11-1851)
Vantrease, John to Adaline Amonet 12-23-1876 (12-24-1876)
Vantrease, Nelson (Robinson) to Milly McKisic 3-29-1877 (no date)
Vantrease, Wm. F. to Mary West 4-2-1874 (4-9-1874)
Vantrees, N. D. to M. J. Driver 9-18-1865 (9-19-1865)
Vantrese, Wm. to Mary Vantrease 4-9-1877? (no return)
Vaughn, Frank to Victory Mullican 5-18-1880 (5-?-1880)
Vaughn, James M. to Jane Caldwell 2-20-1850 (2-21-1850)
Vaughn, Nicholas to Martha Ann Butler 12-20-1856 (12-21-1856)
Vaughn, Samuel R. to Rebeca Glenn 8-18-1862 (8-19-1862)
Vaughn, Wm. H. to Mary A. Martin 5-25-1859 (6-2-1859)
Vernatta, James to Carolina Garrison 1-20-1851 (1-2?-1851)
Vernatta, James to Sarah Pine 9-7-1868
Vernatta, John to Catharine Measels 7-30-1857
Vernatta, John to N. E. Neil 9-2-1867 (9-4-1867)
Vick, Eli to Amandy Eason 10-12-1872 (10-16-1872)
Vick, Eli to Mary J. Ford 12-3-1867 (12-4-1867)
Vick, Henry to Mary Ann Canedy 10-6-1866 (10-7-1866)
Vick, William to Sarah West 4-8-1851
Vickors, W. J. to M. J. Edge 3-26-1874
Vicus, Wm. P. to Parzada M. Newby 3-20-1863 (no return)
Vier, Wm. R. to Nancy T. Adamson 10-18-1879 (no date)
Vire, William to Frances George 7-25-1849 (7-26-1849)
Viss, Thos. to Hannah Prowel 8-7-1858 (8-8-1858)
Wadde, John to Eliza Childers 9-30-1850 (10-1-1850)
Wade, Charles to Margret J. Markam 10-26-1874
Wade, Charley to Jane Johnston 5-31-1877 (no return)
Wade, P. M. to M. A. Easthert 3-1-1866
Wade, T. W. to Jennie Hayes 9-21-1878 (9-23-1878)
Wade, W. W. to Bettie Crowley 3-21-1872
Waford, David to Vicktory Willoby 6-23-1877 (6-24-1877)
Walden, J. C. to E. J. Elkins 11-3-1862 (11-4-1862)
Waldon, Stephen to Sarah J. Tramel 7-25-1874 (7-30-1874)
Waldredge, J. H. to M. E. Wilkinson 2-4-1878 (2-5-1878)
Walkar, John M. to Louisa F. Foutch 8-1-1867 (8-2-1867)
Walker, A. D. to Mary F. Taylor 12-19-1873

Walker, E. C. to Matilda Page 7-16-1879
Walker, F. A. to Calona Bane 2-3-1875 (2-18-1875)
Walker, G. W. to Roda Bain 11-8-1871 (11-12-1871)
Walker, J. D. to Sophia Grissom 7-25-1871 (7-26-1871)
Walker, James to Jane Cotten 1-4-1869 (1-5-1869)
Walker, John H. to Tabitha Noris 1-8-1868 (no return)
Walker, John to Cyrena Puckett 12-22-1870
Walker, John to Eran Jones 1-4-1869 (1-5-1869)
Walker, O. D. to Jain Chisam 1-2-1866 (1-15-1866)
Walker, R. D. to A. D. Allen 6-1-1874 (6-5-1874)
Walker, Samuel L. to Hicksey Taylor 3-3-1879 (solemzd?)
Walker, Samuel to Mary Alnage ?-23-1861 (no return)
Walker, Samuel to Mary J. Taylor 8-2-1871 (8-5-1871)
Walker, Samuel to Sarah H. Glenn 2-7-1880 (2-8-1880)
Walker, T. R. to Tennessee C. Clark 2-14-1874 (no return)
Walker, W. W. to B. Z. Robinson 4-29-1876 (4-30-1876)
Walker, W. W. to Malvina Jones 2-1-1873 (2-3-1873)
Walker, William to Jane Linder 6-18-1870 (6-21-1870)
Walker, Wm. L. to Elizabeth J. Blunt 1-5-1864 (1-6-1864)
Wall, J. E. to M. L. Walker 10-30-1876 (11-1-1876)
Wall, J. K. P. to Malvina Fisher 9-21-1874 (9-27-1874)
Wall, L. D. to S. E. Anderson 10-1-1879 (10-2-1879)
Wall, T. M. T. to Rebecca Elexandra 8-19-1875 (8-22-1875)
Wall, Thos. to Melessa J. Laseter 8-17-1864 (8-19-1864)
Waller, T. J. to Eva Magard 10-21-1879 (10-22-1879)
Waller, Thos. A. to Mary C. Lee 5-1-1850 (5-2-1850)
Waller, William to Jain W. Anderson 6-21-1865
Waller, William to M. W. Anderson 6-20-1865 (no return)
Walling, Andrew to Rachel Fuson 9-24-1874
Walls, Jackson to Rebecca Garrison 3-12-1855
Walls, Wm. L. to Martha E. Tramel 1-13-1871 (1-18-1871)
Walston, J. to Mary Scurlock 7-25-1863 (no return)
Walton, Jessee to Elliot Kerley 8-26-1858 (9-2-1858)
Wamack, A. M. to Mary Ann Cantrell 10-5-1854
Wamack, B. H. to M. E. Potter 2-5-1855 (2-8-1855)
Wamack, G. M. to Ester W. Griffith 8-20-1870 (8-28-1870)
Wamack, Solomon to Rebecca Noris 10-22-1855
Wamack, William C. to Reboc Dunham 12-13-1853
Ward, J. F. to Betta Dass 3-27-1878
Ward, J. W. to J. F. Dodd 1-3-1870 (1-27-1870)
Ward, T. M. to E. R. Acuff 4-13-1871
Ward, Thomas G. to Bathena C. Turney 8-3-1857 (8-5-1857)
Ward, Thomas G. to Elizabeth Barger 12-23-1872 (12-26-1872)
Ward, Wesley to Nancy Twoney 11-14-1876 (11-25-1876)
Ware, Isaac to Mary Ware 1-1-1866 (2-3-1866)
Warford, A.? to Helen Hays 9-12-1866 (9-7?-1866)
Warford, Davies? J. to Malinda J. Crook 7-3-1849 (7-4-1849)
Warford, Francis B. to Rachel White 2-5-1849 (1?-11-1849)
Warford, Saml. to Rachael McCullough 5-25-1872 (5-26-1872)
Warford, Samuel to Josephin Malone 6-25-1856 (6-26-1856)
Warford, Wm. to Rebecca Driver 3-11-1869
Warren, Alexandria to Rutha Tinsley 11-6-1872
Warren, E. to S. E. Lisk 10-13-1870 (10-14-1870)
Warren, Edmund to Martha Ann Parsley 12-21-1870
Warren, Emond H. to Nancy P. Jenkins 9-10-1873
Warren, F. D. to M. A. Tinsley 12-8-1869 (12-9-1869)
Warren, George W. to Elizabeth Kennedy 12-20-1853 (12-21-1853)
Warren, George to Elizabeth Warren 1-25-1857
Warren, J.? E.? to Emma Wheeller 7-20-1871
Warren, John to Mary Waker omitted (7-12-1838)
Warren, Joseph to Tennessee Given 11-22-1866 (11-23-1866)
Warren, Squire to Margrett J. Evins 2-26-1874
Warren, Wm. to L. J. Parelli 5-18-1876
Washer, John to Mary F. Johnson 10-14-1868 (no return)
Watkins, J. D. to Amanda M. Phelps 10-3-1840 (no return)
Watson, Ezekiel to Margaret Robinson 8-26-1854 (8-31-1854)
Watson, H. J. to Mary Reynolds 12-30-1869
Watson, R. H. to M. J. Terry 3-2-1878 (3-3-1878)
Watson, S. W. to Ethel Helum? 10-4-1876 (10-5-1876)
Watson, W. M. C. D. to Martha J. Nelson 1-3-1857 (1-4-1857)
Watson, William J. to Catharine Conner 1-7-1857
Watts, Pleasant to Polly Elender Atnip 11-29-1855
Watts, Plesant to Nancy H. Patterson 4-9-1869 (4-11-1869)
Weasnor, William O. N. to Elizabeth Hayse 11-28-1854 (11-30-1854)
Webb, B. M. to Helan Hare 1-8-1867 (no return)

Webb, Daniel to L. E. Redmon 11-25-1876 (no return)
Webb, E. W. to Elizabeth Magness 8-7-1873
Webb, Jacob to Delia Spurlock 6-13-1880 (no return)
Webb, James to Mary Ann Adcock 12-2-1859 (12-3-1859)
Webb, John B. to Angalina Rankhorn 10-14-1852
Webb, John to Eliza Pack 5-13-1856 (2?-14-1856)
Webb, L. R. to A. Potter 10-8-1866 (10-10-1866)
Webb, Wm. to E. Fisher 12-21-1876 (no return)
Weble, Even W. to Sarah Martin 11-6-1851
Welch, J. M. to P. A. Agee 8-21-1869 (8-26-1869)
West, Francis to Martha Smith 2-9-1850 (no return)
West, J. B. to Mary A. Grindstaff 11-7-1858 (11-11-1858)
West, J. R. to Amanda Foutch 3-12-1864 (exec. no date)
West, Jackson to Adaline Edens 3-2-1852 (retnd w/o cft.
West, John to M. J. Young 7-27-1878
West, Johney to Juley Berry 11-7-1877 (11-8-1877)
West, Joseph B. to Luisa V. Ray 9-12-1854 (exec. no date)
West, Joseph B. to Soph Grindstaff 11-29-1865 (12-7-1865)
West, Newton to Dicey Christian 5-17-1879 (5-18-1879)
West, R. B. to Sarah E. Whitten 11-2-1869 (no return)
West, Robert B. to Hattie Norman 6-10-1874 (6-11-1874)
West, Solomon W. to Josephine Meritt 4-6-1868 (4-8-1868)
West, T. P. to Sarah Taylor 7-29-1879 (7-30-1879)
West, Thomas E. to Elizabeth M. Bowers 1-8-1853 (1-12-1853)
West, Tilmon to M. F. Jones 8-8-1876 (8-9-1876)
Whaley, E. M. to Eliza Bethell 1-2-1868 (1-2-1868)
Whaley, Isaac to Nancy D. Boren 7-21-1849 (no return)
Whaley, John D. to M. A. C. Harvy 4-3-1875 (4-4-1875)
Whaley, S. B. to Parthena M. Bell 3-21-1855
Whaley, W. A. to Canny Overall 9-9-1876 (no return)
Whaley, Wm. H. to Martha E. Jones 12-11-1852 (12-13-1852)
Whaley, Wm. to Margaret J. Neal 4-2-1849 (4-4-1849)
Whaly, Lemuel M. to Margrett C. Evins 1-24-1874 (1-25-1874)
Wheeler, John B. to Mary T. West 12-19-1849
Whit, John J. to Sarah H. Jones 9-6-1865 (9-10-1865)
White, F. C. to Elizabeth Williams 11-20-1872 (11-21-1872)
White, Francis M. to Dulana McInteer 6-30-1855 (7-1-1855)
White, Isaiah Jr. to Lucy Atwell 9-8-1860
White, James B. to Sarah E. Whilliby 4-6-1867 (4-10-1867)
White, James B. to Sarah Wiloby no dates (w/Jan)
White, James H. to Nancy P. Williams 11-6-1865 (11-9-1865)
White, James M. to Lyda Malone 7-23-1854
White, James T. to Cintha P. Calvin 1-29-1864 (2-3-1866)
White, James to Talitha P. Close 1-16-1855
White, T. J. to N. E. Preston 11-15-1876 (11-19-1876)
Whitely, Eliga to Susan Markes 12-18-1874
Whitely, John to Vina Tyree 11-13-1875 (11-14-1875)
Whitely, Sam to Betta Markes 2-20-1878 (2-2?-1878)
Whitesal, James to Mary E. Hays 7-16-1867
Wilbern, George to Eliza Ann West 9-22-1867 (no return) [B]
Wilder, David H. to Sarah H. Fare 1-9-1862 (no return)
Wilder, Wiley to Elizah Forister 10-16-1850 (no return)
Wilkerson, B. C. to Elizabeth Potter 3-23-1859 (3-24-1859)
Wilkerson, John B. to Hannah Potter 11-30-1853 (12-19-1853)
Wilkinson, Benjamin J. to Darthouly Atnip 7-27-1870
Wilkinson, H. B. to Mallie West 1-3-1878
Will, Anderson to Mary Nole 4-18-1871 (no return)
Willes, Mat to May Hayes 7-16-1879
William, James M. to Tera Sellars 10-27-1865 (10-29-1865)
William, R. L. to H. M. Hill 3-4-1875
William, Thomas J. to L. J. Stern 6-23-1849 (6-25-1849)
Williams, A. C. to Mary Washer 12-19-1877 (12-27-1877)
Williams, Aaron to Eliza Simpson 6-20-1869 (7-12-1869)
Williams, Andrew to Conder? Cheek 2-14-1874 (2-15-1874)
Williams, Barnet to Elizabeth Jones 8-26-1853 (8-28-1853)
Williams, Bethel to Carline Hacher 9-22-1869 (no return)
Williams, Bethell to Caroline Washer 9-22-1869 (9-23-1869)
Williams, C. M. to Malisa Tubb 2-3-1873 (2-13-1873)
Williams, C. M. to S. E. Mitchel 9-14-1874
Williams, Charles M. to Sarah Fouch 2-13-1873
Williams, Francis M. to Palmirey G. Lowery 9-20-1873 (9-21-1873)
Williams, Frank to Feby Curtis 10-19-1868 (no return) [B]
Williams, Georg W. to Deliley Fitts 1-3-1872 (1-4-1872)
Williams, Hezekiah W. to Mary L. Adamson 1-29-1857
Williams, J. C. to Delpha Vier 10-26-1859 (10-27-1859)

Williams, J. H. to M. J. Stacy 7-13-1878 (7-14-1878)
Williams, J. N. to Elizabeth Kidwell 2-21-1867 (2-22-1867)
Williams, James S. to Mary J. Cantrell 4-12-1865 (4-14-1865)
Williams, John A. to Phrosannah Florda 7-22-1857 (7-23-1857)
Williams, John A. to Rachel Ferrell 9-6-1852 (9-7-1852)
Williams, John A. to Saphronia Florid 7-22-1863 (no return)
Williams, John W. to Orpha Simpson 4-12-1853 (4-14-1853)
Williams, Joseph to Jane Mitchel 10-17-1874 (10-18-1874)
Williams, Lafait to Jane Bates 3-28-1868 (3-29-1868) [B]
Williams, Leroy to Cansady Sellers 8-8-1849 (no return)
Williams, Licurgus to Adline Malone 7-29-1872 (7-31-1872)
Williams, Matthew to Darthuly Gray 3-26-1851
Williams, P. M. to C. E. Barger 3-9-1877 (3-11-1877)
Williams, Richmond to Margaret Collins 2-12-1849 (2-15-1849)
Williams, Robert to Lucy B. A. Fotrece? 2-27-1872 (3-17-1872)
Williams, Samuel to Elizabeth Wright 3-20-1869 (no return)
Williams, Sebastin to Paralee Pistole 12-15-1862
Williams, Simeon L. to Arrilla J. Evins 1-10-1874
Williams, Simeon to Mary J. Bennett 5-1-1879 (5-4-1879)
Williams, Sol. to C. F. Cantrell 10-12-1875
Williams, Van to Lidy Lock 7-9-1879 (7-10-1879)
Williams, Vance M. to Moring Fisher 7-18-1872
Williams, Wm. C. to Elizabeth Bentele 4-1-1850 (4-2-1850)
Willowby, Monroe to Bettie Parkerson 3-2-1876 (4-6-1876)
Wills, Wm. A. to Nancey J. Brensley 3-30-1872 (4-2-1872)
Wilmoth, Jackson to Rody Adcock 12-30-1852
Wilmoth, Wm. to Martha Jane Adcock 7-12-1855 (7-18-1855)
Wilson, Henry W. to Polly Ann Gates 1-6-1852
Wilson, Isaiah D. to Susan Berks 10-17-1854
Wilson, Wm. N. to Frances M. Alexander 8-24-1850 (12-25-1850)
Winchester, Eli to Mary J. Lith 8-15-1872
Winchester, John C. to Mariah Ponder 1-19-1867
Windham, J. H. to Nancy F. Chrisian 7-9-1874
Winfree, Gabriel M. to Edily H. Jones 7-2-1855 (no return)
Winfree, John to Sarah Taylor 4-1-1858
Winfree, Wm. to Elizabeth Barnes 5-1-1860
Winfrey, Eli to Leatha New 1-17-1878 (1-20-1878)
Winfrey, H. S. to Josie Brock 7-25-1879 (8-6-1879)
Winfrey, T. L. to Emily J. Diver 11-9-1869 (no return)
Winfrey, Wm. T. to Thursy C. McGuffey 10-15-1872 (10-17-1872)
Winfry, J. L. to Nancy A. Fitts 3-16-1874
Winnard, E. H. to Charlotty McGuire 5-23-1852
Winord, Thomasj E. to Mary Donnelly 3-10-1880
Wisdom, Shemp to Elizabeth Morris 2-8-1872 (2-13-1872) [B]
Witt, A. M. to Louisa Bratten 3-24-1857 (3-25-1857)
Witt, Abraham to Talitha Whaley 4-3-1866 (exec. no date)
Witt, George W. to Margaret E. Fite 12-24-1855
Wodsides, James to Frances Dale 12-22-1849 (12-24-1849)
Womack, W. D. to Palina Titsworth 8-9-1864 (8-12-1864)
Womack, W. W. to Mary F. Wood 2-14-1874 (2-15-1874)
Wood, Hany to Eliz. Markum 1-22-1865 (1-24-1865)
Wood, J. T. to M. A. Vernon 2-13-1872 (2-14-1872)
Wood, James L. to Julis F. Bowers 5-19-1853 (exec. no date)
Wood, James to Tennie Bennett 9-22-1877
Wood, Jefferson to Mary Grindstaff 10-30-1866 (11-1-1866)
Wood, P. L. to Amanda Roy 11-6-1866 (11-8-1866)
Wood, P. L. to C. L. Roy 3-9-1861 (3-14-1861)
Wood, T. L. to E. C. Griffeth 1-18-1865 (1-19-1865)
Wood, T. L. to Elizabeth Griggith 11-23-1871 (no return)
Wood, W. B. to Mary E. Smith 12-16-1875
Wood, W. D. to M. J. Lasiter 1-31-1863 (2-1-1863)
Wood, Yandle to Harriette A. Sneed 2-5-1850 (2-13-1850)
Wooden, Henry to Elizabeth Markum 6-22-1865 (no return)
Wooddist, John to Mary Scurlock 9-28-1870
Woode, T. L. to Eliz. W. Bennette 1-22-1876 (1-23-1876)
Wooden, John to Louizia E. Wanford 5-15-1873
Wooden, John to Parilie Clack 2-15-1860? (2-15-1861)
Wooden, Thomas to Mary Foutch 7-6-1853 (exec. no date)
Woods, Edward E. to Susan Turner 5-8-1856
Woodside, John F. to Milliey Ellis 11-5-1865 (no return)
Woodside, L. N. to Tennessee Evans 2-1-1860 (2-2-1860)
Woodsides, F. to Hollie C. Edmonson 7-1-1865 (no return)
Woodsides, J. K. to C. E. Allen 9-10-1868 (no return)
Woodsides, John F. to Sarah S. Terry 1-13-1857 (1-14-1857)
Woodsides, Wm. H. to Tricy Ann Huggins 9-21-1854

Woodward, J. Fletch to Emma Edmonds 6-4-1872
Worley, D. B. to Mary E. Blankenship 12-26-1869
Worley, David B. to Martha A. Hooper 1-4-1858 (1-9-1858)
Wright, B. M. to Bettie Gilbert 12-8-1877
Wright, Benj. F. to Jane Wright 12-5-1878
Wright, C. C. to Martha Goodson 11-25-1879 (no return)
Wright, David to Mary Ann Brim 2-6-1851
Wright, E. D. to Rutha Fisher 1-3-1865 (no return)
Wright, George H. to America J. Troglin 10-29-1873 (10-30-1873)
Wright, Hatten to Josie Cope 4-20-1880 (no return)
Wright, R. V. to Harriet E. J. Botts 4-9-1857
Wright, S. F. to A. J. Fisher 1-3-1865 (no return)
Wright, Thomas E. to Lucretia McDowell 9-30-1870 (10-3-1870)
Wright, W. J. to E. B. Fisher 2-9-1866 (2-10-1866)
Wright, Wm. B. to Juy Comfergher 1-23-1872 (1-25-1872)
Wroe, Thomas C. to Lucinda Breverman? 10-10-1849 (exec. no date)
Yanson, David A. to Harriett Lasiter 2-25-1867 (2-26-1867)
Yeargan, Henry to Rachael Hays 1-24-1861 (2-14-1861)
Yeargan, John B. to Parale Goodner 2-28-1854
Yeargin, W. C. to Margret Night 1-10-1877 (1-16-1877)
Yeargoin, A. S. to Mollie H. Williams 2-20-1872 (2-22-1872)
Yearigin, Charles T. to Florence Rutland 2-25-1871 (2-26-1871)
Yergan, A. J. to Tabitha Robinson 11-20-1849 (11-22-1849)
Yergan, C. C. to Sarah Warfon 1-20-1849 (1-5-1849)
Yergan, James A. to Luisa C. Miner 4-17-1850 (4-19-1850)
Yergan, R. C. to L. E. Gothard 9-22-1877 (9-25-1877)
Yergin, Robert to Salina Vick 3-5-1852 (3-9-1852)
York, Rubin to M. Fowler 12-22-1879 (no return)
Yorke, Isack to Olivia Corby 2-26-1875 (2-28-1875)
Young, Almon D. to Mary J. Turner 3-1-1873 (3-2-1873)
Young, David C. to Lucisa Braswell 7-25-1877 (no return)
Young, David to Jennie Flowers 1-23-1879 [B]
Young, Ed to M. J. Turner 10-29-1874 (no return)
Young, Isaac to Ellennora Petty 12-23-1871 (12-24-1871)
Young, Isaac to Marth J. Davis 5-25-1858 (exec. no date)
Young, James to Ireny F. Vaughn 2-22-1868 (2-23-1868)
Young, James to Parrile Bellins 9-19-1866
Young, James to Sarah Billings 2-4-1870 (no return)
Young, John F. to Elizabeth Pinager 7-22-1871
Young, John L. to Udora A. Russell 12-30-1872 (12-31-1872)
Young, John to Sarah Fowler 2-6-1860 (2-7-1860)
Young, John to Udora A. Russell 11-6-1872 (12-3-1872)
Young, S. R. to N. E. Moore 8-8-1878
Young, Samuel S. to Rebecca Forrest 9-21-1864 (no return)
Young, Thomas M. to Zany Petty 10-21-1867 (10-27-1867)
Young, W. P. to Samantha Neel 8-30-1877
Young, Welden to Sarah Driver 9-23-1867
Young, Wiley to Elis. Driver 7-24-1868 (7-25-1868)
Young, Wm. to Eliza. Brock 8-31-1859 (no return)
Young, Wm. to Martha Braswell 2-14-1878 (2-15-1878)
Young, Wm. to Mary Love 10-5-1850 (10-7-1850)
Youngblood, J. F. to Elizabeth Ward 9-9-1876 (9-10-1876)
Youngblood, J. F. to N. T. Hollingsworth 12-28-1859
Youngblood, James H. to Nancy Dejournet 8-14-1854 (8-17-1854)
Youngblood, Josiah to Charrity Self 9-22-1871 (9-24-1871)
Younge, Joseph to Catharine Johnson 3-17-1875 (no return)
Youngour, W. C. to Adah E. West 1-20-1873 (1-23-1873)
Zachary, W. C. to Harrett Zachary 11-27-1879 (12-3-1879)

-----, Bettie to Thomas Mc----- 12-22-1879 (no return)
-----, Sefilia to S. M. Davis 2-1-1875
Aalsup, Susan P. to Wm. Foster no date
Abner, Louisa M. to James Bush 6-3-1851
Acole?, Jennie to Thomas Belcher 4-28-1873 (no return) [B]
Acuff, E. R. to T. M. Ward 4-13-1871
Acuff, Emily to William Heptanstall 1-7-1875
Adams, Jane to Thomas Hayse 12-23-1872 (12-25-1872) [B]
Adams, Nancy T. to John C. Overall 1-11-1868 (1-23-1868)
Adams, S. C. to James D. Owen 1-14-1880 (2-15-1880)
Adamson, Alcey E. to John A. Dirting 12-17-1873 (12-18-1873)
Adamson, Ann C. to John A. J. Nelson 12-24-1854
    (endrsd, no prop)
Adamson, Ann to John Vandagriff 4-15-1855
Adamson, Charlotte J. to Wm. H. Noaks 8-26-1861 (8-27-1861)
Adamson, Elisa to Joseph Pistole 8-7-1868 (no return)
Adamson, Jane to Torrence O'Conner 8-2-1873 (8-3-1873)
Adamson, Lakey to Allen Johnson 10-13-1855 (11-18-1855)
Adamson, M. A. to John Rhody 10-23-1877 (10-29-1877)
Adamson, Mary L. to Hezekiah W. Williams 1-29-1857
Adamson, Nancy T. to Wm. R. Vier 10-18-1879 (no date)
Adamson, Nancy to James Romines 4-5-1872 (4-7-1872)
Adamson, Rachal J. to John W. Adamson 1-21-1876
Adamson, Rachel to Henry Conner 9-9-1874 (no return)
Adamson, Sarah Jane to Simeon T. J. Hunt 5-14-1859
    (5-15-1859)
Adcock, Annie to Isaac Anderson 7-26-1879 (7-27-1879)
Adcock, Anny to Napoleon Parker 11-17-1856 (no return)
Adcock, Arteby to Chestly Turner 2-8-1873 (2-9-1873)
Adcock, Cassander to George Long 1-5-1860 (not endorsed)
Adcock, Catharine to Tona Adcock 2-1-1875 (2-2-1875)
Adcock, Catherine to Alvin R. Anderson 9-18-1873 (9-19-1873)
Adcock, Fancy to Isaac Tubb 5-25-1876 (no return)
Adcock, Florence to S. B. Martin 3-2-1874 (3-24-1874)
Adcock, Frances to Elijah Allen 9-30-1851 (10-5-1851)
Adcock, Harriet to Paton Turner 5-11-1866 (5-13-1866)
Adcock, L. M. to G. N. Northrell 6-28-1865 (no return)
Adcock, L. to S. K. Holder 3-15-1875 (3-18-1875)
Adcock, Lodemia to Filling Truitt 7-25-1865 (no return)
Adcock, Lucinday to James E. Adcock 4-21-1870 (4-22-1870)
Adcock, M. E. to Wm. Simpson 3-12-1871
Adcock, Margrett A. to Calvin W. Anderson 8-2-1871
Adcock, Marth to John Bayn 10-6-1865 (no return)
Adcock, Martha Ann to Edward Adcock 3-8-1852 (3-11-1852)
Adcock, Martha Jane to Wm. Rigsby 9-27-1869 (10-3-1869)
Adcock, Martha Jane to Wm. Wilmoth 7-12-1855 (7-18-1855)
Adcock, Mary Ann to James Webb 12-2-1859 (12-3-1859)
Adcock, Mary C. T. to John Taylor 1-18-1872
Adcock, Mary D. T. to David Pittman 12-21-1859 (12-22-1859)
Adcock, Mary F. to James Jones 2-6-1875 (2-7-1875)
Adcock, Mary to W. T. Brian 2-16-1871
Adcock, Moetta to T. A. Cantrell 12-13-1856 (12-14-1856)
Adcock, Nancy to William Dunham 3-29-1849 (ret,no cert.)
Adcock, Oma C. to Davis Penegar 10-21-1866
Adcock, Polly to Gabrel Slaton 10-19-1853
Adcock, Rody to Jackson Wilmoth 12-30-1852
Adcock, Sarah C. to Amasa Jones 9-12-1855
Adcock, Sophrona to William Fisher 2-11-1874 (2-12-1874)
Adcock, Veta to David Bayne 1-16-1860 (1-11?-1860)
Addcock, Marth to John Bayn 10-6-1865 (10-25-1865)
Adge, Mary to C. Scott 1-10-1878 (1-14-1878)
Adimson, Vina to A. B. Drury 10-26-1866 (no return)
Adkins, Alice A. to Erastus Jaco 1-21-1880 (1-20?-1880)
Adkins, Elizabeth to Andrew Alexander 10-27-1867 (no return)
Adkins, Elizabeth to John Neel 6-19-1879
Adkins, Huldy J. to Peter J. Hunroe 8-20-1860 (8-24-1866?)
Adkins, Martha to Martin Jones 12-7-1851
Adkins, Mary Ann to Isam Keeton 7-29-1852
Adkins, Nancy to Farris Hendrixon 6-5-1869 (6-6-1869)
Adkins, Rebecca to James R. Spencer 2-22-1865
Adkins, Ruth to Berry Mangrum 6-21-1860 (exec. no date)
Adkins, Sallie to Thomas N. Smith 5-24-1866 (5-27-1866)
Agee, Louisa to John H. Pharmer 3-5-1856 (4-15-1856)
Agee, P. A. to J. M. Welch 8-21-1869 (8-26-1869)
Aken, Caroline to Wm. Sewell 1-31-1863 (2-1-1863)

Albert, Mandy C. to George R. Dobbs 12-6-1871 (12-7-1871)
Alcorn, Salley to James M. Borin 3-20-1873
Aldrege, Martha to Joel Kerklen 3-15-1853
Aldridge, Lucinda to William Taylor 7-1-1850 (7-21-1850)
Aldrige, Biddy M. to Andrew McGinness 9-4-1852 (9-5-1852)
Aldrige, Liny to John T. Stokes 12-28-1868 (12-29-1868)
Aldrige, Lucinda to John Fisher 10-17-1865 (10-11-1865)
Alexander, A. E. to B. G. Hendrix 12-23-1866 (no return)
Alexander, Eliza Jane to Wm. P. Hawker 9-16-1858
Alexander, Frances M. to Wm. N. Wilson 8-24-1850
    (12-25-1850)
Alexander, M. J. to J. S. Denby 10-19-1869 (10-24-1869)
Alexander, Mandy E. to James Alexander 8-6-1873 (no return)
Alexander, Margaret to Moses Robinson 2-28-1855 (3-1-1855)
Alexander, Matilda to Hardy Johnson 9-11-1862 (9-12-1862)
Alexander, Nancy C. to Thomas Hart 10-11-1855
Alexander, Nancy C. to W. A. Bain 1-5-1863 (1-8-1863)
Alexander, Nancy to Henry Bennett 10-4-1848 (10-6-1848)
Alexandria, Martha to Alm.on L. Frazier 1-28-1874
Alexandria, Sarah to Alex Holland 6-11-1873
Allen, A. D. to R. D. Walker 6-1-1874 (6-5-1874)
Allen, Adah to James A. Marks 3-30-1870 (3-31-1870)
Allen, Amanda F. to W. C. Jennings 8-30-1861 (9-1-1861)
Allen, Amandy E. to Nelson Page 12-16-1873 (12-18-1873) [B]
Allen, Babe to John Truett 12-28-1878 (no return) [B]
Allen, Bettie to W. B. Carnes 5-10-1877
Allen, C. E. to J. K. Woodsides 9-10-1868 (no return)
Allen, Cora to E. E. Sheals 12-23-1876 (12-24-1876)
Allen, Dilila to Wm. Fish 8-29-1873 (9-5-1873)
Allen, Elenora to Isaac Drake 3-11-1861 (no date)
Allen, Eliza to Carroll Taylor 7-10-1854 (7-12-1854)
Allen, Elizabeth to M. Fitts 2-20-1869
Allen, Emma V. to A. T. Phillips 12-4-1866
Allen, Isabeler to Abner Self 4-16-1855 (4-17-1855)
Allen, Jane to John W. Cluson 9-21-1857 (10-4-1875)
Allen, Jane to Kay Gayin 5-3-1866 (no return)
Allen, Jane to Reny Gain 5-13-1866
Allen, Jenymae? to Joshua W. Picket 4-6-1858
Allen, Juley M. to James Truitt 11-13-1867
Allen, Lou to John H. Gray 10-2-1875 (10-3-1875)
Allen, Manda to W. T. Righte 2-28-1878 (3-3-1878)
Allen, Margaret to B. B. Nichouls 8-25-1866
Allen, Margaret to Robert Newby 5-24-1879 (5-25-1879)
Allen, Marth to Tom Beasley 10-5-1867 (10-6-1867)
Allen, Martha Ann to Enoch Atnip 7-12-1853
Allen, Martha J. to John T. Taylor 5-18-1872
Allen, Martha J. to Wm. C. Cantrell 10-7-1862 (10-17-1862)
Allen, Martha to Benjamir. Thomas 5-21-1855 (5-22-1855)
Allen, Marthena to John H. Allen 9-21-1857 (no return)
Allen, Marthena to John H. Ford 9-?-1857 (9-22-1857)
Allen, Mary Ann to W. H. Smith 2-19-1861 (2-20-1861)
Allen, Mary E. to Lemon Hale 7-1-1859 (7-3-1859)
Allen, Mary J. to John Mcore 9-18-1866 (9-12?-1866)
Allen, Mary T. to John L. Stark 9-12-1873 (9-14-1873)
Allen, May to James Sims 8-2-1855
Allen, Mical to J. J. Harney 11-20-1867 (11-21-1867)
Allen, Minney to James Tubb 3-17-1866 (3-18-1866)
Allen, N. W. to W. D. Carnes 8-29-1876
Allen, Nancy F. to Jorden W. Goggins 1-6-1872 (1-7-1872)
Allen, Nancy Jane to Luther G. Love 10-14-1858
Allen, Nancy to William S. Eastham 9-13-1854
Allen, Paralee to Dempsy Braswell 9-21-1872 (9-22-1872)
Allen, Partheny to John Roggers 1-9-1851 (1-1?-1851)
Allen, Philis? to J. W. Kennedy 8-26-1849
Allen, Rebecca F. to J. J. Mullican 2-18-1875 (no return)
Allen, S. to James L. Mullica 4-28-1858 (4-29-1858)
Allen, Sarah to Dempsey Taylor 8-19-1871 (8-20-1871)
Allen, Sarah to Joseph Starn 3-29-1863 (no return)
Allen, Sarah to Wm. Capshane 2-27-1868 (2-28-1868)
Allen, Susan to Amous Neel 6-2-1858 (6-3-1858)
Allen, Susan to H. C. Easthan 2-23-1861 (2-24-1861)
Alnage, Mary to Samuel Walker ?-23-1861 (no return)
Alvis, S. F. to R. A. Lawrence 10-2-1872 (10-10-1872)
Amery, Nancy M. to Henry Vansur 7-23-1851 (8-9-1851)
Amonet, Adaline to John Vantrease 12-23-1876 (12-24-1876)

Anderson, Amanda J. to James M. Durlin 12-29-1866
   (no return)
Anderson, Caroline to Book Rich 9-28-1875
Anderson, Cintha to Joe Cantrell 8-24-1875 (8-25-1875)
Anderson, E. C. to Joseph S. Owen 9-10-1870 (9-11-1870)
Anderson, Emilly D. to G. L. Robinson 9-6-1851
Anderson, Fanny to Jessee Garner 4-5-1869 (4-16-1869)
Anderson, Helan to J. J. Billins 8-28-1878 (no return)
Anderson, Jain W. to William Waller 6-21-1865
Anderson, Jane to C. A. Cantrell 11-20-1875 (11-21-1875)
Anderson, Julia to George Foutch 8-24-1878 (9-8-1878)
Anderson, L. A. C. to C. E. Adamson 8-23-1870 (8-25-1870)
Anderson, Lina to Wm. Cumins 8-4-1879
Anderson, M. W. to William Waller 6-20-1865 (no return)
Anderson, Martha to Fay M. Stuk? 1-29-1867 (1-31-1867)
Anderson, Mary E. to S. C. Hale 10-3-1866 (10-5-1866)
Anderson, Nancy C. to Ebaneser Snow 1-24-1866 (no return)
Anderson, Nancy to James Bennett 12-18-1875 (12-19-1875)
Anderson, Parlee to James Ownes 8-26-1873
Anderson, S. E. to L. D. Wall 10-1-1879 (10-2-1879)
Angleman, Martha to Joseph Nunley 3-18-1872 (3-19-1872)
Argo, Jane to Elijah Chamlins 5-1-1851
Arnell, Dorinda to Anderson Taylor 12-24-1878 (no return)
Arnell, Malinda to James M. Page 5-19-1880 (5-20-1880)
Arnold, Martha J. to N. J. Patty 12-12-1862 (no return)
Arnold, Nancy E. to Lawson Cantrell 1-5-1864 (1-14-1864)
Arnold, Sarah to Johnathan Griffith 11-4-1872 (11-8-1872)
Arnold, Susan F. to David Neale 4-12-1873 (4-13-1873)
Ashford, Twendy to J. P. Farller 3-24-1866 (3-25-1866)
Ashworth, Betsy to James Manson 11-7-1874 (11-9-1874)
Ashworth, Elizabeth to Wm. Hunt 5-21-1867 (no return)
Ashworth, Fanney to Young Stokes 10-17-1873 (10-18-1873) [B]
Ashworth, Mary to Francis Turner 1-18-1860 (1-19-1860)
Askew, Caroline to Wm. Sewell 1-31-1863
Askew, Eliza to John Hunter 9-27-1865 (9-28-1865)
Askew, Mary to James M. Fouch 6-10-1872 (6-16-1872)
Askew, Mary to Sanal Bellow 12-25-1864
Atnip, Adaline to J. T. Manier 7-21-1860 (7-28-1860)
Atnip, Cindy to Ninavey Mullican 7-6-1854
Atnip, Darthouly to Benjamin J. Wilkinson 7-27-1870
Atnip, Elizabeth to Garrison Taylor 7-15-1852
Atnip, Frances to Thomas Shields 5-11-1876
Atnip, Gemima to Hugh Page 2-3-1863
Atnip, M. A. to J. H. Hayes 1-16-1869
Atnip, Malisy to H. H. Cantrell 3-27-1875 (3-29-1875)
Atnip, Mandelia to Andrew Jackson 3-15-1867 (3-16-1867)
Atnip, Martha to John Turner 8-23-1879 (8-24-1879)
Atnip, Mary to G. B. Rankhorn 12-29-1857
Atnip, Olive to Tilmon D. Cantrell 11-17-1868 (11-21-1868)
Atnip, Polly Elender to Pleasant Watts 11-29-1855
Atnip, Virginia to J. B. Cantrell 8-26-1868 (8-27-1868)
Atwell, Eliza to Samuel Casey 7-23-1857
Atwell, Lucy to Isaiah Jr. White 9-8-1860
Atwell, Susan to Jacob Drewery 3-16-1870 (no return)
Atwell, V. F. to F. P. Lee 3-21-1869
Ausbey, Tennessee to Jessee A. Jennings 5-25-1872 (5-26-1872)
Austen, Dosha to John W. Botts 12-11-1852 (12-13-1852)
Austin, Illinois to Owen Meadly 12-17-1872 (12-18-1872)
Auston, Susan to Mat Martain 12-21-1878 (12-22-1878)
Avant, Delia to Robert L. Scruggs 6-1-1874 (6-3-1874)
Avant, Josie to W. M. Johnson 12-2-1878 (12-26-1878)
Avant, M. H. to W. C. Potter 11-10-1869
Axem, Mandy to Alexandria Maner 3-17-1868 (3-22-1868)
Badger, D. A. to James A. Hathaway 10-29-1876
   (exec. no date)
Bailif, M. A. to S. Fisher 12-24-1877
Bailiff, Mary A. to James R. Newsom no date (exec.2-16-1854
Bailiff, Nancy to James R. Jones 5-1-1855 (no return)
Bain, Emaline to H. L. Hale 10-21-1865 (10-22-1865)
Bain, Frances to Wm. Striclin 2-19-1867
Bain, Lucindy F. to Benjamin Atnip 4-15-1868 (no return)
Bain, Mary Ann to Bethel A. Adamson 11-22-183?
Bain, Melvina to Hiram Hildreth 8-16-1862 (9-17-1862)
Bain, Roda to G. W. Walker 11-8-1871 (11-12-1871)
Baine, Anna to Levey Robinson 1-13-1873

Baine, Delila to R. A. Trammell 4-30-1875 (5-2-1875)
Baine, M. J. to M. L. Green 10-21-1867 (10-24-1867)
Bains, Elizabeth to John Stephens 11-25-1862 (11-26-1862)
Bains, Mary M. J. to John S. Stephens 7-30-1856 (no return)
Bains, Matilda Ann to Henry Pipkin 9-10-1851 (no return)
Baird, M. B. to C. B. Barton 2-1-1876 (no return)
Baird, Oppelia to B. F. Bell 12-21-1875 (no return)
Baits, Martha J. to John Oakley 9-7-1867 (no return)
Baker, Callie to Jacob Neale 2-21-1874 (2-22-1874) [B]
Baker, Doke to Jack Davis 9-2-1878
Baker, Manorvey to James A. Briggs 12-3-1856
Baker, Mary to J. M. Lefever 12-25-1878 (12-26-1878)
Baker, Susan to Washington Purtle 7-17-1856
Baliff, Roxanna to John B. Claiborn 12-24-1879 (no return)
Baliss, M. C. to W. A. Trammel 1-11-1876 (1-13-1876)
Bane, Adiline to Wm. Alen 1-29-1867
Bane, Calona to F. A. Walker 2-3-1875 (2-18-1875)
Bane, Delila J. to S. J. Hilaritt 12-2-1861 (12-3-1861)
Bane, Harriette M. to James Spencer 9-27-1849
Bane, Nancy Ann to Moses Pack 1-25-1860 (1-29-1860)
Bane, Norcissa to John Pack 1-29-1853 (1-30-1853)
Banks, Annie J. to Wm. Etheridge 12-4-1872 (12-5-1872)
Banks, Margaret to Wm. P. Johnson 8-3-1855
Banks, Margrett to Y. L. Hirendon 2-14-1871 (2-20-1871)
Banks, Martha to Thomas J. Hoss 7-19-1870 (7-21-1870)
Banks, Mary to Joseph L. Banks 2-16-1876
Banks, S. M. to G. M. Mears 8-29-1877 (no return)
Banskan, Elizabeth to Cristerfer Adkins 10-12-1865 (no return)
Barens, Martha to M. C. Colewich 8-16-1856
Barens, Mary to Isaac W. Eledge 1-5-1855 (1-11-1855)
Barens, Mary to John Ferrell 11-10-1856 (11-13-1856)
Barger, C. E. to P. M. Williams 3-9-1877 (3-11-1877)
Barger, Eliza J. to Joseph H. Blackbun 7-30-1861 (8-8-1861)
Barger, Elizabeth to Thomas G. Ward 12-23-1872 (12-26-1872)
Barger, M. C. to J. C. Evans 10-18-1876 (10-19-1876)
Barger, Martha to Edward Evans 10-14-1851
Barger, Mary to Henry M. File 9-30-1851 (10-1-1851)
Barger, Sarah E. to Moses A. Stark 11-16-1865
Barks, Jane to William Herrin 3-6-1854 (3-7-1854)
Barnes, Elizabeth to Wm. Winfree 5-1-1860
Barnes, Fanny to Allen Fuson 7-25-1871 (7-30-1871) [B]
Barnes, Frances P. to Mathew Jones 12-26-1853 (12-27-1853)
Barnes, H. E. to Welcum Adcok 10-23-1876 (no return)
Barnes, Josephine to Benjamin F. Tooney 2-4-1873 (2-6-1873)
Barret, Rachal to Trandus? Rosa 6-27-1865 (no return)
Barrette, Nancy to John Keef 4-30-1849 (5-1-1849)
Barry, Mary to James Groomes 9-4-1876
Bascum, Malcina to Lemuel H. Fite 10-21-1862 (10-26-1862)
Bass, Elizabeth to Wm. Griffith 1-11-1872 [B]
Bass, Elizabeth to Wm. Philips 11-9-1862
Bass, Mary Ann to James P. Tichle? 4-22-1851 (4-23-1851)
Bass, Rachel to Samuel Hickey 6-27-1874 [B]
Bates, Didady to Wm. Crook 10-27-1877 (10-28-1877)
Bates, Hannah to David Smith 10-12-1870 (no return) [B]
Bates, Jane to Lafait Williams 3-28-1868 (3-29-1868) [B]
Bates, Locky J. to Dallas Malone 2-1-1867 (no return)
Bates, Margret to Charles Came 2-1-1867 [B]
Bates, Marthey R. to Bird Bates 10-28-1870 (10-30-1870)
Bates, Mary to Thomas Selvedge 8-13-1863 (no return)
Bates, Nancy to William Hennsley 1-29-1872 (1-30-1872)
Batey, Algelina to Jackson Brimer 1-15-1859
Bats, Dedama to George W. Lambertson 8-25-1866 (no return)
Batton, Amandy C. to E. P. James 9-9-1867
Batton, M. F. to D. James 2-10-1868 (2-11-1868)
Batton, Martha M. to Matthew S. Olovers 8-17-1849
   (exec. no date)
Batts, Elizabeth to John S. Holley 9-30-1862 (10-2-1862)
Baty, Catherine to Wm. R. Goodman 5-20-1869
Baty, Hannah E. to Isaac L. Davis 10-23-1871
Baty, Jane to Rufus Pain 10-3-1874
Baty, Mary to Randle Hile 1-16-1869
Baughan, Supprona J. to John T. Robinson 11-16-1853
Bayliff, Rebekee to John Chapman 12-18-1866 (12-24-1866)
Bayne, Sallie to John Burnett 10-2-1871
Bayne, Sarah to John Striclin 2-8-1860

Bayne, Sarah to Robert Johnson 9-24-1875 (9-26-1875)
Bayne, Sarah to Wm. Brent 5-26-1880 (no return)
Beal, Irenia A. R. to B. C. Roland 8-18-1860 (8-19-1860)
Bean, Nancy to Wm. Hawker 6-19-1876 (6-21-1876)
Beanbush, Martha to Alford Baker 4-18-1866 (4-22-1866)
Becker, Catherine to Jessee F. Lafever 3-22-1860 (3-28-1860)
Beckwitt, Harriet to George H. Hill 11-30-1852
Been, Elizabeth to D. A. Parker 11-30-1871 (12-1-1871)
Bell, Parthena M. to S. B. Whaley 3-21-1855
Bellins, Parrile to James Young 9-19-1866
Bennett, Amanda to Levi Foutch 3-11-1876
Bennett, Eliza to McAdo Sandlin 5-11-1867
Bennett, Emma to Patrick Bussell 4-12-1876 (4-13-1876)
Bennett, Lucinda T. to J. H. P. Parkerson 11-2-1872
          (11-3-1872)
Bennett, Lucity to John Scott 1-13-1849 (1-14-1849)
Bennett, Margaret F. to James F. Hooper 9-25-1860
          (9-26-1860)
Bennett, Mary J. to Simeon Williams 5-1-1879 (5-4-1879)
Bennett, Mary to Thomas Pipkins 4-3-1876 (4-5-1876)
Bennett, Mary to W. Hendrexan 3-30-1863
Bennett, Matilda to Wm. Alexandra 3-13-1878 (3-15-1878)
Bennett, Melissa Ann to Wm. Scott 10-14-1850 (10-20-1850)
Bennett, Nancy to John Parkerson 9-7-1857 (9-8-1857)
Bennett, Parile to Luke W. Neal 4-3-1861 (exec. no date)
Bennett, Permelia E. to James Sandlin 1-15-1866
Bennett, Polly Ann to Wm. Scott 2-26-1862 (3-2-1862)
Bennett, Tennie to James Wood 9-22-1877
Bennette, Eliz. W. to T. L. Woode 1-22-1876 (1-23-1876)
Bennette, Matilda to Henderson Hill 3-14-1853
Bentele, Elizabeth to Wm. C. Williams 4-1-1850 (4-2-1850)
Benton, Mary A. to G. W. Pickett 8-12-1873 (8-14-1873)
Berks, Susan to Isaiah D. Wilson 10-17-1854
Berry, Bettie J. to C. C. Avant 10-12-1872 (10-13-1872)
Berry, Frances to A. H. Thomas 8-31-1875 (7-8-1875)
Berry, Juley to Johney West 11-7-1877 (11-8-1877)
Berry, M. T. to J. H. Stephens 8-23-1872 (9-8-1872)
Berry, Mattie to John A. Fuson 12-3-1872 (12-19-1872)
Berry, Nancy A. to Thomas H. Stark 9-11-1872 (9-12-1872)
Berry, Zorof to N. E. Hayes 11-14-1877 (no return)
Bery, M. to William Cantrell 11-27-1866
Beshears, Lucinda to Wm. Aggie 11-13-1875 (11-17-1875)
Bess, Caroline to Alexander Besheres 7-18-1867
Bess, Martha to Martin Officer 8-13-1870 (no return) [B]
Bethel, Madre to Isaac M. Fite 9-6-1856 (no return)
Bethel, Mary to Monroe Hill 9-22-1875 (9-23-1875)
Bethell, Eliza to E. M. Whaley 1-2-1868 (1-2-1868)
Bethell, Sary P. to Samuel C. Duncan 9-4-1870 (9-5-1870)
Bethells, Elizabeth to Eli Rowland 1-27-1849 (1-31-1849)
Bevert, Mary to John D. Simmons 3-9-1863 (no return)
Biford, Jane to Wm. H. George 1-18-1864 (no return)
Biggs, Mary to Robert Floide 1-10-1876
Bigsby, Frances M. to Francis Fergerson 6-14-1851
          (exec. no date)
Billings, Sarah to James Young 2-4-1870 (no return)
Billings, Sarah to John W. Shaw 7-2-1873 (7-8-1873)
Bing, Mary Frances to James J. Bennett 1-18-1866
Biss, Parilee to Jasper Manning 1-8-1870 (1-9-1870)
Bixley, Sarah to W. W. Colley omitted (8-4-1866)
Blackburn, Esnoria H. to T. W. Eason 4-26-1873 (4-27-1873)
Blackburn, Jain to John Madin no date (exec.9-6-1866)
Blackburn, Sarah A. to M. M. Floyd 3-29-1865
Blair, Elizabeth to Thomas Rugle 5-10-1871 (5-14-1871)
Blakship, Martha to Francis Baker 4-18-1866 (no return)
Blankenship, Mary E. to D. B. Worley 12-26-1869
Blare, Elender J. to Berry Y. Cantrell 1-15-1852
Bluhm, Rebecca to M. C. Hayes 2-4-1880
Blunt, Elizabeth J. to Wm. L. Walker 1-5-1864 (1-6-1864)
Bly, Nancy to Wm. Tafley 9-20-1876 (9-21-1876)
Blye, Mary to W. N. Johnson 12-19-1863 (no return)
Boatwright, Judah Ann to Wm. G. Foster 10-2-1861 (10-3-1861)
Bohanan, Martha to W. T. Coggin 11-4-1875 (11-7-1875)
Bond, George Ann to James M. Harper 4-14-1880 (4-15-1880)
Bond, Mary to John Hail 5-7-1866 (5-13-1866) [B]
Bond, R. F. to W. S. Burton 3-1-1877 (3-22-1877)

Bond, Tennessee to John T. Hallerin 11-23-1872 (11-24-1872)
Bond, Tossa to Wm. E. Burton 4-3-1865 (4-17-1865)
Bonds, Elisabeth M. to George Marks 6-17-1868 (6-18-1868)
Bone, Mary N. to James P. Doss 1-19-1866 (1-29-1866)
Bone, Mary to Jefferson Hail 5-7-1866 (5-10-1866)
Book, Winey to John Jones 9-21-1865
Boren, Nancy D. to Isaac Whaley 7-21-1849 (no return)
Bota?, Fanny to James Beatey 4-25-1873
Bottes, Elizabeth to A. J. Kersey 6-17-1876 (6-18-1876)
Botts, Eliza to Wm Keltey 10-19-1854
Botts, Harriet E. J. to R. V. Wright 4-9-1857
Botts, Matta to Monroe F. Doss 12-27-1857 (12-28-1857)
Botts, Nancy to Isaac Hutcheson 11-11-1852
Bottums, Mariah to Henry Garison 6-16-1863 (6-18-1863)
Boughers, Martha to Wm. Crips 8-22-1872
Bowers, Elizabeth M. to Thomas E. West 1-8-1853 (1-12-1853)
Bowers, Julis F. to James L. Wood 5-19-1853 (exec. no date)
Bowers, Malcina to L. H. Fite 10-21-1862 (10-26-1862)
Bowers, Mary J. to B. F. Stephens 5-5-1857 (5-6-1857)
Bowers, Rosannah to Jacob Pack 1-27-1850
Boyd, Catherine to John J. Lane 8-30-1853 (no return)
Boyd, Cathrine to James Ray 3-9-1854
Boyd, Emiline to Wily Chapman 1-16-1859
Boyd, Varnetta to L. B. Fisher 6-1-1863 (no return)
Boyne, Liley to Jackson B. Hayse 7-28-1873
Bozart, Mary to George Smith 11-26-1856 (12-27-1856)
Bozarth, Angaline to James M. Bozarth 7-13-1872 (7-14-1872)
Bozarth, Julia to R. T. Frisly 12-4-1864
Bozarth, Phelee to G. E. Baker 8-?-1857 (8-11-1857)
Bozarth, S. L. to Wm. Medlin 10-25-1875 (11-3-1875)
Bozorth, Helen to C. C. Smith 9-12-1860 (no return)
Bozorth, Sarah to G. W. Gorman 10-20-1864
Bracher, Tabitha to Madison Keaton 9-30-1858
Bracken, Rachel to Wesly Mash 9-18-1851
Bradd, Mary J. to J. W. Crook 10-6-1869 (no return)
Bradford, Sarah to Josiah Hollinsworth 1-9-1868 (1-9-1868)
Bradley, Elizabeth to J. M. Hall 2-18-1862 (2-20-1862)
Bradley, Nancy to James Garrison 7-16-1857 (7-17-1857)
Bradly, Angelea to Thomas W. Goodner 2-26-1867 (3-10-1867)
Bradly, Kanzady to Benjamon Ellis 8-22-1879
Brady, Mary Ann to A. M. Preston 9-19-1869 (no return)
Braidy, Sarah E. to John Monroe Crook 2-6-1867
Brand, Julian to Alfred Jones 3-18-1851 (3-20-1851)
Braswell, Anna to E. D. Tish 10-1-1866 (no return)
Braswell, Charity to James Cutchins? 12-12-1855 (12-17-1855)
Braswell, Clary to Henry Stokes 1-3-1870 (no return)
Braswell, Demares to George Cathcart 1-15-1856
Braswell, Elizabeth to Edward W. Edge 8-1-1877 (8-5-1877)
Braswell, Elizabeth to Harry Killy 10-9-1858 (no return)
Braswell, Elizabeth to Wm. B. Shehane 1-13-1875 (1-14-1875)
Braswell, Harret to Isaac Shehun 2-12-1866 (2-13-1866)
Braswell, Harriett A. to William Edge 2-23-1871
Braswell, Jane to Wm. B. Barnes 8-28-1862
Braswell, Louiza to Zacheriah Smith 10-18-1861 (no return)
Braswell, Louizah to Jack Sulens 4-29-1866 (no return) [B]
Braswell, Louizah to Join Fuller 5-23-1866 (5-29-1866)
Braswell, Lucisa to David C. Young 7-25-1877 (no return)
Braswell, M. C. to Mathew B. Bayne 12-28-1870
Braswell, M. L. to C. C. Jarerel? 12-1-1873 (12-18-1873)
Braswell, Mahaly to Henry Joins 6-6-1870
Braswell, Martha to P. L. Braswell 10-16-1858 (no return)
Braswell, Martha to Wm. Young 2-14-1878 (2-15-1878)
Braswell, Mary J. to Shane L. Malone 10-4-1870 (10-9-1870)
Braswell, Mary to George Neal 6-28-1861 (6-31-1861)
Braswell, Mary to George Snotgrass 10-14-1876 (10-15-1876)
Braswell, Mary to Jacob A. King 9-19-1873
Braswell, May L. to W.H. Blackburn 9-14-1874
Braswell, Nancy to R. V. Smith 1-29-1857
Braswell, Parilla to Alexander Milligan 8-2-1860
Braswell, Priscilla to A. W. Patterson 2-2-1864 (no return)
Braswell, Rebecca to Wm. Staren 6-12-1858 (6-13-1858)
Braswell, Sarah to George W. Norton 8-12-1869
Braswell, Sintha J. to Nathaniel H. Cradoc 1-20-1864
          (no return)
Braswell, Verginia to J. H. Davis 11-25-1876 (11-26-1876)

Braswell, Vina to J. M. Paity 9-25-1875
Bratten, E. to W. R. Cooper 3-17-1876 (3-19-1876)
Bratten, Louisa to A. M. Witt 3-24-1857 (3-25-1857)
Bratten, Nancy E. to Allen C. Vandigreft 7-29-1874 (7-3-1874)
Bratten, Nancy L. to James Allen 10-29-1868 (10-30-1868)
Bratton, Hulda Ann to A. S. Smith 1-13-1857 (1-15-1857)
Bratton, Mary to James H. Lamberson 9-2-1853 (9-8-1853)
Bratton, Mattie E. to G. W. Turney 8-3-1870
Bratton, Nancy to Robert L. Clark 1-24-1852 (1-28-1852)
Bratton, Sarena to Mikael Mingle 1-14-1860 (1-18-1860)
Bratton, Sopha J. to John A. Carol 1-31-1850 (2-5-1850)
Brensley, Nancey J. to Wm. A. Wills 3-30-1872 (4-2-1872)
Breverman?, Lucinda to Thomas C. Wroe 10-10-1849
          (exec. no date)
Brewington, Nancy to Wm. H. Marcrum 1-9-1852
Briant, Jane to Obediah Barrett 10-6-1857 (1-3-1858)
Briant, Margarett to John R. Adamson 8-14-1875 (8-19-1875)
Briant, Marth to Wash Briant 1-24-1866 (1-25-1866) [B]
Briant, Nancy Ann to G. W. Adamson 12-30-1868 (12-31-1868)
Briant, Nancy M. to William L. Driver 1-23-1856 (1-24-1856)
Briant, Rachel to Wills Baret 1-26-1855 (1-3?-1855)
Bridges, Elizabeth to Wm. Estes 11-11-1854
Bridges, F. J. to J. M. Driver 3-7-1877 (3-15-1877)
Bridges, Mary T. to Joseph T. Lawrence 1-14-1868
Bridges, Parila to Samuel Luckey 9-16-1859
Brien, Martha A. to Eliel Tubb 7-11-1852 (7-15-1852)
Briggs, Elizabeth to Wm. Floyd 7-12-1862 (7-13-1862)
Briggs, Mary A. to A. B. Hollemen 9-6-1854 (9-7-1856?)
Brim, Elizabeth to James L. Allen 9-9-1854 (9-1?-1854)
Brim, Mary Ann to David Wright 2-6-1851
Brimm, Nancy to John Marcum 4-20-1866 (no return)
Britten, Mary to George Goodner 2-25-1868 (no return) [B]
Britton, Jennie to David Owens 11-28-1879 (no return)
Brock, Eliza. to Wm. Young 8-31-1859 (no return)
Brock, Ella to Wm. Sertain 10-17-1874 (10-18-1874)
Brock, Josie to H. S. Winfrey 7-25-1879 (8-6-1879)
Brooks, Erman to Goolsbury Kerby 4-1-1858 (4-10-1858)
Broseley, Teley to James W. Brown 8-28-1872 (no return)
Brow, Mary to Governor McClenin ? (no return) [B]
Brown, Caroline to Abner Carter 12-27-1875 (12-28-1875)
Brown, Gincey to Britton Barnes 1-20-1865 (no return)
Brown, Mary to John Frazor 2-25-1854
Brown, Morindy K. to Abslom? Carter 1-13-1873 (date omit.)
Brown, Nancy to Wm. Liles 1-30-1859 (1-31-1859)
Brown, Pink to John Bayne 9-8-1873
Brown, S. C. to Britten Barnes 4-27-1871
Brown, Sarah A. to Henry L. Puckett 3-9-1874 (3-12-1874)
Bryant, H. E. to J. W. Gilbert 12-15-1856 (12-18-1856)
Bryant, Roda E. to George Bonds 9-22-1870
Buckly, Josephine D. to George Marks 12-29-1870
Buckner, Eliza to Richard Pedigo 11-3-1869 (12-4-1869)
Buckner, Sarah T. to Samuel Heron 5-22-1855 (5-24-1855)
Bulington, Aseneth to Benjamin Ravelin 12-21-1867 (no return)
Bullard, E. L. to W. P. Harmon 8-24-1870 (9-11-1870)
Bullard, Eliza to Jackson Goodwin 8-6-1852 (8-7-1852)
Bullard, Frances to John Hilliard 9-18-1855
Bullard, I. J. to Thomas Suthin 8-17-1870 (8-18-1870)
Bullard, Macy Ann to Hyram Johnson 2-20-1868
Bullard, Margrett J. to Wm. Barnes 8-1-1872
Bullard, Mary E. to Daniel Mathis 7-23-1864 (7-24-1864)
Bullard, Rachel P. to Joseph Hibden 4-3-1869 (4-4-1869)
Bullard, Rachel to Simpson Estridge 1-27-1855
Bung?, Rexey A. to Francis M. Spurlock 12-4-1856
Bunton, Mary to Bransford Evans 4-3-1866 (4-6-1866)
Burden, L. L. to Jerry Turner 2-11-1869 (2-12-1869) [B]
Burnette, Elizabeth E. to Wm. C. Hendrickson 12-7-1851
Burton, Amanda W. to W. R. Huddleston 7-16-1879 (7-20-1879)
Burton, Angaline to Ezekial Maynor 2-5-1865
Burton, Catharine to James Parker 1-2-1852 (1-4-1852)
Burton, Martha J. to B. A. Martin 4-21-1880
Burton, Martha to J. L. Terry 3-14-1876 (3-16-1876)
Burton, Martha to Jefferson Dyer 8-7-1848 (8-17-1848)
Burton, Martha to Wade Jones 1-2-1878 (1-3-1878)
Burton, Sarah V. to J. S. Close 1-4-1869 (1-14-1869)
Buson, Sarah to Seazer? Hayes 8-23-1876

Bussel, Jane to Hiram W. Coole 2-5-1850
Bussel, Sarah E. to Marton Dalton 4-13-1853 (4-14-1853)
Buster, M. C. to E. R. Atnip 8-16-1875 (8-17-1875)
Butington, Asanith to Benjamin Roveland 12-21-1867 (12-22-1867)
Butler, Martha Ann to Nicholas Vaughn 12-20-1856 (12-21-1856)
Buttram, Josie to John E. Drury? 1-20-1880
Byd, Mary E. to Samuel H. Camron 5-7-1856 (5-8-1856)
Cadd, Martha An to L. D. Braswell 4-1-1877
Cader, Eliza to Fuller Sandlin 10-26-1876
Calcot, Jane to Jackson Hunter 9-7-1874 (9-8-1874) [B]
Caldwell, Jane to James M. Vaughn 2-20-1850 (2-21-1850)
Caleps, M. A. to J. B. Mitchel 9-11-1877 (9-13-1877)
Calhoone, Fanney to W. L. Bethel 4-1-1859 (no return)
Calicot, Nancy to Andrew Reynolds 5-7-1866 (5-9-1866)
Calicut, Nancy to Andy Reynolds no dates (w/ '66 entries [B]
Callicut, Lucy Jane to Winket Robinson 9-20-1854 (9-21-1854)
Calvert, Eliza to V. D. Blankinship 9-30-1865 (10-1-1865)
Calvin, Cintha P. to James T. White 1-29-1864 (2-3-1866)
Calwell, Cyntha to James Fisher 1-7-1862
Calwell, Mary to Wm. J. Fisher 3-22-1861 (3 = 24 = 1861)
Camden, Batheana to James Powel no date (exec. 4-22-182
Cameron, Sarah M. to W. J. Isbell 2-1-1861 (2-3-1861)
Cameron, Susan to James Hayes 12-22-1865
Cammeron, Emily to Andy Glenn 5-19-1871 (5-18?-1871)
Camron, Erun to Matthew T. Dozier 5-28-1856 (5-29-1856)
Canady, Emma to J. S. Dunlop 6-11-1871
Canady, Josie to Rubin C. Bomer 4-20-1871
Cancin?, Mary E. to A. L. Foster 2-5-1860
Canedy, Mary Ann to Henry Vick 10-6-1866 (10-7-1866)
Cannady, Amanda to J. H. Seawell 7-30-1876
Cannon, Mary E. to Thomas J. Adamson 4-8-1861
Cannon, Nelly E. to Samuel M. Keeton 8-6-1860 (8-7-1860)
Cannon, Sarah Ann to John L. Boyd 3-13-1856
Cantrel, Fany to Clay Bary 3-19-1866 (no return)
Cantrel, Kenie to Henry Judkins 12-21-1859 (12-30-1859)
Cantrell, America A. to Foderick J. Titsworth 7-18-1855 (7-19-1855)
Cantrell, B. E. to J. A. Taylor 9-24-1873 (9-28-1873)
Cantrell, Barby to James M. Moore 10-16-1856 (no return)
Cantrell, C. F. to Sol. Williams 10-12-1875
Cantrell, C. M. to L. D. Cantrell 6-4-1866 (no return)
Cantrell, Callie to Henry Show 1-23-1879
Cantrell, Canzady to A. English 10-2-1852
Cantrell, Catharin to S. T. Britt 5-25-1871 (no return)
Cantrell, Charity to John D. Hill 9-18-1851
Cantrell, E. J. to S. B. Davis 10-18-1876
Cantrell, Elisa to Archabald Redmon 11-15-1852
Cantrell, Eliza E. to J. R. Reeder 12-11-1875 (12-16-1875)
Cantrell, Elizabeth to J. B. Cantrell 10-25-1876 (no return)
Cantrell, Elizabeth to John M. Linder 9-14-1859 (9-20-1859)
Cantrell, Elizabeth to Nathan Z. Jenkins? 8-14-1855 (8-20-1855)
Cantrell, Elizabeth to Wm. M. Anderson 11-25-1867 (no return)
Cantrell, Ellennora to Wm. Thomas Keel 11-25-1871
Cantrell, F. M. to B. F. Flanders 5-15-1863
Cantrell, Famia to Wm. T. Griffeth 10-30-1866 (10-31-1866)
Cantrell, H. A. to J. L. Button 7-3-1877
Cantrell, H. to J. Fanan 7-15-1865 (no return)
Cantrell, Hannah to David Delong 2-11-1875
Cantrell, Hannah to John H. Roberts 8-26-1871 (8-27-1871)
Cantrell, Honriah B. to John H. Hayese 9-27-1873 (9-29-1873)
Cantrell, Jane to James Oakes 3-23-1850 (3-24-1850)
Cantrell, Jennie to J. C. Jones 6-1-1880 (no return)
Cantrell, Josey to David Isbell 11-12-1868 [B]
Cantrell, Julia Ann to Wm. Linder 9-5-1859 (not endorsed)
Cantrell, Keziah to James Roberts 11-10-1863
Cantrell, L. A. to John L. Cockrum 3-16-1878 (3-17-1878)
Cantrell, L. A. to S. D. Thompson 12-26-1876 (no return)
Cantrell, Lavina to Cheslew W. Cantrell 5-2-1850
Cantrell, Lucey to David Griffith 2-2-1879
Cantrell, M. A. to C. P. Lowerey 1-27-1877 (1-29-1877)
Cantrell, M. E. to A. C. Mulican 12-15-1877 (12-16-1877)
Cantrell, M. E. to J. P. Culwell 12-15-1877 (12-16-1877)
Cantrell, M. E. to J. P. Hennafree 7-19-1866
Cantrell, M. J. to A. P. Cantrell 12-21-1868
Cantrell, Malissa to James L. Fuson 8-3-1857 (9?-3-1857)
Cantrell, Manerva to Larkin Bane 1-1-1853 (2-2-1853)

Cantrell, Marth to Archable Barnes 10-10-1878 (10-15-1878)
Cantrell, Martha A. to L. G. Bing 2-3-1863 (2-4-1863)
Cantrell, Martha Ann to James W. Melton 3-20-1851
Cantrell, Martha J. to Caleb Anderson 10-13-1852
Cantrell, Martha J. to J. M. Redman 8-18-1864
Cantrell, Martha J. to Starkey Cotton 6-30-1857 (no return)
Cantrell, Martha to Elias N. Green 5-3-1864 (5-5-1864)
Cantrell, Martha to John M. Elkins 3-20-1869
Cantrell, Mary Ann to A. M. Wamack 10-5-1854
Cantrell, Mary E. to Joseph Bryant 4-23-1879 (no return)
Cantrell, Mary E. to Louis K. Cantrell 1-20-1868 (1-22-1868)
Cantrell, Mary J. to James S. Williams 4-12-1865 (4-14-1865)
Cantrell, Mary J. to William Parker 4-4-1874 (4-5-1874)
Cantrell, Mary S. to J. W. C. Holland 4-7-1875
Cantrell, Mary to John M. Cotten 12-12-1848 (12-14-1848)
Cantrell, Mary to Levy Laxitor 11-5-1862 (11-9-1862)
Cantrell, Mary to P. G. Looney 9-15-1869 (9-16-1869)
Cantrell, Mary to Walker Moore 1-21-1871 (1-22-1871)
Cantrell, Mary to Wm. Benson 12-27-1864 (12-28-1864)
Cantrell, Nancy Ann to Thomas A. Blair 4-23-1851 (5-1-1851)
Cantrell, Nancy to George Adams 3-27-1849 (3-?-1849)
Cantrell, Nancy to H. L. C. Moore 3-30-1867 (3-31-1867)
Cantrell, Nancy to James M. Dulaney 4-8-1869
Cantrell, Nancy to James P. Greer 9-19-1873 (9-24-1873)
Cantrell, Nancy to Wm. A. Poller 7-24-1852 (7-27-1852)
Cantrell, Nancy to Wm. Pollard 8-25-1849 (no return)
Cantrell, Narcissa to John H. Evans 7-9-1874
Cantrell, Narcissy to John Evans 10-8-1853 (10-10-1853)
Cantrell, Nelly to Newton Avery 7-4-1866 (7-5-1866)
Cantrell, Permelia to James A. Rigsby 7-27-1852 (no return)
Cantrell, Polly to Anthoney Satterfield 9-27-1873 (9-29-1873)
Cantrell, R. G. to B. A. Davis 2-24-1876
Cantrell, R. J. to E. J. Laster 9-25-1876
Cantrell, Rosajane? to Azariah Lasiter 7-18-1866 (7-19-1866)
Cantrell, S. A. to J. N. Donnell 12-27-1875
Cantrell, S. T. to G. W. Childress 9-27-1877
Cantrell, S. to O. D. Potter 1-7-1860 (1-9-1860)
Cantrell, Samanth to Wesley Sanders 12-27-1865 (12-28-1865)
Cantrell, Sarah C. to Newton T. Adcock 1-7-1874 (1-8-1874)
Cantrell, Sarah J. to John K. Garham 4-28-1863 (4-30-1863)
Cantrell, Sarah to J. B. Durham 6-22-1871
Cantrell, Sarah to James L. Cantrell 5-18-1871 (5-24-1871)
Cantrell, Sarah to John Davis 3-2-1868 (3-3-1868)
Cantrell, Sarah to Thomas Moore 7-10-1879 (no return)
Cantrell, Sarah to William M. Pack 12-9-1867
Cantrell, Sharlott B. to Franklin P. Byars 3-12-1874
Cantrell, Susan to James P. Stoner 9-27-1855
Cantrell, Talitha to Thomas Blare 1-1-1852
Cantrell, Talitha to Wesley Sanders 11-23-1848
Cantrill, Catharine to E. J. Lassiter 9-3-1874 (9-4-1874)
Caphshaw, Adline to A. D. Hathway 9-7-1866 (8?-15-1866)
Capshaw, Elenor to Levi Haney 3-24-1857
Capshaw, F. C. to D. W. Capshaw 3-6-1875 (no return)
Capshaw, F. E. to C. A. Taylor 12-24-1875 (12-26-1875)
Capshaw, Hester to Joseph Grammer 2-5-1852
Capshaw, Mary to Wm. Rankhorn 4-23-1859 (4-27-1859)
Capshaw, Paralee to Wm. Haney 10-13-1853
Capshaw, Rebecca to John Fisher 10-23-1862 (10-24-1862)
Capshaw, Sarah to Walter Batts 7-1-1874 (7-2-1874)
Carder, Elizabeth to Thomas Crips 11-4-1858
Carder, Mandy to Rily McCheaver 8-19-1867 (8-20-1867)
Carder, Mary to James L. Robinson 12-6-1854 (no return)
Cardwell, Sarah to Wm. Gambrell 1-3-1850
Carmicle, Susan to James Buckner 5-17-1873 (5-18-1873)
Carte, Margaret to Zenith Crips 12-5-1866 (12-6-1866)
Carter, Barthena to James Scott 2-29-1852 (3-1-1852)
Carter, Eliza to James P. Etherage 8-25-1873 (8-28-1873)
Carter, Mary F. to Sylvanus Puckett 2-14-1874 (2-16-1874)
Carter, Mary to F. P. Rowland 9-4-1879
Carter, Nancy M. to Wm. S. Kurr 3-3-1871 (3-4-1871)
Carter, Parly to G. E. Lafever 3-13-1877 (3-18-1877)
Carter, Rebecca to E. M. Garrison 9-11-1850 (no endorsmnt)
Carter, Serena to Wm. C. Green 6-6-1866 (no return)
Carter, Susan E. to J. Sylvanus Puckett 5-10-1861 (5-16-1861)
Carter, Susie to Jesse McBrian 10-15-1859 (no return)

Cartright, Martha to D. A. Buck 6-9-1866 (no return)
Caskey, Elizabeth M. to Daniel Gilbert 1-13-1851 (not executed)
Caskey, Elizabeth to Daniel G. Hill 3-16-1852 (3-18-1852)
Caskey, Ester to James Tramel 12-2-1857
Caskey, Nancy M. to Thomas N. Close 2-24-1857
Casper, Sinty J. to Isaac A. Dale 12-19-1849 (12-30-1849)
Cates, Sarah E. to Rufus B. Underhill 10-17-1848 (10-19-1848)
Cathcart, Parmelia to James H. Fuson 6-29-1875 (exec. no date)
Cathcate, Luca to Andrew Johnson 12-1-1877 (12-20-1877)
Catnrell, Jane to A. J. Fry 3-29-1856 (3-20?-1856)
Catton, M. L. to P. G. Cantrell 1-14-1875
Ceartin, Elizabeth to James Billings 2-10-1866 (2-11-1866)
Certain, Becky to William Tenney 8-21-1866 (8-22-1866)
Certain, Frances E. to T. M. Anderson 11-7-1859 (no return)
Certain, Martha to Ozious D. Robinson 12-19-1867
Certain, Mary E. to George Johnson 10-15-1874
Certain, Sarah to Wm. T. Clouse 10-22-1857 (no date)
Ceton, Emmis to C. N. Parker 2-28-1878
Chain, Barbara to Thomas Alexander 12-5-1866 (12-6-1866)
Chambers, Hariet to Alex Baker 3-4-1868 (3-7-1868) [B]
Chapman, Allis to J. M. Griffith 7-14-1877 (7-15-1877)
Chapman, Bitha to James Sandlin 12-18-1868 (12-20-1868)
Chapman, Darthula to Wm. Jones 8-16-1860
Chapman, Eliza J. to Wm. Keith 2-18-1867 (2-20-1867)
Chapman, Eliza Jane to W. H. Bennette 11-4-1854
Chapman, Lucinda T. to Elijah Neal 9-16-1870 (9-18-1870)
Chapman, Malinda J. to Thomas J. Malone 10-9-1872
     (no return)
Chapman, Mary Jane to Thomas E. Chumley 7-1-1874 (7-5-1874)
Chapman, Matilda to Wm. Neel 10-29-1858 (10-31-1858)
Chapman, Rody Frances to Levi Neal 8-28-1867
Chapman, Sarah B. to James Scott 3-29-1879 (3-30-1879)
Chapman, Sarah to Wm. Coffee 8-31-1870 (9-1-1870)
Chapman?, Susan F. to John M. Parker 8-8-1872
Chapthorn, Hariet to William Close 12-23-1874
Cheatam, Marth to Lemuel Cawley 2-24-1877 (9-28-1877)
Cheatham, Elizabeth to Z. B. Pratt 10-11-1860
Cheatham, Mary J. to A. J. Ferrell 1-16-1850
Cheatham, Permelia to George W. Bond 3-8-1855
Cheatham, Roda W. to T. C. Allen 1-17-1871 (1-21-1871)
Cheek, Caladonia to Jason Fouch 9-20-1867 (9-22-1867)
Cheek, Conder? to Andrew Williams 2-14-1874 (2-15-1874)
Childers, Eliza to John Wadde 9-30-1850 (10-1-1850)
Childers, Elizabeth to Almon R. Medlin 1-2-1851 (1-7-1851)
Childers, Nancy to Wm. Elrod 1-9-1851
Childress, Sarah to James Huchins 9-12-1864 (no return)
Childress, Susan to Hiram Robinson 4-2-1870 (no return)
Chinly, Sary to Thomas Hale 9-21-1866 (9-22-1866)
Chisam, Jain to O. D. Walker 1-2-1866 (1-15-1866)
Chrisian, Nancy F. to J. H. Windham 7-9-1874
Christen, Judia to Joseph Exum 7-22-1875 (7-23-1875)
Christian, Admonda to Coleman Corley 8-26-1872 (8-21?-1872)
Christian, Amandy to Henry Suttles 5-17-1869 (5-23-1869)
Christian, Catharine to James Rowland 2-21-1871 (2-23-1871)
Christian, Dicey to Newton West 5-17-1879 (5-18-1879)
Christian, Harriet E. to Jackson Malone 3-24-1858 (3-25-1858)
Christian, Mary to C. F. Brock 5-31-1879 (6-1-1879)
Christian, Sarah Ann to Colman Curley 1-18-1855 (1-24-1855)
Claborn, Sarah to Wm. Oneal 7-2-1867 (7-3-1867)
Clack, Parilie to John Wooden 2-15-1860? (2-15-1861)
Clark, Amonet to Lambered Eavens 4-2-1866 (4-7-1866) [B]
Clark, Delilea to Moses Cantrell 9-26-1866 (10-1-1866)
Clark, Druciler to G. W. Hayes 9-1-1879 (9-4-1879)
Clark, M. C. to D. W. Ballinger 12-29-1877 (12-30-1877)
Clark, Mary to John Atrip 10-24-1850
Clark, Mary to Richard McGinis 12-4-1867 (12-5-1867)
Clark, Paralee to Wm. D. Evans 1-21-1852 (1-22-1852)
Clark, Rebecca F. to Alexander Hays 10-30-1849 (2-2-1850)
Clark, Rosy to Isaac Richardson 4-2-1866 (4-6-1866) [B]
Clark, Tennessee C. to T. R. Walker 2-14-1874 (no return)
Clarke, Mariah to Hansford Merrit 1-3-1857 (1-4-1857)
Clarke, Mary E. to Joshua L. Hollansworth 1-15-1856 (1-16-1856)
Clarke, Mary to George Dabbs 9-23-1857 (9-24-1857)
Clause, Martha to W. J. Lewis 9-7-1853
Clayborn, Mary J. to Lemuel D. Hendrickson 4-28-1852 (4-29-1852)

Clayborn, Matildy to James McCaffrey 6-20-1878
Cleaborn, Pheby A. to Sylvanus Crook 8-18-1871 (8-19-1871)
Clemmons, Levona to H. B. Kelley 2-2-1880 (2-4-1880)
Clemmons, Mary to Wm. Medley 10-19-1876 (10-20-1876)
Clemmons, Nancy J. to J. L. Jones 10-27-1870 (10-28-1870)
Cleyborn, Catharine to Jasper B. Scott 12-24-1851
Close, Elizabeth P. to T. D. Cantrell 12-20-1879 (12-22-1879)
Close, Frances to Leroy A. Lane 12-9-1862 (no return)
Close, Hannasah to Wm. Anders 6-26-1875 (6-27-1875)
Close, Jane to Elijah Self 12-28-1861 (12-31-1861)
Close, Josephina to W. T. Griffith 8-13-1874 (8-15-1874)
Close, Mary P. to Wm. L. Moore 10-12-1878 (10-14-1878)
Close, Mary to W. K. Cantrell 10-24-1878
Close, R. J. to John Moss 12-31-1868
Close, Talitha P. to James White 1-16-1855
Clouse, L. J. to Charley Robinson 3-25-1876 (no return)
Clouse, Rebecca Ann to David Lasitor 8-11-1854
Coalmon, Mary to J. W. Tuck 11-17-1879
Coape, Etter to W. B. Cawley 1-28-1876 (2-1-1876)
Coble, Mary Jane to Jackson Minor 12-17-1850 (12-18-1850)
Coble, Sintha to John A. Fite 7-11-1872 (7-14-1872)
Cochran, Elizabeth to William Tolbert 8-31-1871
Coffee, Fanny L. to John D. Bone 2-26-1857
Coffee, Lelia to G. W. Lewis 9-1-1877 (9-3-1877)
Coggin, Louisa Ann to Charles Pullen 12-13-1858
Coggin, Louizey E. to John F. McHord 1-13-1874 (1-20-1874)
Coggin, M. H. to B. F. Starnes 9-14-1869 (9-26-1869)
Coggin, M. R. to E. C. Martin 10-9-1879 (10-12-1879)
Cogins, Emenley to John New 6-3-1866 (no return)
Coilly, M. J. to Wm. McDowel 11-10-1877 (11-11-1877)
Coker, Martha to John Cally 2-16-1877 (2-18-1877)
Cole, L. M. to J. M. Hale 3-24-1876 (3-30-1876)
Coleman, Nancy to James Ayrs 2-16-1858 (2-18-1858)
Coleman, Susan to Amon Starnes 8-10-1869
Collins, Margaret to Richmond Williams 2-12-1849 (2-15-1849)
Colrits?, Letty Ann to Robert Cantrell 12-15-1870
Colwell, Cansady to John Johnson 1-28-1856 (no return)
Colwell, Charity to Bartemus Pack 9-24-1859 (9-25-1859)
Colwell, Elizabeth to Archibald Pack 9-5-1860
Colwell, Lusinda to Jonathan Johnson 3-23-1854 (5-5-1854)
Colwell, Martha to James Evans 6-22-1854 (6-21?-1854)
Colwell, Mary to Robert Holt 6-16-1859
Comfergher, Juy to Wm. B. Wright 1-23-1872 (1-25-1872)
Compton, Elizabeth to John W. Hays 7-22-1865 (no return)
Congar, Nancy to James F. Hamilton 10-12-1859 (10-12-1859)
Conger, Martha to Archabald B. Cheatham 11-3-1852 (11-4-1852)
Conger, Martha to Wm. Garner 1-3-1854 (1-5-1854)
Conger, Mary to John Exum 5-12-1874 (4-13-1874)
Coniecel, E. C. to John W. Benner 12-22-1879 (12-24-1879)
Conk, Mary F. to John L. Brown 12-6-1875 (12-7-1875)
Conner, Catharine to William J. Watson 1-7-1857
Conner, Nancy Jane to Francis M. Cubbons 2-4-1851
Conner, Nilly E. to S. M. Keaton 8-6-1860 (no return)
Connor, Elizabeth to James Keeth 1-18-1872
Connor, Pheby C. to Presly Adamson 4-11-1876 (4-13-1876)
Conor, Josephine to Wm. Buland 7-12-1865 (no return)
Cooper, Jane to Wesly Mitchel 2-13-1879 (solmzd no date
Cooper, Lavina to Thomas J. Brady 12-19-1851 (12-23-1851)
Cooper, Norah to Thomas Malone 1-25-1879 (1-26-1879)
Cooper, Tenessee to Isaac Butlar 4-13-1878 (4-14-1878)
Cooper, Tennesse to Asbury N. Hayes 2-20-1872 (2-22-1872)
Cope, Elizabeth to A. P. Irwin 6-6-1864 (no return)
Cope, Josie to Hatten Wright 4-20-1880 (no return)
Cope, Oedema to F. A. Badger 7-3-1866
Cope, S. to J. P. Cantrell 11-28-1870
Cope, Sallie to Isaac D. Griffith 9-11-1871 (9-13-1871)
Corby, Olivia to Isack Yorke 2-26-1875 (2-28-1875)
Corley, B. C. to James B. Jackson 5-15-1880 (5-16-1880)
Corley, Elizabeth to Wm. Deadman 1-12-1872
Corley, Martha to Thomas N. Brent 9-24-1858 (9-26-1858)
Cotten, Jane to James Walker 1-4-1869 (1-5-1869)
Cotten, Mary to Robert V. Gilbert 4-24-1861 (4-25-1861)
Cotton, Amandy L. to George Blankenship 2-24-1873
Cotton, M. Burk to S. Preston 12-25-1866 (no return)
Cozzin, Babe to George McCray 12-30-1878 (6?-2-1878)

Craddock, Lucinda to E. Monroe Adimson 3-23-1875 (3-26-1875)
Craddock, Mary J. to J. W. Vandygrif 4-18-1865 (no return)
Craddock, Parale to Wm. B. Rich 10-18-1871 (10-19-1871)
Craddock, S. A. to J. b. Collin 3-10-1860
Crepps, Julia to Albert Porter 5-12-1866 (5-17-1866) [B]
Crip, Lucretta to Wm. G. Ethridge 11-23-1854 (11-24-1854)
Cripps, Sarah E. to Todivora Edge 7-31-1872 (8-1-1872)
Crips, Elizabeth Ann to Wm. J. Rigsby 8-28-1856 (8-29-1856)
Crips, Elizabeth to Tilmon Joines 10-15-1868
Crips, Martha J. to James Etherage 6-10-1869
Crips, Mary A. to Jackson Carter 3-10-1858 (3-11-1858)
Crips, Sarah to Wm. Maynard 1-22-1880
Cronk, Nelly to Moffet Crowder 12-24-1851
Crook, Elizabeth to William Brent 1-15-1859 (no return)
Crook, Jane to Wm. Bennett 6-17-1878 (solem,no date)
Crook, Lucia to William Brent 10-7-1865 (10-8-1865)
Crook, Malinda J. to Davies? J. Warford 7-3-1849 (7-4-1849)
Crook, Permetia to Y. Malone 4-15-1879 (4-16-1879)
Crook, Sarah E. to John M. Malone 8-15-1877 (8-16-1877)
Crowder, Easter to Isaac Lamberson 5-24-1869 (no return)
Crowder, Johannah to O. D. Goodson 7-16-1858 (8-19-1858)
Crowder, Sarah to Sim Brown 9-24-1871 [B]
Crowley, Bettie to W. W. Wade 3-21-1872
Cubbins, Charity to Josiah Sheham 6-6-1864 (no return)
Cubbins, Jane to Thomas W. Dodd 4-16-1863 (no return)
Cubbins, Mary J. to Andrew Smith 3-8-1879 (sodmnzd no dat
Cubbins, Tavelee to James R. Fuson 7-31-1862 (8-3-1862)
Cubbins, Z. E. to John Cripes 4-3-1878 (4-4-1878)
Cullard, S. E. to Alford Lawrence 2-18-1866
Culwell, Bethany to Jackson Foster 11-23-1870 (11-26-1870)
Culwell, Bethuna to Spencer Sparkman 7-12-1867
Culwell, Elizabeth to Carroll Johnson 3-7-1874 (3-8-1874)
Culwell, Mary to James Billings 3-27-1874
Cumings, Martha J. to Micajah Hamilton 12-24-1859 (12-25-1859)
Cummins, Rutha to William Turner 6-9-1854
Cummons?, Paralee to Martin Delong 7-3-1858 (7-4-1858)
Curtice, Adonorindey to Wm. Fouch 9-28-1870 (9-29-1870)
Curtin, Mary to Wm. Johnson 1-31-1872 (2-1-1872)
Curtin, Sarah A. to James T., Jr. Hayes 12-23-1871 (no return)
Curtis, Artily to Wiley Jones 12-15-1860 (12-17-1860)
Curtis, Faney to Charly Adcock 7-27-1867 (7-28-1867) [B]
Curtis, Feby to Frank Williams 10-19-1868 (no return) [B]
Curtis, Mary E. to Zack Davis 6-30-1868 (no return)
Curtis, Nancy A. to Smith Hendrixson 1-28-1868 (no return)
Cutlar, Sary to Lafayette Adcock 1-1-1858
Cutler, Easter H. to John P. Pettey 11-20-1872 (11-21-1872)
Dabbs, Delila to Thomas Clarke 3-10-1857 (3-11-1857)
Dabbs, Martha to Freling W. Parker 12-18-1855 (12-20-1855)
Dade, Paralle to Enoch George 6-27-1857 (6-28-1857)
Dale, Elizabeth to William J. Pew 11-12-1866 (11-13-1866)
Dale, Frances to James Wodsides 12-22-1849 (12-24-1849)
Dale, Mary to Henry Sellers 3-21-1853 (3-23-1853)
Dale, N. P. to B. F. Hall 2-14-1865
Dale, Vinia to Marion Goodwin 3-15-1873 (3-16-1873)
Dandlee, Nancy to Henry Sewel? 5-24-1855
Danford, Mary J. to Sampson Chapman 10-6-1869 (10-10-1869)
Dass, Betta to J. F. Ward 3-27-1878
Daugherty, Martha Ann to C. F. Bethell 9-28-1848 (9-29-1848)
Daulton, Mary to Jacob Frazier 1-28-1851 (1-29-1850?)
Davault, Eveline to James Green 12-26-1866 (12-27-1866)
David, J. E. to John C. Foutch 9-9-1862 (9-10-1862)
David, M. S. to John H. Fite 8-18-1874 (8-19-1874)
David, Nancy to John R. Lawrence 2-1-1862 (no return)
Davies, Julia Ann to M. L. Deadgrave? 10-9-1861 (no return)
Davis, Amanda E. to A. Edwards 6-28-1860 (no return)
Davis, Amanda to John A. Patton 12-24-1856 (12-?-1856)
Davis, Catherine to Wm. R. Caplinger 5-4-1867 (5-5-1867)
Davis, Dovy to Elijah Scott 8-30-1849 (9-2-1849)
Davis, Elizabeth to David A. Dirting 11-29-1870 (12-1-1871?)
Davis, Elizabeth to James M. Dunlap 12-24-1854
Davis, Emely to James B. Burns 1-22-1855 (2-1-1855)
Davis, Emma to James W. Herd 1-4-1870 (1-5-1870)
Davis, Emma to James W. Herd 1-4-1870 (no return)
Davis, Isabell to Andy Robinson 4-20-1880 (no return)
Davis, Marth J. to Isaac Young 5-25-1858 (exec. no date)

Davis, Martha to Wm. Trusty 1-16-1865
Davis, Mary A. S. to John A. Reynolds 8-24-1876 (8-26-1876)
Davis, Nancy Ann to Wm. W. Griffith 11-20-1852 (11-25-1852)
Davis, Nancy to Alexnder? Turner 10-6-1851 (10-15-1851)
Davis, Nellie to Edmon P. Reeder 2-25-1861 (2-28-1861)
Davis, Olive to George Thomison 3-8-1861 (3-11-1861)
Davis, Rebecca to George R. Smith 5-1-1857 (5-3-1857)
Davis, Sarah to W. J. Parsley 2-27-1860
Davis, Talitha to Thomas Pridy 12-25-1848 (no return)
Davise, Lettie B. to James McMillan 12-21-1878 (12-22-1878)
Dawson, Mary Jane to F. L. Banks 12-31-1857 (1-4-1858)
Deadman, Cynthia to Shay Foutch 2-10-1870 (no return) [B]
Dean, Hariet to Amos Allen 1-12-1865 (1-15-1865)
Dedmon, Safronia to O. B. Staley 1-2-1861
Deems, Elisabeth to Carrel Johnson 12-16-1865 (12-17-1865)
Deen, Lakey to Joseph Adamson 7-6-1854
Dejournet, Nancy to James H. Youngblood 8-14-1854 (8-17-1854)
Delong, America to W. J. Adcock 4-11-1874 (4-12-1874)
Delong, Lucy to J. W. Blunt 12-15-1848 (12-17-1848)
Delong, Nancy to William Bigs 9-12-1853
Deney, Sarah to David E. Hall 8-22-1865 (no return)
Denham, Jane R. to E. N. Trail 7-5-1858 (7-8-1858)
Dennis, Carolina to Patrick Conner 3-17-1851
Dennis, Mary P. to Robert S. Hall 9-18-1869
Dennis, Sarah to Winson Crowder 4-17-1851 (4-19-1851)
Denny, Delia to Joseph Hindsley 2-16-1877 (2-17-1877)
Denny, E. J. to Daniel Midget 11-25-1867 (11-27-1867)
Denny, Ready to John Hendsley 11-24-1875 (11-26-1875)
Derham, Mary to George Robinson 8-29-1879
Devease, Josephine to Jackson Brimer 9-14-1865 (9-20-1865) [*]
Dewease, Mandy C. to Guy Taylor Smith 12-10-1867 (12-12-1867)
Dickson, Mary to Lazeris Johnson 3-13-1878 (3-16-1878)
Dilldine, Callidony to A. P. Rigsby 7-13-1878 (7-14-1878)
Dinnes, D. E. T. to David Emery 9-1-1865 (no return)
Dinwiddle, Jennie to H. Calhoon 2-19-1877 (2-20-1877)
Dinwiddy, Lucy J. to J. M. Hall 2-24-1868 (2-2-1868)
Dinwiddy, S. A. to Stephen Pledger ?-30-1866 (8-2-1866)
Dinwittie, Liza to W. E. Rich 11-27-1879
Dirting, M. F. to Thomas J. Adamson 7-21-1876
Dirting, Mary to Bluford Mathis 12-9-1870 (12-12-1870)
Diver, Emily J. to T. L. Winfrey 11-9-1869 (no return)
Doak, Martha to F. B. Nolner 9-22-1875 (9-23-1875)
Dobbs, Mary to John Johnson 3-31-1870 (4-7-1870)
Dodd, Adline to L. D. Moore 10-26-1870 (10-27-1870)
Dodd, C. E. to S. B. Parker 2-14-1870 (2-16-1870)
Dodd, Caroline to John Parker 4-6-1863
Dodd, Elizabeth C. to Ohu Jones 1-5-1858 (1-7-1858)
Dodd, J. F. to J. W. Ward 1-3-1870 (1-27-1870)
Dodd, Parris to Andrew Spurlock 9-11-1878 (9-12-1878)
Dodson, Lavina to S. T. Nix 7-17-1860
Dollar, Lucia A. to John Arnel 8-23-1876 (8-24-1876)
Dollar, Martha N. to John R. Carter 1-7-1880 (1-11-1880)
Donley, Hixey to Samuel Fuston 5-20-1875
Donnell, A. H. to Wm. L. Judkins 7-22-1865 (7-23-1865)
Donnelly, Mary to Thomasj E. Winord 3-10-1880
Dood, Nancy C. to Jackson Pew 1-8-1865
Dooling, Zenora to Ambrose Robinson 6-21-1859
Doss, Amanda T. to Robert T. Smith 12-12-1854 (no return)
Doss, C. D. to J. T. Quarles 8-14-1857 (no return)
Doss, Darthuly F. to James T. Quarles 10-2-1860 (not endorsed)
Doss, Jenny to Elick Philips 1-5-1872 (no return) [B]
Doss, Josy to Jo Rollins 7-4-1873 (7-13-1873) [B]
Doss, Martha Jane to Joshua L. Jennings 12-10-1850 (no return)
Doss, Rody to Wiat Rollins 1-22-1869 (1-24-1869) [B]
Dougherty, Louisa Jane? to Sampson Hayse 8-27-1849 (8-29-1849)
Dowel, Louisa D. to R. D. Allison 6-22-1858 (6-24-1858)
Dowell, A. J. to W. J. Stokes 1-3-1870 (1-5-1870)
Dowell, Martha E. to James H. Kitchens 1-30-1870 (2-2-1870)
Dowlen, Mary J. to Lorance Carner 8-4-1858
Down, Sarah J. to Wm. Hickman 1-19-1872? (1-25-1870?) [*]
Dozier, Marthy J. to Felix R. Terrey 5-14-1873
Drewrey, Sarah to Jas. E. Drewrey 2-5-1874 (no return)
Drewry, Tennie to T. J. Page 7-17-1879
Driver, Amanda S. to B. H. Copehardt 10-1-1878 (10-6-1878)
Driver, Amanda to Mark A. Malone 9-16-1873 (9-18-1873)

Driver, Arminty to James M. Driver 3-9-1871 (3-11?-1871)
Driver, Asenith to J. M. Pirtle 4-11-1873 (4-13-1873)
Driver, Elis. to Wiley Young 7-24-1868 (7-25-1868)
Driver, Elizabeth to John B. Parker 9-22-1857 (9-30-1857)
Driver, Julia Ann to Jessee Redman 3-4-1858 (3-5-1858)
Driver, M. J. to N. D. Vanfrees 9-18-1865 (9-19-1865)
Driver, Martha to N. B. Bradly 5-22-1868 (5-24-1868)
Driver, Mary Alice to Geo. H. Calvert 3-21-1878 (3-25-1878)
Driver, Mary F. to C. A. Raliff 2-20-1874 (no return)
Driver, Mary to William M. Brent 1-22-1857
Driver, Mary to Wm. Morgan 5-13-1875
Driver, Matilda to Samuel H. Gray 7-16-1851 (7-17-1851)
Driver, Parale to Wm. Crook 3-25-1858 (exec. no date)
Driver, Rebecca to Wm. Warford 3-11-1869
Driver, Sarah E. to Josiah Hullet 12-23-1864 (no return)
Driver, Sarah to Welden Young 9-23-1867
Driver, Susan A. to Benj. Collins 8-6-1868
Drurey, Harriett to James M. Page 1-28-1873 (2-6-1873)
Drurey, Nancey to John B. Taylor 9-4-1865 (9-11-1865)
Drury, M. to J? B. Taylor 1-2-1867 (date obscure)
Drury, Martha to Fedrick J. Hill 6-24-1853
Duham?, Jane to Jessee Standley 3-4-1850 (3-6-1850)
Duke, Elizabeth to Logan Davis 6-27-1877 (6-29-1877)
Duke, Mary to Benjamon Aderson 5-13-1878 (5-14-1878)
Dukes, Ollivia to D. A. Parker 7-29-1874 (7-31-1874)
Dun, Elizabeth to John Johnson 4-4-1857
Dunham, Martha A. P. to Joseph Ray 3-27-1863 (no return)
Dunham, Mary T. to Mathias T. Pinegar 2-11-1873 (2-16-1873)
Dunham, Reboc to William C. Wamack 12-13-1853
Dunham, Susan to Bery Fisher 3-13-1850 (3-15-1850)
Dunlap, Hellen to Henry C. Eastham 8-6-1872
Dunlap, Margaret to Mattha Hunt 9-13-1853
Dunn, Nancy to James Ferrell 5-8-1877 (5-10-1877)
Dunton, S. L. to John Carnes 6-28-1877
Durham, Bettie to W. C. Griffith 4-6-1880 (4-8-1880)
Durham, Elizabeth to John Tramell 5-29-1852 (5-30-1852)
Durham, Lucy Jane to James Ferrell 2-1-1851 (2-9-1851)
Durham, R. A. to Aaron Fletcher 10-13-1861 (no return)
Durham, Rachel to James Ferrell 12-31-1862
Durham, Sally to John Casky 8-18-1864 (no return)
Durham, Virginia to John Donnell 12-25-1852 (12-26-1852)
Duse?, Syrenia A. to Charles Denney 1-25-1872 (1-28-1872)
Dyer, Manerva E. to James S. Palmer 9-5-1859 (9-15-1859)
Dyer, Mary E. to Bird L. Jones 7-24-1869 (7-29-1869)
Dyer, Nancy to Charles D. Hutchins 8-10-1854
Easham, Harriet A. to W. A. Dunlap 10-9-1867
Eason, Amandy to Eli Vick 10-12-1872 (10-16-1872)
Eason, E. T. to G. M. Bowers 1-24-1868 (1-25-1868)
Easthert, M. A. to P. M. Wade 3-1-1866
Eathaly, Mary to Richard Richardson 10-1-1864 (10-2-1864)
Eaton, Eliz. Jane to Wm. W. Foutch 10-2-1868 (10-22-1868)
Eaton, Mary to Wm. Reasonover 9-14-1869 (no return)
Eavens, Frances to Swet Turner 4-2-1866 (4-7-1866) [B]
Eddings, Caroline to Hardy Malone 8-29-1877 (8-30-1877)
Edens, Adaline to Jackson West 3-2-1852 (retnd w/o cft.
Edens, Mary Jane to George Turner 4-6-1853 (4-7-1853)
Edge, C. d. to G. A. Copi 6-25-1874 (6-28-1874)
Edge, Delina to Wm. Bess 2-29-1876 (3-2-1876)
Edge, M. A. to W. T. Tibbs 6-12-1875 (1?-12-1875)
Edge, M. J. to W. J. Vickors 3-26-1874
Edge, Mary J. to Banjamin S. Robinson 5-15-1855 (5-10-1855)
Edings, Heny to Harrey Lawrence 12-20-1876 (12-24-1876)
Edmonds, Emma to J. Fletch Woodward 6-4-1872
Edmonson, Hollie C. to F. Woodsides 7-1-1865 (no return)
Edons, Gabriella to James W. Green 5-17-1853 (exec. no date)
Edwards, C. C. to J. M. Puck 2-29-1872
Edwards, Margrart to John c. Cannady 12-2-1851 (12-5-1851)
Edwards, Mary Jane to Lewis Liles 12-1-1859 (1859?)
Edwards, Uphema to Joseph Pack 11-21-1855 (11-22-1855)
Elexander, Ritta to Samuell Elexander 7-7-1877 (7-8-1877)
Elexandra, Rebecca to T. M. T. Wall 8-19-1875 (8-22-1875)
Elkins, Anjaline to B. R. Judkins 11-3-1862 (11-4-1862)
Elkins, E. J. to J. C. Walden 11-3-1862 (11-4-1862)
Elkins, Elizabeth to A. C. Breadlove 8-30-1878 (8-31-1878)
Elkins, L. V. to A. P. Cantrell 11-26-1864 (11-27-1864)

Elkins, L. V. to A. Pleantice 11-26-1864 (no return)
Elkins, Matilda to J. A. Cantrell 1-28-1869
Eller, Sarah A. to Rowland Terry 3-1-1871 (no return)
Ellis, Lucinda to Harden Hensley 8-28-1867 (no return)
Ellis, Milliey to John F. Woodside 11-5-1865 (no return)
Ellis, Nancy to James Henesley 10-4-1871 (10-5-1871)
Elrod, Amanda A. to John Steele 3-4-1880 (3-5-1880)
Elrod, Elizabeth to Edmon H. Felts 1-2-1851 (1-7-1851)
Elrod, Nancy to Allen Steel 4-1-1850
Elrod, Nancy to Franklin Goff 5-2-1856
Embry, M. J. to Bethal Tittle 6-29-1878 (6-30-1878)
Emery, Nancy R. to I. D. Cantrell 11-23-1878 (11-24-1878)
Emory, Voney E. to Shadrick Clemmons 1-14-1873
English, M. E. to A. C. Jones 1-13-1868 (1-14-1868)
English, Mary E. to Hanry Rodey 12-24-1872 (12-25-1872)
Estes, Elizabeth to Thomas Keff 8-31-1855 (9-2-1855)
Estes, Josie to R. M. Cantrell 2-12-1880
Estes, Tennessee to George Childreth 9-21-1870
Estis, Gennie to G. W. Childres 10-3-1867
Estis, Loura to George Allen 11-25-1872 (11-28-1872)
Estis, Mary to J. Smith 8-24-1862 (no return)
Estus, Jane to Joab Keel 12-28-1874
Etherage, Harrett to John Tomerson 1-4-1872 (1-5-1879)
Etheridge, Chrisasis? to L. H. Hardison 7-18-1878 (7-1?-1878)
Etheridge, Sarah to Henry Crips 9-11-1875 (9-12-1875)
Ethrage, Parilee Jane to Thomas N? Smith 12-8-1859
Ethridge, Emma to James Eli Ingram 1-11-1872 (1-10?-1872)
Ethridge, Malissa to Ezekiel Taylor 12-26-1855 (12-27-1855)
Ethridge, S. A. to J. H. Hickman 9-24-1868 (9-25-1868)
Evans, Elizabeth to Daniel C. Bayne 2-22-1852
Evans, Mary Ann to James Rowland 12-14-1875
Evans, Mary E. to Malshel Hunt 11-5-1851 (11-6-1851)
Evans, Mary to J. B. Hayes 11-19-1877 (11-21-1877)
Evans, Matilda to Thomas R. Huggins 4-3-1855 (7-3-1855)
Evans, Paralee to Aaron Frazor 8-21-1854
Evans, Sarrah Sepha to E. R. Northcut 2-18-1867 (no return)
Evans, Sinthey A. to Washington Rogers 10-30-1879
Evans, Tennessee to L. N. Woodside 2-1-1860 (2-2-1860)
Evans?, Eliza to John H. Allen 11-12-1859 (11-13-1859)
Everett, Emma M. to T. J. Sneed 12-1-1868 (12-2-1868)
Everett, Jessemine to Edward Turner 5-12-1870 (5-15-1870)
Everlin, Nancy to Wm. Arnal 10-18-1865 (10-19-1865)
Evertt, Lizzie to J. D. Fisher 9-16-1878 (no return)
Evins, Arrilla J. to Simeon L. Williams 1-10-1874
Evins, Margrett C. to Lemuel M. Whaly 1-24-1874 (1-25-1874)
Evins, Margrett J. to Squire Warren 2-26-1874
Exan, Manerva to E. R. Teague 12-30-1866
Exum, Amandy to J. C. Keer 2-3-1866 (2-5-1866)
Exum, Eliza to Henry Lancaster 8-22-1878 (9-1-1878)
Exum, Elizabeth to I. N. Hayes 3-8-1880 (3-29-1880)
Exum, Knector? C. to William Hollay 11-13-1857
Exum, Luella to Joseph Moss 1-5-1872 (1-7-1872)
Famer, Louisa to Isaac W. Ricketts 3-13-1860 (3-25-1860)
Fare, M. L. to J. W. Harris 8-2-1860
Fare, Sarah H. to David H. Wilder 1-9-1862 (no return)
Farel, Elizabeth to Ruffin Rackley 2-28-1862 (no return)
Farell, Martha to John M. Baine 1-18-1856 (1-20-1856)
Farler, L. E. to Wm. Riley Taylor 3-3-1878
Farmer, Lucy Ann to James W. Allen 9-6-1860
Farmer, Mary F. to Isaac H. Baim 4-19-1871 (4-20-1871)
Farmer, Susan to J. D. Moore 4-21-1876 (4-23-1876)
Farrell, Sarah to J. K. Marshall 9-10-1872 (9-15-1872)
Farrell, Talitha to Jehue Cantrell 3-8-1873 (3-9-1873)
Fazier, Violet to Frank League 9-16-1867 (9-18-1867)
Felphs, A. to Greenbery Goodson 1-5-1867 (no return)
Felps, Elizabeth to Isaac Taylor 1-10-1879 (1-12-1879)
Felts, Eliza to Wm. Albert 11-29-1871 (11-30-1871)
Felts, Jane to P. c. Brock 11-23-1859
Ferrel, Amanda to J. B. Sellars 2-27-1866 (no return)
Ferrel, Mary to George Purser 8-7-1866 (no return)
Ferrel, Rebeca D. to Samuel Hays 2-23-1866
Ferrel, Sarah E. to Robert W. Melton 10-3-1853 (10-6-1853)
Ferrell, Amanda C. to Greenberry Mullican 10-5-1869 (10-7-1869)
Ferrell, Annie L. to Wm. H. M. Ston? 11-19-1872 (11-21-1872)
Ferrell, Anny to Terry Trapp 4-22-1850 (ret, filed)

Ferrell, Brunetta B. to James T. Lee 9-22-1871 (9-23-1871)
Ferrell, Catharine to John Jordan 9-29-1857
Ferrell, E. A. to W. E. Smith 3-22-1877
Ferrell, Enicy to Francis Kirby 1-11-1859
Ferrell, Hexy C. to Archibald Baynes 11-8-1853
Ferrell, Hixey C. to Wm. J. Graham 3-2-1861 (3-3-1861)
Ferrell, M. F. to J. C. Gilbert 9-25-1869 (9-25-1869)
Ferrell, Mary L. to A. M. Pressly 10-4-1869 (10-6-1869)
Ferrell, Rachel to John A. Williams 9-6-1852 (9-7-1852)
Ferril, M. J. to S. Anderson 11-6-1876 (11-9-1876)
Ferril, Sarah to Elisha McGinnis 3-16-1853 (no return)
Ferrill, S. J. to H. A. Moss 3-28-1873 (3-30-1873)
Fields, Pheby Ann to Newton Scott 2-6-1850 (2-13-1850)
Files, Mary to John Hodge 3-17-1870 (3-18-1870)
Finley, Harriet to James Howard 3-4-1856 (3-6-1856)
Finley, Matilda C. to John E. Hall 6-15?-1850 (6-13-1860?)
Fish, Elizabeth to Wilson Taylor 9-6-1865 (no return)
Fish, Fannie to Albert Taylor 3-22-1876 (3-23-1876)
Fish, Louisa L. to John Spencer 5-10-1875 (5-1?-1875)
Fish, M. D. to T. M. Hooper 8-2-1866 (8-3-1866)
Fish, Malinda to Wm. E. Taylor 8-?-1867 (8-22-1867)
Fish, Mary E. to John T. Tramel 3-30-1867 (no return)
Fish, Mattie to Andrew Tyler 2-2-1878 (2-3-1878)
Fish, Pissilla to Barzel Taylor 5-1-1852 (5-2-1852)
Fish, Rachel D. to Ansell Clemmons 7-2-1860 (7-3-1860)
Fish, Rody G. to Lewis J. Taylor 5-14-1863 (no return)
Fisher, A. J. to S. F. Wright 1-3-1865 (no return)
Fisher, Amandy Jane to Wm. Coggins 2-21-1871 (no return)
Fisher, E. B. to W. J. Wright 2-9-1866 (2-10-1866)
Fisher, E. to Wm. Webb 12-21-1876 (no return)
Fisher, Elisabeth to John Tales 2-13-1866 (2-15-1866)
Fisher, Haseltine to E. Neely 11-10-1879 (11-20-1879)
Fisher, Isabell to Jaswa Goulsby 9-27-1876
Fisher, Jennett to Thomas McDowell 10-16-1871
Fisher, Lucindy J. to L. P. Lane 10-14-1871 (10-16-1871)
Fisher, Malvina to J. K. P. Wall 9-21-1874 (9-27-1874)
Fisher, Molly to E. W. Potter 2-13-1869 (2-16-1869)
Fisher, Moring to Vance M. Williams 7-18-1872
Fisher, Mournin? to Wm. Fisher 10-3-1859 (10-5-1859)
Fisher, Nancy J. to Silvanus Stokes 2-9-1870 (2-10-1870)
Fisher, Palestrene to Alford M. Bond 2-27-1875 (3-1-1875)
Fisher, Pasly to Charles Smith 12-19-1874 (no return)
Fisher, Roselinda to Wm. A. Lane 2-19-1855 (2-20-1855)
Fisher, Rutha to E. D. Wright 1-3-1865 (no return)
Fisher, Samantha to J. B. Kife 12-22-1877 (12-23-1877)
Fisher, Susan to Danel Jones 12-18-1865 (12-24-1865)
Fisher, Susan to Jas. R. Blankinship 2-2-1874
Fisher?, Elizabeth to John Fisher 10-11-1866
Fisk, Mary A. to Nelson Bradford 2-10-1872 (2-12-1872)
Fissen, S. E. to C. Robinson 8-24-1870 (8-25-1870)
Fite, A. E. to John A. Turney 9-1-1874 (9-2-1874)
Fite, Elizabeth to L. G. Hale 9-6-1851
Fite, M. E. to Wm. Jencinkins 1-5-1875
Fite, Manervy Ann to Washington Rackly 11-15-1850
Fite, Margaret E. to George W. Witt 12-24-1855
Fite, Margarett T. to Nathaniel H. Grindstaff 9-13-1872 (9-19-1872)
Fite, Martha C. to John Barge 3-12-1850 (3-14-1850)
Fite, Martha to John Jr. Davis 1-25-1871 (1-26-1871)
Fite, Martha to M. H. McNamer 3-31-1870
Fite, Mary L. to Lemuel J. Bratton 12-26-1871 (12-28-1871)
Fite, Mary V. to John W. Tribble 4-19-1873 (4-20-1873)
Fite, Parlee to James A. Bane 12-23-1848 (12-24-1848)
Fite, Parmelia to W. R. Coggins 2-22-1875 (no return)
Fite, Saphronia to George Pritchet 1-23-1861 (exec. no retur
Fite, Sarah E. to James Smith 7-7-1857 (exec. no date)
Fite, Tempy to J. D. Grindstaff 3-31-1862 (4-2-1862)
Fitts, Deliley to Georg W. Williams 1-3-1872 (1-4-1872)
Fitts, Durena J. to Barnabas Taylor 2-24-1866 (no return)
Fitts, Elizabeth to Wm. Hoover 11-14-1864 (12-23-1864)
Fitts, Nancy A. to J. L. Winfry 3-16-1874
Fitts, Sarah F. to J. R. Hayes 5-5-1877 (no return)
Flippin, Nancy to A. L. Garison 5-10-1868 (5-11-1868)
Florda, Cason to Jackson Foster 10-29-1857
Florda, Phrosannah to John A. Williams 7-22-1857 (7-23-1857)
Flordia, Elizabeth to E. H. Foster 1-5-1874 (1-11-1874)

Florid, Saphronia to John A. Williams 7-22-1863 (no return)
Florida, Rutha to Lason Lee 12-5-1874 (12-6-1874)
Flowers, Alice to Samuel Shaw 2-10-1876
Flowers, Jennie to David Young 1-23-1879 [B]
Floyd, Nancy C. to John F. Goodner 3-5-1849 (3-7-1849)
Floyd, Sophronia C. to William P. Hoskins 1-17-1853 (1-18-1853)
Floyed, Mandy to Philip Pledger 2-25-1868 (3-1-1868)
Folles, Ethelinda to B. B. Druels 10-7-1875 (no return)
Foraster, Talitha C. to Isaac Turner 3-1-1849 (no return)
Ford, C. Victory to Marcus C. Rowland 11-15-1875 (no return)
Ford, Jennie to James H. Blackburn 3-17-1865 (3-19-1865)
Ford, Jennie to John Reynolds 10-24-1870
Ford, Manervey to Henry Stout 12-2-1871 (12-3-1871)
Ford, Martha E. to Nelson Brien 11-22-1859 (11-26-1859)
Ford, Mary Ann to Wm. Right 9-19-1852 (9-23-1853)
Ford, Mary J. to Eli Vick 12-3-1867 (12-4-1867)
Ford, Nancy to Fred Turner 1-5-1871 (no return) [B]
Forde, M. J. to Levi Hodge 10-8-1876
Forester, Katy to James Mullican 4-27-1865 (5-3-1865)
Forgerson, Mary E. to Samuel Hicks 1-24-1849 (1-25-1849)
Forister, Elizah to Wiley Wilder 10-16-1850 (no return)
Forrest, Rebecca to Samuel S. Young 9-21-1864 (no return)
Forrester, Martha A. to Monroe Cantrell 3-8-1860 (3-11-1860)
Foster, Calley to Thomas Parcly 6-24-1876 (no return)
Foster, Cariline to James Burton 7-1-1861 (7-2-1861)
Foster, Casander to John S. Holley 2-17-1869 (2-18-1869)
Foster, Elizabeth to Benjamin M. Meritt 12-17-1868 (no return)
Foster, Elizabeth to Stith H. Lane 11-1-1848 (11-2-1848)
Foster, Juley A. to Harmon B. Culwell 1-1-1874 (1-11-1874)
Foster, Malinda H. to John W. Miller 12-31-1858 (1-2-1859)
Foster, Martha E. to W. P. Conger 9-24-1878 (9-24-1878)
Foster, Martha to Alex E. Ferrell 4-3-1862 (4-5-1862)
Foster, Martha to James Leage 5-19-1877
Foster, Mary J. to George Close 5-26-1870 (no return)
Foster, Mary to George Gorden 6-11-1859 (6-14-1859)
Foster, Matilda to W. H. Huggins 1-23-1862
Foster, Nancy Jane to Samuel Florida 11-24-1874 (11-25-1874)
Foster, Nancy T. B. to Joseph L. Patton 9-29-1865 (no return)
Foster, S. C. to Z. Culwell 12-11-1869 (12-2?-1869)
Foster, Sarah J. to Granville Lane 1-25-1859 (1-31-1859)
Foster, Virginia to G. B. Pedigo 12-9-1868
Fotrece?, Lucy B. A. to Robert Williams 2-27-1872 (3-17-1872)
Fouch, Elizabeth to Isaac H. Brown 9-14-1865 (no return)
Fouch, Elizabeth to Joab Baliff 3-9-1853 (3-?-1853)
Fouch, Rebecca M. to Wm. G. Crowley 7-4-1853
Fouch, Sarah to Charles M. Williams 2-13-1873
Fouch, Susan to George Henly 1-16-1872 (no return)
Foutch, Adah to Jackson McClaine 12-25-1873 (no return) [B]
Foutch, Amanda to J. R. West 3-12-1864 (exec. no date)
Foutch, Elisabeth to Wesley Higenbottom 7-30-1868 (7-31-1868)
Foutch, Harriet to John Jones 12-18-1857
Foutch, Louisa F. to John M. Walkar 8-1-1867 (8-2-1867)
Foutch, Lucy to Nace Stokes 5-11-1876 (5-12-1876)
Foutch, Mahala J. to Ishmael Grigston 7-9-1855 (7-12-1855)
Foutch, Mary A. to W. H. Neal 6-15-1877 (6-17-1877)
Foutch, Mary J. to Isaac M. Sandlin 3-31-1860
Foutch, Mary to Thomas Wooden 7-6-1853 (exec. no date)
Foutch, Mary to W. D. Taylor 10-4-1875 (10-7-1875)
Foutch, Nancy E. to James Henly 9-22-1873 (no return)
Foutch, Sarah E. to W. R. Adkinse 5-17-1879 (6-10-1879)
Foutch, Sarah P. to H. C. Flippin 10-8-1869 (no return)
Foutch, Supphonia to John Crowder 8-31-1869 (9-2-1869)
Foutch, Susan C. to John Balue 2-28-1859 (3-3-1859)
Foutch, Talitha C. to C. A. Balliff 4-13-1870 (4-24-1870)
Foutch, Thena to R. W. Nesmith 12-18-1869 (12-26-1869)
Fowler, Elenor to Benjamin Redmon 11-8-1852
Fowler, Jane to George W. Clouse 1-11-1855 (no return)
Fowler, Jane to Rufus Fuson 2-10-1857
Fowler, M. C. to Wm. J. Edge 8-29-1878
Fowler, M. to Rubin York 12-22-1879 (no return)
Fowler, Rachel to Jason J. Certain 10-14-1854 (10-15-1854)
Fowler, Sarah to John Young 2-6-1860 (2-7-1860)
Francis, Rebeca to Samuel M. Mellin 5-16-1861 (no return)
Franklin, Mahaly to W. C. Dier 7-23-1866 (7-24-1866)
Franklin, Martha to Wm. Henly 5-20-1874 (5-28-1874)

Frazer, Martha T. to Watler Botts 11-14-1859
Frazer, Mary Ann to George Lever 8-19-1850 (8-20-1850)
Frazier, Haley S. to Benjamin Baker 10-3-1874 (10-4-1874) [B]
Frazier, Harriett to S. S. Craddock 5-1-1873
Frazier, Helen A. to Wm. N. Rose 10-22-1879 (10-23-1879)
Frazier, Hellen to Isaac Alexandria 10-7-1871 (10-8-1871)
Frazier, Inda to Arrison Shaw 12-19-1878
Frazier, Martha to M.H. Pack 4-6-1871
Frazier, Nancy to Wm. Roady 8-1-1861
Frazier, Parelee to Wm. Pack 7-7-1875 (7-11-1875)
Frazor, Ann to L. W. Roady 7-14-1853
Frazor, Margart to Samuel Neel 10-11-1850 (10-12-1850)
Friffith, M. J. to W. H. Griffeth 10-14-1875
Frisly, America to James Elrod 4-5-1879 (4-6-1879)
Frist, P. to Biral Stalks 3-19-1866 (no return)
Fry, Charlott to John Crook 12-17-1848
Fucell, Betty to Alexander Parsley 9-29-1871 (10-1-1871)
Fults, Allis to Isaac Hutchison 3-18-1869
Fultz, Harriett M. to Leroy Nunnelly 4-24-1876
Furgerson, Elily to John Capshaw 2-25-1859
Fuson, Avaline to T. J. Davis 5-4-1878 (5-5-1878)
Fuson, Eleener to Isaac H. Hayse 8-21-1849
Fuson, Eliza to Thomas Francis 10-30-1867 (10-30-1867)
Fuson, Elizabeth to Jessee Cantrell 1-3-1853
Fuson, Lucy J. to C. H. McAfferty 11-23-1869 (11-24-1869)
Fuson, Margaret to Benjamin Merrett 7-13-1854
Fuson, Margret to M. M. Allen 4-28-1877 (no return)
Fuson, Mary E. to Isaac N. Fite 11-24-1875 (no return)
Fuson, Mary J. to Samuel Fish 12-9-1872 (12-22-1872)
Fuson, Matilda to David W. Right 10-7-1850 (10-13-1850)
Fuson, Nancy C. to James Gothard 12-19-1860 (12-20-1860)
Fuson, Rachel to Andrew Walling 9-24-1874
Fuson, Sarah M. to M. Allen 1-6-1878
Fuson, Sarah to Ambros Corley 7-13-1868
Fuson, Sarah to Bethel Noris 10-19-1852
Fuston, Elizabeth to Stephen Carty 8-22-1873
Fuston, Sintha to James Allen 10-16-1866 (10-18-1866)
Gambell, Martha J. to Alexander C. Earheart 4-27-1872 (4-28-1872)
Gamble, Minerva to Alexander Harris 9-4-1869 (9-5-1869)
Gann, Catherine to Jerry Crook 12-11-1867
Gann, Elizabeth to George W. Adkins 9-17-1855
Gann, Mary Jane to Henry Adamson 4-18-1877 (4-19-1877)
Gann, Matilda to John Ashford 1-28-1862
Gardner, Louisa to Wm. Austin 2-2-1855 (2-4-1855)
Garison, Elizabeth C. to Jno. B. Butler 8-20-1877 (8-21-1877)
Garner, Elmina to Fred Starnes 5-17-1879 (5-18-1879)
Garner, Jane to Nep McLellin 3-8-1875 (3-11-1875)
Garner, M. E. to J. L. Hale 1-31-1877 (2-1-1877)
Garner, Mary F. to James F. Hamelton 10-11-1858 (10-13-1858)
Garner, Sarah E. to Thomas J. M. Lee 12-5-1868 (12-6-1868)
Garriette, Elizabeth to John Taylor 1-8-1850 (1-10-1850)
Garrison, Carolina to James Vernatta 1-20-1851 (1-2?-1851)
Garrison, Elenor to John C. Bennette 10-13-1852 (10-14-1852)
Garrison, Elizabeth E. to John T. Johnson 6-20-1872 (6-30-1872)
Garrison, Elizabeth M. to Elijah J. Bratton 9-20-1854 (9-21-1854)
Garrison, Emley to Thomas Keeton 4-7-1879 (4-9-1879)
Garrison, Martha T. to Thomas Bratton 3-22-1854 (3-30-1854)
Garrison, Mulvina to John Casky 3-22-1854 (3-23-1854)
Garrison, Rebecca to Jackson Walls 3-12-1855
Gates, Polly Ann to Henry W. Wilson 1-6-1852
Gayin?, Jane to Martin Spark 5-3-1866 (no return)
Geln?, M. E. to W. H. McClellen 4-30-1877 (no return)
George, Frances to William Vire 7-25-1849 (7-26-1849)
George, Kesiah to Wm. L. Hale 10-17-1857 (10-18-1857)
George, Mary to Thomas J. Hale 12-18-1858 (12-19-1858)
George, Rebecca to John Estes 10-22-1864
Gilbert, Arrena to G. W. Gilbert 12-28-1862 (12-29-1862)
Gilbert, Bettie to B. M. Wright 12-8-1877
Gilbert, Elen to F. W. Raymond 7-22-1869
Gilbert, Eliza to Milton Morgan 3-19-1867
Gilbert, Josey to David Burtram 8-12-1876 (no return)
Gilbert, Martha to Francis Christphine 4-5-1863 (no return)
Gilbert, Mary A. to G. D. Guy 10-19-1878 (sol. no date)
Gilbert, Mary to H. L. Haney 9-12-1874
Gilbert, Mary to Wm. Hodges 9-24-1862

Gilbert, Rachel L. to D. M. Gay 3-6-1880 (3-7-1880)
Gilbey?, Hattie to Wm. Nunley 1-19-1878
Gillahan, E. J. to J. C. Adamson 10-17-1877 (10-20-1877)
Gipson, Eliza J. to Joseph M. Vanhooser 9-15-1874 (9-16-1874)
Givan, Emaline to Pery G. Cantrell 2-14-1859 (2-15-1859)
Givan, Virginia F. to J. W. Goggin 9-12-1873 (9-14-1873)
Givans, Sarah M. to B. L. Johnson 11-17-1850
Givans, Talitha to Edward Gothard 2-8-1854 (2-9-1854)
Given, Mary E. to William A. Turner 11-8-1854
Given, Nancy to John B. Stark 1-17-1860 (1-19?-1860)
Given, Sarah C. to Wm. M. Fite 7-29-1861 (7-30-1861)
Given, Sarah J. to Jasper N. Hayes 5-26-1880
Given, Tennessee to Joseph Warren 11-22-1866 (11-23-1866)
Givens, Palmer to R. B. Sumars 1-25-1875 (1-28-1875)
Giveon, Angie to J. S. Measle 12-15-1878 (no return)
Givin, Tennessee to Wm. B. Preston 11-9-1861 (12-1-1861)
Givines, Mary E. to Eliga Robinson 9-19-1865 (9-21-1865)
Givven?, Nannie to Lou? Tubb 12-15-1876 (12-17-1876)
Glavans?, S. to J. H. Ashburn 1-6-1876 (1-7-1876)
Glenn, Rebeca to Samuel R. Vaughn 8-18-1862 (8-19-1862)
Glenn, Sarah H. to Samuel Walker 2-7-1880 (2-8-1880)
Glenn, Sarah M. to Joshua D. Edmons 12-15-1853
Glover, Evaline T. to John S. Jarvis? 2-17-1856 (exec. no date)
Glover, Martha Ann to John Clemmons 12-14-1854
Goad?, Ruthana to Robert S. Sutton 1-24-1861
Gogars, Jane to Martin Starks 5-30-1866
Goggin, Allis to Samuel Malone 10-4-1855 (no return)
Goggin, Mary H. to J. M. Hale 12-16-1879 (12-18-1879)
Goggin, Nancy E. to Jasper Owen 11-1-1864 (11-3-1864)
Gogin, Mandy to George Findley 12-14-1853
Goin, M. A. to Jackson Goin 11-14-1876 (11-5-1876)
Goodin, Ele to Wm. P. Pickett 10-19-1866 (no return)
Goodman, Mary Ann to Lewis W. Day 12-1-1859
Goodner, Amanda R. to James M. Baird 11-21-1848 (11-23-1848)
Goodner, Caroline to Wm. Garrison 1-16-1873 (1-19-1872?)
Goodner, Elizabeth to John Martin 12-22-1865 (12-24-1865)
Goodner, Malissa to Benjamin Mullinax 3-5-1873 (3-6-1873)
Goodner, Parale to John B. Yeargan 2-28-1854
Goodner, Phillip to George Corsel 3-19-1866 (3-20-1866)
Goodner, Tennessee to Denis Ray 7-11-1867 (no return) [B]
Goodson, Martha to C. C. Wright 11-25-1879 (no return)
Goodson, Nancy to J. C. Stanley 7-18-1856 (7-20-1856)
Goodson, Rebecca to James Marshell 6?-29-1849
Goodson, Sarah to Charles Ferrell 1-29-1861 (1-30-1861)
Goodson, Sophronia to E. W. Capshaw 11-27-1874 (11-29-1874)
Goodson, Susanah to W. W. Ford 1-8-1859 (1-9-1859)
Goodwin, Susanah to N. I. Alexander 8-14-1862
Gordon, Fanny to Wood Allen 12-21-1868 (12-24-1868)
Goreme, Sarah E. to Jo. Kimbrow 4-25-1879 (4-26-1879)
Gorss, Mina to Bejamon Doss 6-6-1877 (no date)
Gosset, Virgina A. to John Turner 12-3-1856
Gothard, Charlotta to Alexander Pitly 8-23-1861 (8-24-1861)
Gothard, L. E. to R. C. Yergan 9-22-1877 (9-25-1877)
Gothard, M. E. to G. M. Fuson 12-20-1877
Gowans, Polley to Lucian Preston 2-17-1869 (2-19-1869) [B]
Gowen, Susan M. to E. K. Atwell 5-12-1877 (5-13-1877)
Gracy, Mary S. to Hyram Childress 2-26-1870 (2-27-1870)
Graham?, Mary J. to C. Ferrell 3-29-1862 (3-30-1862)
Gray, Darthuly to Matthew Williams 3-26-1851
Grayham, Hixa to Archibald Moore no date (exec. 5-22-186
Green, Carlain to George W. Self 8-20-1853 (8-21-1853)
Green, Catharine to Thomas Self 10-17-1855 (10-18-1855)
Green, Charloty to Winship Petty 2-12-1863
Green, Eliza to Thomas Floid 11-17-1877 (11-28-1877)
Green, Elizia to Charles Preston 9-4-1870 (no return) [B]
Green, Gabriala to Crocket Adcock 10-21-1865
Green, Jane to B. F. Bratcher 1-9-1878 (1-3?-1878)
Green, Lidia to Enoch Ferril 6-27-1865 (6-29-1865)
Green, Martha to William W. Cantrell 1-22-1867
Green, Sarah E. to Elias Taylor 1-31-1869
Greene, Frances to Wm. Smith 11-11-1870 (11-13-1870)
Greer, Mary to Isaac J. Conger 2-22-1873 (2-25-1873)
Greer, Sarah Ann to James Alexander 11-15-1855
Grifeth, Mary to Samuel Henley 1-2-1866 (1-4-1866)
Griffeth, E. C. to T. L. Wood 1-18-1865 (1-19-1865)

Griffeth, Mary Ann to Martin Cantrell 4-25-1861
Griffeth, Mary J. to James E. Jones 10-27-1866 (11-1-1866)
Griffin, Jane to Wm. C. McGann 8-14-1856
Griffith, A. M. to H. C. Dodd 1-11-1866 (1-14-1866)
Griffith, Darthula to T. J. Crips 4-23-1869 (4-25-1869)
Griffith, E. F. to Joseph Scott 12-14-1876 (exec. no date)
Griffith, Edith to James M. Hayes 11-3-1864
Griffith, Elizabeth J. to Isaac Cantrell 10-2-1855
Griffith, Elizabeth to Danel Vanatta 8-21-1879 (no return)
Griffith, Elizabeth to Reuben Davis 9-17-1855 (exec. no date)
Griffith, Ester W. to G. M. Wamack 8-20-1870 (8-28-1870)
Griffith, Jenna to N. H. Grindstaff 4-30-1877 (5-6-1877)
Griffith, Josie to G. W. Moss 10-22-1879
Griffith, Lidy to Benjamin F. Davis 9-9-1852 (9-16-1852)
Griffith, Malinda to George W. Davis (date omitted) (exec.10-28-1852)
Griffith, Malvina to Jasper N. Harps 7-14-1853
Griffith, Marth to Joshua B. Scott 9-8-1855 (9-20-1855)
Griffith, Martha to John W. Sandlin 7-4-1855 (7-14-1855)
Griffith, Mary to Levi Parkerson 6-29-1872 (6-30-1872)
Griffith, Nancy to Martin Cantrell 3-26-1868
Griffith, P. T. to R. B. Trail 12-20-1876 (no return)
Griffith, Parilee to Francis Hall 1-13-1860 (1-15-1860)
Griffith, Santhia? C. to James Griffith 8-10-1872 (8-18-1872)
Griffith, Sarah to Obediah Jenkins 7-22-1850 (7-23-1850)
Griffith, Serah E. to Johnathan Patten 10-27-1866 (11-1-1866)
Griffitt, Mary to Jonathan Agee 2-19-1866
Griggith, Elizabeth to T. L. Wood 11-23-1871 (no return)
Grindesstaff, Mary to Wm. Harden 11-9-1876
Grindstaff, Catherine to James Parker 7-7-1877
Grindstaff, Elizabeth to George Measles 11-27-1865 (11-29-1865)
Grindstaff, Kallie to W. B. Kile 12-19-1877
Grindstaff, Mary A. to J. B. West 11-7-1858 (11-11-1858)
Grindstaff, Mary to Jefferson Wood 10-30-1866 (11-1-1866)
Grindstaff, Sarah W. to Thomas E. Bratton 12-14-1868 (no return)
Grindstaff, Soph to Joseph B. West 11-29-1865 (12-7-1865)
Grissom, Sophia to J. D. Walker 7-25-1871 (7-26-1871)
Groom, Luisa to Stephen Roy 4-4-1870 (4-8-1870)
Groomes, Elizabeth to George McElroy 12-22-1875 (12-23-1875)
Gross, Sarah to Isam Lawrence 2-23-1879 (no return)
Guarner, M. J. to Zachariah Prichard 11-9-1870 (11-10-1870)
Guinn, Mary to W. P. Smith 2-8-1854 (2-9-1854)
Hacher, Carline to Bethel Williams 9-22-1869 (no return)
Haile, Margret J. to Sterling B. Harmon 9-10-1873 (9-11-1873)
Haines, Mary to Samuel Gay 5-14-1864 (no return)
Hale, Emaline to Peter Connor 12-12-1867 (12-13-1867)
Hale, M. E. to J. M. Butler 12-25-1865 (no return)
Hale, M. E. to J. M. Butler 4-28-1865 (3?-16-1865)
Hale, M. E. to J. R. Butcher 12-13-1876 (10-14-1877)
Hale, M. L. to L. P. Coggin 3-15-1876 (3-31-1876)
Hale, Mahala to Thomas Curtis 2-15-1852
Hale, Mary Jane to William Hullet 11-11-1852 (11-12-1852)
Hale, Mary T. to James Neal 1-9-1879
Hale, Nancy E. to J. B. Linney 3-3-1874 (3-4-1874)
Hale, Nancy E. to J. B. Turney 3-3-1874 (3-4-1874)
Hale, Paticents to Allen Baites 1-9-1869  [B]
Halemontallar, Elizabeth to Wm. T. Curtis 1-24-1880
Hales, Miscellaney to T. H. Starnes 12-18-1876 (12-19-1876)
Hales, Sarah Jane to Thomas C. Harper 1-21-1852 (1-22-1852)
Haley, Angelina to Coleman Green 4-22-1876 (4-23-1876)
Haley, Delila J. to Jacob A. Jennings? 10-10-1862 (10-15-1862)
Hall, A. E. to James M. Hayes 4-3-1874
Hall, Amandy J. to John C. Garritson 9-15-1872 (9-24-1872)
Hall, Elizabeth to Jessey Reynolds 8-4-1866 (8-5-1866)
Hall, Fanney P. to Elias Lane 1-3-1873 (1-5-1873)
Hall, Frona to J. T. Turner 9-29-1877 (no return)
Hall, Mary E. to Bazzel Anderson 3-13-1872 (3-14-1872)
Hall, Mathe to Thomas Parker 8-13-1879 (8-15-1879)
Hall, Mattie to Thomas Parker 8-13-1879 (8-15-1879)
Hall, Nancy L. to James A. Ewell 12-10-1875 (12-12-1875)
Hall, Sarah to John Clemmons 2-14-1874 (2-16-1874)
Hall, Sarah to R. M. Dodd 1-22-1870 (1-23-1870)
Hall, Sariah An to James Pitts 1-20-1859
Hall, Tassie to Andrew Lockheart 1-17-1874 (1-18-1874)

Hall, Tempy to Wm. Smith 1-22-1859 (1-23-1859)
Hallam, Rachel to Elisha Titsworth 4-14-1858 (4-4?-1858)
Hallum, Fannie to J. T. Driver 5-13-1879
Hallum, Malinda M. to Wm. M. Hale 2-14-1870 (2-19-1870)
Hamilton, L. A. to T. C. Fry 4-13-1870 (4-23-1870)
Hamilton, Louisa J. to Benjamin Terril 1-7-1858
Hamleta, Mary F. to Wm. Allen 3-24-1866 (3-25-1866)
Hammons, Mary to Benjamin Bullard 9-24-1858
Hammons, Spicy to Wm. Holly 11-23-1863
Hancock, Sinda to Thomas Hayes 2-26-1877 (2-29-1877)
Hancock, Vira to James Simens 2-3-1870 (2-5-1870) [B]
Haney, Hannah to Huston Brim 5-20-1856 (5-21-1856)
Haney, M. E. to H. K. Driver 4-5-1880 (4-6-1880)
Haney, Mary Ann to Wm. Kerbey 8-28-1856
Haney, Susan to James C. Hodge 3-11-1853
Hany, Martha to J. Malone 1-5-1864 (1-6-1864)
Hap?, Tennessee to James H. Moris 9-12-1865 (no return)
Harben, Martha to John Simpson 3-19-1851
Hare, Helan to B. M. Webb 1-8-1867 (no return)
Harget, Matilda M. to Henry Joines 6-19-1868 (no return)
Hargis, Emaline to Allen Cantrell 7-13-1852
Hargret, Oma to C. W. Colman 8-7-1869 (no return)
Hariss, Ader to Henry Moore 2-27-1878 (2-28-1878)
Harmon, Nancy to Elisha Hibden 10-24-1869 (10-29-1869)
Harnould, Elizabeth to John M. Murphy 10-29-1873 (10-30-1873)
Harp, M. C. to A. Barnes 4-14-1877 (3?-28-1877)
Harper, M. E. to E. Smith 7-19-1876 (7-26-1876)
Harper, Martha Ann to Wm. Snow 6-23-1849 (6-25-1849)
Harper, P. F. to Felty Colwell 12-30-1865 (12-31-1865)
Harrington, Susan to Matthew Hunt 11-29-1856 (11-30-1856)
Harris, Isabel to John Jones 11-1-1851 (11-2-1851)
Harvel, Elisa to G. H. Murdock 3-10-1870
Harvy, M. A. C. to John D. Whaley 4-3-1875 (4-4-1875)
Harwell, Rebecca J. to James Thrucote? 12-3-1848
Hass, Susa to Wm. Connelly 3-9-1877 (3-11-1877)
Hatfield, H. T. to J. W. Adkins 7-7-1868 (no return)
Hathaway, Elizabeth E. to John G. Fowler 11-19-1851 (11-20-1851)
Hathaway, Lucy to James Murphy 9-13-1875
Hathaway, Lusinda to James K. Pope 9-1-1855 (9-2-1855)
Hathaway, M. C.? to T. J. Fuson 1-27-1875 (2-4-1875)
Hathaway, Mary to T. J. Fuson 1-27-1875 (no return)
Hathaway, S. D. to J. W Johnson 2-12-1877
Hathaway, S. Jane to Thomas W. Vandigrift 12-6-1871 (12-7-1871)
Hathaway, Tennessee to James Jacobs 6-18-1878 (6-30-1878)
Hathway, Hariett to Braswell Brown 6-22-1866 (solemnized)
Hayes, Amanda to Monro Hayes 5-8-1866 (no return) [B]
Hayes, Aney to Phelix G. Cantrell 10-13-1865 (10-15-1865)
Hayes, Elizabeth J. to John W. Hopkins 8-9-1872 (8-11-1872)
Hayes, Elizabeth to Timothy McCorkle 1-7-1869
Hayes, Elizabeth to Wm. Adkins 2-14-1872 (2-18-1872)
Hayes, Jennie to T. W. Wade 9-21-1878 (9-23-1878)
Hayes, Louisa to Wm. J. Kelly 5-14-1851 (5-15-1851)
Hayes, Mary to Wils Adams 5-11-1866 [B]
Hayes, May to Mat Willes 7-16-1879
Hayes, Milley to Wm. Parker 11-3-1871 (11-5-1871)
Hayes, Molley to J. B. Groomes 11-14-1877 (11-18-1877)
Hayes, Sefrona to James Bratcher 12-15-1878
Hays, Ann to Horace Turner 10-18-1873 (10-20-1873) [B]
Hays, Araminta J. to Samuel Grinstaff 7-30-1860 (7-31-1860)
Hays, Betty to Benson? Martin 2-1-1878 (no return)
Hays, Harriett to George Gasaway 10-6-1869 (10-7-1869) [B]
Hays, Helen to A.? Warford 9-12-1866 (9-7?-1866)
Hays, Helon to Samul Hanford 9-12-1866 (no return)
Hays, Louvina to Horas Hick 5-7-1866 [B]
Hays, Mary Ann to Alexander Cannon ommitted (10-26-1843)
Hays, Mary E. to James Whitesal 7-16-1867
Hays, N. P. to J. D. Robertson 9-1-1865 (9-3-1865)
Hays, Rachael to Henry Yeargan 1-24-1861 (2-14-1861)
Hays, Samantha to Thomas Dables 9-12-1877 (no return)
Hayse, Arraminta J. to Wm. F. Allen 9-11-1856
Hayse, Eliza F. to Hanry Mandlebame 11-3-1858
Hayse, Elizabeth to Barzelia Taylor 3-23-1858 (no return)
Hayse, Elizabeth to William O. N. Weasnor 11-28-1854 (11-30-1854)
Hayse, Elizabeth to Wm. H. Adcock 10-14-1848 (10-18-1848)
Hayse, Josephine to John Kelley 1-3-1856

Hayse, Lucinda C. to Allen Page 3-27-1850 (3-28-1850)
Hayse, M. J. to A. M. Parker 10-3-1874 (10-31-1874)
Hayse, Nancy C. to Joseph J. Pepkin 3-14-1849 (3-15-1849)
Hayse, Paralee to Joshua Trammel 3-27-1851 (no return)
Hayse, Sarah to Haris Hendrixson 4-10-1872 (4-11-1872)
Hearn, J. R. to N. T. Foutch 5-24-1870 (5-26-1870)
Heaven, Eliza to Samuel Baird 2-18-1868 (2-23-1868)
Heddrick, Jane to James Hicks 9-25-1869 (no return)
Hedgecock, Eliz. A. to J. D. Stephenson 1-17-1849 (1-18-1849)
Hedgecock, Emily J. to David S. Stephenson 1-31-1849
Heflin, Harret to Thomas Roberson 5-2-1867 (5-4-1867)
Hegwood, D. J. to David Hall 6-11-1870
Hellum, Mary Jain to Samuel A. Carter 5-16-1865 (5-19-1865)
Hellums, Elizabeth to James Lawrence 4-20-1870 (5-3-1870)
Helum?, Ethel to S. W. Watson 10-4-1876 (10-5-1876)
Hendix, Syntha to Felix Crips 9-4-1879 (no return)
Hendricks, Susan to George Drewry 10-5-1849
Hendrickson, Nancy M. to E. H. Fish 1-27-1857
Hendrickson, Samantha Jane to John Ethridge 3-16-1853 (3-18-1853)
Hendrix, Amandy to John Taylor 8-19-1874 (8-20-1874)
Hendrix, Elizabeth to Thomas Fusan 7-21-1864 (no return)
Hendrix, Elizebeth to David J. Taylor 11-6-1867
Hendrix, Frances M. to Borzela Taylor 12-13-1873 (12-14-1873)
Hendrix, M. J. to Criss Vandagriff 7-14-1877 (no return)
Hendrix, Margrett to John Trustey 5-5-1879 (5-6-1879)
Hendrix, Nancy to John Hodge 5-25-1876 (5-26-1876)
Hendrix, Rean to Horres Thomas 11-11-1879 (11-10?-1879)
Hendrixon, Martha to Wiley Hendrixon 1-13-1870
Hendrixon, Sarah H. to Francis M. Ethridge 1-21-1873 (1-24-1873)
Hendrixson, Elizabeth E. to Wm. Culwell 5-8-1879
Hendrixson, Sarah to Lusion Calwell 5-15-1880 (5-16-1880)
Hendrixson, Susan S. to A. J. Bennett 5-7-1856 (5-8-1857?)
Hendrixson, Tennessee to Wm. Hanes 11-9-1874 (2-9-1875)
Henesly, Malissia to Wm. R. Bates 8-12-1871 (no return)
Henley, Martha to Micager Maynard 11-15-1856
Henly, Mary J. to Andrew Rigsby 6-25-1869
Henly, Nancy to Joseph Pack 8-7-1874 (8-9-1874)
Henrixon, Mary J. to James H. Fuson 10-5-1862
Herd, Margaret E. to Eli Lawson 7-27-1864 (no return)
Herd, N. E. to John S. Green 10-3-1867
Heren, Angeline to George Palmer 6-8-1870 (6-9-1870)
Herenton, Martha to Thos. W. Tyree 12-6-1878 (12-8-1878)
Herington, Louiza to Jesse Haris 4-4-1868 (4-5-1868)
Herington, Polly to John Reynolds 10-30-1869 (10-31-1869)
Herndon, Liza A. to Rubin Martan 11-18-1876
Herndon, Loucinda to Smith Tomlin 1-23-1878 (6-24-1878)
Herren, Sarah to Lewis Maynard 5-12-1856
Herrin, Sally L. to Isaac Lafever 3-19-1861 (3-27-1861)
Herrin, Sarah to John Hill 1-17-1857 (no return)
Herrod, Julia to Bartley Carter 8-23-1854 (8-24-1854)
Herron, Malinda to Almon Henley 4-14-1870
Hess, Jane to Wm. Alexandria 10-28-1870 (10-22?-1870)
Hess, Nancy to William Hullett 6-18-1871
Hibden, Elizabeth to Elijah Hicks 7-7-1875 (7-8-1875)
Hibdon, M. H. to S. B. Heriman 5?-8-1880 (no return)
Hibdon, S. C. to J. D. Evans 3-24-1877 (3-25-1877)
Hickison, Mary E. to William C. Pack 2-20-1875
Hickman, Carolina to John Ross 8-20-1856
Hickman, Cynthia M. to Samuel Vanatta 7-13-1860
Hickman, Mary Jane to D. D. Driver 5-25-1861
Hickman, Tabitha to Asa Driver 9-25-1850 (10-1-1850)
Hicks, America to Harvey Patterson 12-21-1853 (12-22-1853)
Hicks, Ann to Thomas Martin 3-10-1855
Hicks, Hannah to Alexander Mands 11-3-1848 (11-5-1848)
Hicks, Mary J. to Luke Neale 6-24-1871 (6-25-1871)
Hicks, Nancy M. to Wm. Colwell 1-7-1863 (no return)
Hicks, S. J. to J. A. Simmons 2-1-1879 (2-2-1879)
Hicks, Sarah to Andrew Emory 2-10-1850
Hicks, Sarah to John Pitts 1-6-1878
Hicks, Winny to Wm. Jones 11-16-1864 (no return)
Higgins, Sarah to John Hancock 7-5-1870 (no return) [B]
Higgins, Susan to John Fitspatric 6-29-1858 (7-1-1858)
Hildreth, Alzena to John Smitson 12-27-1874
Hildreth, Caroline to G. W. Byford 12-15-1873 (12-19-1873)
Hildrith, Canzady to John English 4-24-1880 (4-26-1880)

Hildrith, Sarah P. to Jno. Estes 8-4-1877 (8-5-1877)
Hill, Carline A. to James T. McIntire 2-10-1864 (2-11-1864)
Hill, Elizabeth to A. Foster 10-6-1866 (no return)
Hill, Elizabeth to James Brown 4-26-1853 (4-28-1853)
Hill, Elizabeth to Jobe Trapp 11-9-1877
Hill, H. M. to R. L. William 3-4-1875
Hill, Louisa to James Lee 10-5-1857 (10-6-1858?)
Hill, Mary to Eligah Scott 9-24-1875 (9-26-1875)
Hill, Mary to Thomas Henderson 3-27-1864
Himbrel, Matilda M. to James C Underwood 6-27-1850
    (no return)
Hindsley, Amanda to W. A. Crawford 1-28-1880
Hinson, Jane to Joseph Aamson? 9-9-1852
Hix, Math F. to James Griffith 1-22-1867
Hobbs, Bellsora to H. A. Overall 10-7-1878 (10-8-1878)
Hodge, Anna to John H. Stone 5-23-1877 (5-24-1877)
Hodge, Mary D. to John Tarply 6-4-1874 (6-9-1874)
Hodges, Susanah to Wm. C. Kirby 10-31-1862 (9?-1-1862)
Holand, Mallissia A. to James L. Seay 9-2-1870
Holinsworth, Tarvy to James Turney 11-21-1868 (11-22-1868)
Holland, Nancy J. to Benj. Christen 2-22-1865 (no return)
Hollen, Parlee to H. C. Vandergrift 11-15-1879 (11-17-1879)
Hollingsworth, N. T. to J. F. Youngblood 12-28-1859
Hollinsworth, Mary E. to Henry C. Vandigrift 12-9-1868
    (no return)
Hollinsworth, Nancy E. to J. T. Rogers 10-29-1864 (10-31-1864)
Holly, Amandy R. to John K. Starnes 10-15-1859 (10-26-1859)
Holly, Mary M. to John Atnip 4-1-1869
Holly, Rebecca to Marion Hayes 12-20-1879 (no return)
Holly, Sophia to M. D. Ferrell 10-3-1877 (10-4-1877)
Hooper, M. F. to J. D. Philips 10-14-1865 (10-22-1865)
Hooper, Martha A. to David B. Worley 1-4-1858 (1-9-1858)
Hooper, Mary J. to Asiah Driver 1-4-1858 (1-6-1858)
Hooper, Sarah to Jack Pettigo 3-22-1879 (3-23-1879)
Hooton, Susan to John Turner 5-24-1860 (5-25-1860)
Hornel, Malindy to John J. Page 1-27-1872 (1-28-1872)
Hornes, Mary to James P. Keele 4-3-1872
Horney, Sarah M. to T. L. D. Ferrell 1-27-1880 (1-29-1880)
Horton, Matilda to James Rucker 10-16-1854
Hoskins, Alis to A. P. Smith 4-5-1875 (4-8-1875)
Hoss, Charity Ann to Wm. C. Self 10-29-1869
Hoss, Rebecca to John Keely 8-28-1869 (8-29-1869)
Howard, Dempsy W. to Joseph Hathaway 7-14-1871 (7-15-1871)
Huggins, Sarah to Joseph Hendrickson 7-16-1853 (7-17-1853)
Huggins, Tricy Ann to Wm. H. Woodsides 9-21-1854
Hughes, Mary to Richard Orton 6-11-1880 (6-13-1880)
Hull, Talitha to John Davis 3-22-1854 (3-24-1854)
Hullett, Mary Jane to Wm. H. Tramel 7-18-1856
Hunt, Elizabeth to James Payne 1-28-1851 (1-29-1851)
Hunt, Elizabeth to Monroe Eles 7-31-1876 (8-6-1876)
Hunt, Elizabeth to Wm. Rigsby 4-17-1852
Hunt, Ellen to Isaac N. Johnson 1-15-1873 (no return)
Hunt, Kissey C. to George W. Spurlock 7-26-1859? (8-8-1859)
Hunt, Martha E. to John A. Robinson 1-13-1875
Hunt, Mary A. to Christopher C. Prichard 9-12-1872
Hunt, Mary to John Gann 8-7-1862
Hunt, Sarah J. to James M. Malone 9-18-1873
Hunter, Harriett to Allen Crowder 1-23-1872 (1-24-1872) [B]
Hunter, Lucy R. to Joseph Lockhart 3-18-1864
Hunty, Elizabeth to Pleasant Hale 9-6-1852
Hutchins, Susan to W. L. Fitts 10-6-1869 (no return)
Hutson, Narcissa to William Childress 2-6-1861 (no return)
Ingram, Elizabeth to Wm. Pack 1-3-1865
Inland, Sarah to D. W. Bayors 5-30-1866 (6-3-1866)
Irvin, M. C. to F. G. Foster 1-9-1878 (1-10-1878)
Irwin, Sariah to Isaac T. C. Chrisman 1-8-1849 (1-9-1849)
Isabell, Emily A. to Weldon Terry 5-16-1849
Jackson, Celia C. to Thomas Crook? 3-22-1872 (3-23-1872)
Jackson, Manervy to Samuel Neal 4-11-1866 (no return)
Jackson, Nancy to Amous Fautch 2-5-1849 (2-8-1849)
Jacobes, Tennessee to T. J. Malvane 7-15-1876 (7-16-1876)
Jacups, Mary to Lee? Curtice 12-17-1874
James, Amanda to P. G. Cantrell 7-26-1864
James, Elizabeth to Logan Garrison 1-13-1860 (no return)
James, Elly Ann to Andrew J. Lafever 12-17-1859 (12-20-1859)

James, Jeny A. to John Lafever 3-16-1865
James, M. A. to J. W. Dorsey 8-16-1879 (8-21-1879)
James, M. A. to J. W. Parsly 8-16-1879 (8-21-1879)
James, Marta to Jesse F. Finley 3-31-1852
James, Polly Ann to J. W. Raney 10-14-1868 (10-18-1868)
James, Susannah to J. M. Stephenson 3-2-1857 (3-5-1857)
James, Tennessee to B. S. Elrod 12-14-1853 (12-15-1853)
Jenkins, Candis to E. L. Bradly 4-17-1880 (no return)
Jenkins, Jennie to Thomas Roberts 10-29-1874 (no return)
Jenkins, Nancy P. to Emond H. Warren 9-10-1873
Jennings, L. J. to Calvin Blyth 2-17-1869 (2-18-1869)
Jennings, Tennessee to Samuel M. Bratcher 5-23-1874 (5-24-1874)
Jessee?, Sary to Lawrence Hutchens 7-28-1866 (10-11-1866)
Joblose?, Martha to Elicia Celf 8-24-1875 (8-26-1875)
Johnson, Ann to George Hudelston 2-3-1877 (2-4-1877)
Johnson, Ann to Henry Allen 4-2-1866 (4-6-1866)
Johnson, C. E. to John Miller 10-9-1869 (10-12-1869)
Johnson, Canzada to G. W. Maxwell 1-12-1876
Johnson, Cardelia to Furstman Lawson 8-21-1875 (no return)
Johnson, Catharine to J. R. Ferrill 8-6-1877
Johnson, Catharine to Joseph Younge 3-17-1875 (no return)
Johnson, Catharine to Sidney Stogin? 6-2-1877
Johnson, Dednea to John Anderson 8-16-1866 (exec. no date)
Johnson, Elicetta to Francis Neet 4-2-1875 (4-4-1875)
Johnson, Elizabeth to Charles Robinson 9-25-1878 (9-29-1878)
Johnson, Elizabeth to Elial? Durham 11-6-1849 (12-6-1849)
Johnson, Elizabeth to Esau Pack 6-23-1855 (6-25-1855)
Johnson, Elizabeth to James Pendleton 2-7-1880 (4-21-1880)
Johnson, Elizabeth to Solomon Goodman 12-22-1856 (12-25-1856)
Johnson, Ellen F. to Thomas J. Sneed 6-22-1858 (7-1-1858)
Johnson, Em to George Officer 3-19-1866 (7-14-1866) [B]
Johnson, Emily J. to John B. Tubb 7-7-1873 (7-12-1873)
Johnson, F. C. to Loranzo Brashars 3-4-1879 (3-5-1879)
Johnson, G. F. to Thomas K. David 1-11-1873 (1-12-1873)
Johnson, Letha to Robert Alcorn 11-29-1876 (11-30-1876)
Johnson, Lousa to George W. Maynard 10-12-1860 (10-16-1860)
Johnson, Lowezia to James Nickson 4-9-1877 (4-19-1877)
Johnson, Lucinda to Hezekiah Love 10-22-1856 (10-23-1856)
Johnson, Lucinda to Hezekiah Love 10-22-1856 (no return)
Johnson, M. E. to J. D. Philips 11-25-1868 (11-26-1868)
Johnson, M. J. to J. F. Barnes 10-31-1877 (10-30?-1877)
Johnson, Margrett to Joseph Pack 1-11-1871
Johnson, Mariah E. to Joshua G. Neale 2-9-1874 (2-12-1874)
Johnson, Marth to Thomas Magan 1-5-1880 (no return)
Johnson, Martha E. to David C. Daller 7-11-1874 (7-14-1874)
Johnson, Mary Ann Jane to Elisha Chambers 11-19-1850 (11-20-1850)

Johnson, Mary E. to B. M. Titsworth 2-25-1861 (3-3-1861)
Johnson, Mary F. to John Washer 10-14-1868 (no return)
Johnson, Mary F. to William Thompson 2-3-1874 (2-5-1874)
Johnson, Mary J. to Henry C. David
Johnson, Mary to Giles Sr. Driver 7-15-1855
Johnson, Mary to Taylor Swyscher 9-28-1864
Johnson, Matildy A. to Thomas P. A. Miller 1-23-1872 (1-24-1872)
Johnson, N. J. to James M. Holis 2-16-1865 (2-19-1865)
Johnson, Nancy E. T. to Isaac G. Tenney 11-4-1873 (11-6-1873)
Johnson, Nancy J. to David Curtis 4-27-1869 (no return)
Johnson, Nancy to A. Ivey 2-3-1856 (2-5-1856)
Johnson, Nancy to J. A. Foutch 2-9-1875 (exec. no retrn)
Johnson, Paralee to John Fowler 11-1-1866
Johnson, S. E. to Miles W. Driver 9-26-1876 (9-28-1876)
Johnson, S. E. to Thomas Bain 2-23-1869 (2-25-1869)
Johnson, Sarah A. to Samuel H. Malone 10-3-1878
Johnson, Sarah F. to Wm. Merrit 10-6-1860 (10-11-1860)
Johnson, Sarah J. to Henry Hale 12-8-1849 (12-9-1849)
Johnson, Sarah to Gorge H. Prim 12-26-1850 (12-26-1850)
Johnson, Sarah to John Hildrith 6-23-1880 (6-24-1880)
Johnson, Silvana to General Bates 1-30-1875 (2-4-1875)
Johnson, Susan to Americus Allen 11-11-1857
Johnson, Susan to Thomas Maynard 9-4-1879
Johnson, Sylvia to Robert Bohannon 9-6-1873 (no return)
Johnston, Jane to Charley Wade 5-31-1877 (no return)
Joines, Martha to Isaac Murry 5-13-1869 (5-15-1869)
Joines, Nancy to Benjamin T. Kegle 9-25-1872 (10-5-1872)
Joins, Mary J. to James Fish 11-2-1862 (no return)

Joins, Sarah to Levi Mason 5-31-1869 (no return)
Jones, Caroline to Henry Malone 3-22-1849
Jones, Darthula to Wm. Maning 2-12-1874
Jones, Eady to Thomas D. Oakley 1-4-1866
Jones, Edily H. to Gabriel M. Winfree 7-2-1855 (no return)
Jones, Elisabeth to Thomas Powel 8-16-1867 (8-18-1867)
Jones, Eliza J. to W. R. Baliff 12-13-1862 (12-14-1862)
Jones, Elizabeth to Barnet Williams 8-26-1853 (8-28-1853)
Jones, Elizabeth to James Barnes 7-20-1860
Jones, Elizabeth to S. R. Trammell 8-6-1878 (no return)
Jones, Elizabeth to Wm. Jenkins 12-21-1868 (12-25-1868)
Jones, Emeline to Ples Johnson 11-24-1869 (11-26-1869) [B]
Jones, Eran to John Walker 1-4-1869 (1-5-1869)
Jones, Farasetta to J. T. Hayes 12-15-1864 (12-16-1864)
Jones, Frances to James Swinegane 3-19-1858 (no return)
Jones, Frances to Joseph S. Tisdale 2-28-1872 (2-29-1872)
Jones, Hariet to Hezekiah Jones 2-22-1865 (2-25-1865)
Jones, M. E. to C. T. Jones 10-1-1875 (10-2-1875)
Jones, M. F. to Tilmon West 8-8-1876 (8-9-1876)
Jones, Mahala to Obediah Jenkins 12-17-1857
Jones, Malvina to J. H. Cantrell 12-21-1869 (12-22-1869)
Jones, Malvina to W. W. Walker 2-1-1873 (2-3-1873)
Jones, Martha E. to William S. Palmer 1-10-1859 (no return)
Jones, Martha E. to Wm. H. Whaley 12-11-1852 (12-13-1852)
Jones, Martha T. to J. D. Bane 8-29-1867 (9-1-1867)
Jones, Martha to Benjamon Cantrell 12-15-1874 (12-16-1874)
Jones, Mary (Hooker) to Erwin Sanders 12-6-1848 (12-7-1848)
Jones, Mary J. to Wm. L. Malone 10-1-1873 (no return)
Jones, Mary to S. J. Parson 7-5-1875 (7-8-1875)
Jones, N. E. to T. A. Bogle 9-2-1876
Jones, Nancy A. to James R. P. Brimer 2-11-1867 (2-14-1867)
Jones, Rebecca to Thompson Allison 12-22-1858 (12-23-1858)
Jones, Sarah An to J. J. Griffith 5-13-1869 (no return)
Jones, Sarah H. to John J. Whit 9-6-1865 (9-10-1865)
Jones, Sarah to Wm. F. Turner 1-2-1877 (no return)
Jones, Semantha E. to H. E. Stones 11-12-1874
Jones, Susan to Lenard Cantrell 9-29-1876 (10-1-1876)
Jones, Susannah to L. Chapman 1-17-1850
Jones, Victoria to J. B. Ledford 9-11-1877 (no return)
Jones, Viney Ann Tennessee to John Allen 6-13-1866
Judkin, Elizabeth to Sampson Martin 12-11-1873
Judkins, Isabella to John Trapp 1-8-1869 (1-10-1869)
Judkins, Lou to J. G. McGuines 8-22-1878 (8-24-1878)
Julin, Mary Ann to Hammelton Reeves 10-6-1848 (10-8-1848)
Kagle, Salley to Wm. Phillipes 5-7-1878
Keath, Jane to John Pistole 3-19-1851
Keath, Julian to Cornelias Keeton 8-22-1855 (8-26-1855)
Keath, Melviny to Wm. B. Spradly 6-26-1860 (no return)
Keath, Susan Ann to John Davis 8-22-1849 (8-24-1849)
Keath, Susannah to Wm. Keaton 9-6-1855
Keaton, Malvina F. to Leander Dougherty 9-5-1873 (9-7-1873)
Keaton, Melvina to Joseph Pipkin 7-5-1877
Keaton, Nancy to James Jenings 2-26-1877
Keaton, Sarah A. to Francis M. Snood? 5-20-1874 (5-24-1870)
Keaton, Susan to Riley Garison 2-1-1865
Keef, Nancy to Thomas Davis 5-5-1877
Keel, Nancy Jane to James Redman 4-15-1873
Keerald, Mary to D. P. Murdock 1-30-1880 (2-1-1880)
Keeth, S. G. to Peter Cowen 3-2-1878 (3-9-1878)
Keeton, Mary D. to Henry T. Saddler 8-8-1879 (8-10-1879)
Keeton, Mary E. to Thomas J. Conner 5-21-1861
Keith, Edame to Josiah Jared 8-7-1869 (no return)
Keith, M. J. to J. C. Johnson 5-19-1877 (no return)
Kelley, Gabell? to A. D. Driver 12-24-1870 (12-29-1870)
Kelley, Milley to Leander Jackson 7-26-1852 (8-2-1852)
Kelley, Rebecca to Joseph Bates 9-11-1875 (9-12-1875)
Kelly, Elizabeth to Daniel Lasitor 9-20-1850 (9-28-1850)
Kelly, Mary Ann to Alexander A. Smith 3-21-1853
Kelly, Nancy to George W. Close 2-9-1870 (3-13-1870)
Kennedy, Elizabeth J. to N. W. J. Sims 8-16-1853 (no return)
Kennedy, Elizabeth to George W. Warren 12-20-1853 (12-21-1853)
Kerby, Elliot J. to Ausly Stephens 11-6-1860 (11-7-1860)
Kerby, Ellit to Yancey Stephens 1-23-1856 (no return)
Kerby, Mary L. to James R. Dale 1-19-1864 (no return)
Kerby, Mary to Napoleon Parker 1-6-1849 (1-7-1849)

Kerby, Oliva to John M. Gilbert 6-24-1868 (6-25-1868)
Kerby, Susan to Sampson Braswell 2-28-1861
Kerklin, Martha to Noah W. Maynard 12-4-1856
Kerley, Amanda to J. M. Braswell 3-10-1866 (3-11-1866)
Kerley, Elliot to Jessee Walton 8-26-1858 (9-2-1858)
Kersey, Louisa to James J. Martin 1-4-1854
Keton, Catharine to Tarence O.l Conner 10-16-1850 (10-17-1850)
Keton, Mary Ann to James N. Green 4-3-1852 (4-4-1852)
Kidwell, Elizabeth to J. N. Williams 2-21-1867 (2-22-1867)
Kidwell, Mary to G. S. Davise 10-10-1878
Kidwell, Sue E. to T. W. Shields 12-2-1875
Kiel, Madcid to Monro Neel 2-15-1878 (2-20-1878)
King, Judah to Westly Hathaway 10-16-1873 (10-17-1873)
King, Nancy to James Brown 5-20-1870 (5-21-1870)
King, R. E. to James W. Cooper 3-16-1870 (3-24-1870)
King, Tennessee to A. J. Hays 2-3-1876
Kirk, S. J. to W. Davis 10-12-1870 (10-16-1870)
Kisey, Sarah to John A. J. Nelson 8-5-1857 (8-6-1857)
Koger, Margaret L. to J. A. Barnes 5-25-1858 (5-26-1858)
Kyle, Arbell to Samuel Malone 8-9-1879 (8-17-1879)
Lack, Elizabeth to H. G. Kerly 11-15-1859 (11-16-1859)
Lack, Martha A. to Friley Martin 1-7-1851 (1-9-1851)
Lack, Martha to Henry Kathcart 1-17-1871 (1-18-1871)
Lack, Mary to George B. Cantrell 8-9-1879 (8-10-1879)
Lack, Palmetia to Danial Quillin 11-30-1872 (12-8-1872)
Lafever, Judia to J. L. Brown 6-19-1867 (6-20-1867)
Lafever, Martha E. to Samuel H. Malone 3-15-1871 (3-16-1871)
Lafever, Sarah to Alexander Pedigo 4-14-1869 (4-15-1869)
Lafever, Sarah to James Hartwell 10-17-1874
Lafevers, Lucy to Dime? Dewease 11-1-1869 (no return)
Lamberson, Amanda N. to John A. Bratton 2-24-1857 (2-25-1857) [*]
Lamberson, Delilah to W. J. Carroll 3-31-1876 (4-6-1876)
Lamberson, Easter to Pleasant Grindstaff 1-31-1874
          (2-1-1874) [B]
Lamberson, Emiline to Alonzo Reynolds 6-1-1867 (6-7-1867)
Lamberson, M. A. to G. A. Smith 2-27-1876
Lamberson, Mary E. to Wm. G. Gosset 8-20-1854 (no return)
Lamberson, Sarah A. to Isaac Bates 5-20-1873 (5-22-1873)
Lane, Blanchy Ann to Wm. E. Foster 10-18-1848 (10-19-1848)
Lane, Mary J. to Johnathan D. Thweatt 11-17-1859
Lane, Mary Jane to T. L. Cotton 10-1-1864 (10-3-1864)
Lane, R. to R. B. Lane 5-16-1868 (no return)
Lane, Virginia Ann to George W. James 2-3-1859 (2-8-1859)
Laseter, Elizabeth to Jacob Pack 11-5-1862
Laseter, Melessa J. to Thos. Wall 8-17-1864 (8-19-1864)
Laseter, Sarah to E. N. Trail 2-20-1862 (2-27-1862)
Lasiter, Harriett to David A. Yanson 2-25-1867 (2-26-1867)
Lasiter, M. J. to W. D. Wood 1-31-1863 (2-1-1863)
Lassater, Rua to Starkley Adcock 2-7-1876 (2-9-1876)
Laster, C. A. to E. W. Patterson 10-20-1876 (10-22-1876)
Laurence, Susan F. to Joseph L. Hearn 12-21-1863 (12-22-1863)
Lawrance, Elizabeth to Wm. B. Pitman 5-17-1873 (exec. no date)
Lawrence, Artemisa to Samuel Simpson 7-30-1867
Lawrence, Dela to Thomas Davis 12-28-1861 (12-29-1861)
Lawrence, Dicy M. to Antony Bass 12-24-1863 (no return) [B]
Lawrence, Elizabeth A. to Wm. M. Bankston 3-13-1854 (3-14-1854)
Lawrence, Elizabeth to John Reynolds 10-3-1858 (10-5-1858)
Lawrence, Fanney to Isaac Clark 6-19-1876 (6-22-1876)
Lawrence, Helen to James H. Close 3-22-1851 (3-27-1851)
Lawrence, Laura to Dawson Oakley 12-8-1872 (12-6?-1872)
Lawrence, Lee to James N. Bridges 2-20-1861 (2-21-1861)
Lawrence, Leuvea E. to Johnson Tramel 2-21-1855 (2-22-1855)
Lawrence, Malinda to Wm. Ned Smith 6-28-1855
Lawrence, Mary E. to John G. Houston 6-2-1856 (6-3-1856)
Lawrence, Mary to Jacob Lawrence 12-25-1872 (no return) [B]
Lawrence, Mary to James M. Malone 5-3-1853
Lawrence, P. to James Baty 2-11-1849
Lawrence, Susan F. to Joseph S. Kerr 12-21-1863 (12-22-1863)
Lawrence, Susan to Samuel Simpson 2-6-1850 (2-7-1850)
Lawson, Mary C. to John E. Johnson 3-17-1879 (3-20-1879)
Lawson, Mary to Wm. F. Botts 12-7-1870 (no return)
Lawson, Zelpha to Elias Besheares 11-17-1865
Lay, Mary Jane to Levi Johnson 12-26-1859 (12-27-1859)
League, Chernine to Isaac Bozarth 9-13-1879 (no return)
League, Cora A. to Henry Ealsy 7-11-1872 [B]

League, Elizabeth to Levy Nixon 3-21-1878 (3-24-1878)
League, Mary Ann to Wade H. Migginson 4-7-1849 (4-12-1849)
League, Nancy to Elias Stokes 10-24-1878 [B]
League, Sarah to Charles Burton 6-19-1868 (6-21-1868)
Leaguel, Oma to John S. Meggerson 1-12-1876 (1-17-1876)
Leay, Elizabeth to John Palinor 11-2-1853 (11-4-1853)
Lecur, Marge to N. J. Cobb 6-17-1867 (6-20-1867)
Ledford, Adelia to Robert Maning 4-11-1868 (4-19-1868)
Lee, Almyra to John Conger 8-19-1868 (8-19-1868)
Lee, Amanda to C. B. Cantrell 11-25-1870 (11-27-1870)
Lee, Carry I. to Joseph P. Stephens 5-9-1879 (5-11-1879)
Lee, M. A. to F. N. Patterson 5-10-1866 (no return)
Lee, Mahala to H. H. Pistole 8-31-1861
Lee, Mary C. to Thos. A. Waller 5-1-1850 (5-2-1850)
Lee, Parasetta F. to Nelson C. Davis 8-5-1864 (8-6-1864)
Lee, S. E. to J. J. Page 10-4-1876
Lee, Sarah C. to James P. Terry 12-18-1858 (12-19-1858)
Leek, Sarah M. to Wm. T. Rhea 9-10-1850
Lefeaver, Fanny to Isaac Thomas 3-5-1849 (3-11-1849)
Lefer, Elizabeth Ami to Buel Mansel no date (exec. 8-12-184
Lefever, Amanda to W. H. Pedigoe 10-30-1867 (10-31-1867)
Lefever, Jane to Robert Pedigoe 3-26-1857
Lefever, Mary Ann to B. J. Parsley 11-16-1854
Lefever, Mary to William Elrod 1-24-1850 (11-24-1850)
Lefever, Talitha to Jud S. Parsley 4-18-1854 (4-19-1854)
Lewis, Delila to Samuel T. Rigsby 8-31-1853 (9-3-1853)
Lewis, Elizabeth to James Rankhorn 9-5-1860
Lewis, Lula B. to W. T. Hale 4-4-1876 (4-6-1876)
Lewis, Mary J. to Ansel Clemsons 2-5-1862 (no return)
Lewis, Mary to James Steel 3-7-1872 (3-10-1872)
Lewis, Paralle to Lewis Durham 4-6-1850 (4-11-1850)
Liles, Mary J. to James Munroe Pack 11-4-1867
Liles, Sarh to Archable D. Green 9-26-1872
Lillus, Parilee to W. J. Hale 6-8-1861 (6-9-1861)
Linder, Jane to William Walker 6-18-1870 (6-21-1870)
Linder, Mary to Smith Cantrell 10-9-1856 (10-23-1856)
Lisk, M. H. to L. D. Crowder 12-24-1879
Lisk, Rosa A. to Lewis Scale 12-22-1873 (no return) [B]
Lisk, S. E. to E. Warren 10-13-1870 (10-14-1870)
Lith, Martha J. to Eli Winchester 8-15-1872
Little, Mary to Thomas Davis 5-15-1871
Livertak?, Elizabeth to Wm. Malone 7-14-1879 (7-20-1879)
Lochart, Mary to Hezakiah Pickett 10-6-1874 (10-11-1874)
Lock, Lidy to Van Williams 7-9-1879 (7-10-1879)
Lockhart, Elizabeth to Gibson Maynord 12-4-1876 (11?-7-1876)
Lockhart, Rebecca to Wm. R. Philips 2-8-1852
Lockheart, Rebeca to John W. Gay 12-10-1870 (12-11-1870)
Loggin, Oleevy L. to Charley E. Duke 12-20-1859 (no date)
Loona, Martha J. to Wm. B. Phillips 10-29-1872
Looney, Acksey to William G. Chisam 8-16-1856 (8-17-1856)
Looney, Elizabeth to John Megginson 3-31-1854 (4-2-1854)
Looney, Mary Ann to Wm. A. Cotton 12-20-1859 (12-30-1859)
Looney, Nancy to John Gibbs 10-20-1858 (10-21-1858)
Looney, Sarah C. to Henry Turner 10-6-1869 (10-7-1869)
Loss?, Sarah to Aron Cantrell 3-17-1866 (3-18-1866)
Love, Amanda to E. Hutchison 10-12-1866 (10-15-1866)
Love, Ann to E. E. Lane 12-2-1875
Love, Louisa to John W. Lefever? 12-30-1865 (no return)
Love, Martha J. to L. J. Lowery 11-1-1879 (11-2-1879)
Love, Mary to Wm. Young 10-5-1850 (10-7-1850)
Love, Nancy to Wm. Magerson 5-30-1857 (5-31-1857)
Love, Rachel to Andrew J. Robins 2-17-1880 (2-19-1880)
Love, Rebeca to Richard E. Certain 10-14-1858 (10-16-1858)
Love, Sarah to David P. Taylor 5-6-1873
Love, Vilet to Sirus Dunn 1-15-1853 (no date)
Lowery, Milley to E. N. Moores 11-29-1871 (11-30-1871)
Lowery, Palmirey G. to Francis M. Williams 9-20-1873 (9-21-1873)
Lowery, S. C. to J. R. Spurlock 10-30-1879
Lowrey, Elizabeth to H. B. Cope 11-8-1872 (11-10-1872)
Luckey, Amanda to W. B. Briges 12-25-1858 (exec,no date)
Luckey, Lillie to T. P. Davis 4-27-1880 (4-29-1880)
Lucky, Jennie to Lemuel? Lucus 12-25-1871 (12-28-1871)
Luna, Hariet to H. L. Barnes 4-15-1875
Luna, J. D. to J. B. Allen 5-13-1875 (5-20-1875)
Luna?, Martha to Joseph Atnip 10-24-1848

Luny, M. C. to James T. Adcock 8-15-1877 (8-6-1877)
Lyles, Martha to Monroe Green 12-4-1872 (12-5-1872)
Madelly, Mary C. to Samuel Dreese 6-14-1873 (6-26-1873)
Magan, Eliza to Bartle James 7-29-1865 (no return)
Magard, Eva to T. J. Waller 10-21-1879 (10-22-1879)
Maginest, Talmy to Eli Eavins 12-29-1874
Maginis, Ann to Green B. Pedigo 1-14-1858
Magnes, S. F. to M. M. Pillips? 11-18-1876 (11-21-1876)
Magnes, S. J. to Wm. Cope? 1-12-1876 (1-13-1876)
Magness, C. A. to M. D. Smallman 5-26-1868
Magness, Charlott B. to Wm. Odem 10-3-1854
Magness, Dicey to Thomas Beasley 5-12-1872 [B]
Magness, Elizabeth to E. W. Webb 8-7-1873
Magness, Hannah N. to J. B. Lack 4-12-1871
Magness, Hannah to J. B. Lock 4-12-1871 (no return)
Magniss, Mary E. to Georgea. Bery 8-22-1866 (8-23-1866)
Maler, Malinda to George Malone 5-7-1866 (no return)
Mallun, Mary H. to John C. Stewart 9-12-1861 (9-14-1861)
Maloane, Liza to Columbus Johnson 2-3-1877 (2-4-1877)
Maloane, M. to Joseph Curtis 1-9-1878 (1-13-1878)
Maloane, Phroney to J. D. Curtis 2-24-1875 (2-27-1875)
Malone, Adline to Licurgus Williams 7-29-1872 (7-31-1872)
Malone, Anna E. to Thomas Nixon 1-12-1875 (1-14-1875)
Malone, Anny to John M. Jones 5-4-1865 (5-7-1865)
Malone, Elizabeth J. to Clint Jacobs 8-30-1876 (9-3-1876)
Malone, Josephin to Samuel Warford 6-25-1856 (6-26-1856)
Malone, Lyda to James M. White 7-23-1854
Malone, Marildy J. to Jackson Malone 3-17-1866 (sol. no date)
Malone, Martha to John Bennette 2-6-1856
Malone, Mary J. to Pallis M. Hardcastle 9-27-1869
Malone, Mary Jane to Joseph Jones 6-25-1852 (6-29-1852)
Malone, Mary to H. T. Hawkins 1-11-1878 (1-13-1878)
Malone, Mary to Samuel M. Christian 3-6-1861 (no return)
Malone, Melviney to Monroe Eddings 1-18-1873 (1-19-1873)
Malone, Nancy E. to John S. Roberts 12-26-1871 (12-27-1871)
Malone, Susanah to Rufus Johnson 10-16-1872 (10-20-1872)
Malone, Thena to A. M. C. Robinson 9-14-1858 (9-16-1858)
Malone, Torry A. to Spencer Price 4-19-1879 [B]
Manaleburn, Ida to Robt. Black 9-8-1875
Mandlebaum, Alice to J. Q. Seawell 10-7-1875 (10-8-1875)
Manford, M. J. to J. W. Redmon 6-1-1878 (6-2-1878)
Mangrum, Eliza to Jasper Fowler 8-27-1868
Mangum, Tabitha C. to Isaac D. Titsworth 1-24-1871
Maning, Caroline to George Johnson 8-14-1873 [B]
Mannan, Polly to James Jones 11-20-1853
Manning, Sarah to W. B. Bates 12-4-1875 (12-5-1875)
Mannon, Lela to Wm. Bankhorn 10-17-1865
Marcrum, Ora to Curtis Garner 6-29-1849 (no return)
Mares, Sarah to John Stiles 1-7-1861 (not filled in)
Markam, Margret J. to Charles Wade 10-26-1874
Markes, Betta to Sam Whitely 2-20-1878 (2-2?-1878)
Markes, Susan to Eliga Whitely 12-18-1874
Marks, Martha J. to Encory Cubbins 8-15-1861
Markum, Eli J. to Peter Clark 11-16-1860 (11-18-1860)
Markum, Eliz. to Hany Wood 1-22-1865 (1-24-1865)
Markum, Elizabeth to Henry Woodden 6-22-1865 (no return)
Marler, C. to Dock Bates 12-1-1877 (12-12-1877)
Marler, N. to M. A. Baits 12-26-1868 (12-30-1868)
Marshel, Rachel to Alex Prichard 12-25-1868 (12-27-1868)
Martain, Mattie to N. B. Bozarth 11-27-1878 (12-18-1878)
Martain, N. E. to J. R. Taylor 9-27-1876 (9-28-1876)
Martin, Amanda J. to D. W. Sewell 10-18-1860 (no return)
Martin, Catharine to Jacob Griffin 6-7-1858
Martin, Cintha to John R. Hale 4-16-1856 (4-17-1856)
Martin, E. to Benjamin Bullard 1-2-1871 (1-5-1871)
Martin, Elizabeth to Isaac Gibbs 2-28-1874 (3-4-1874)
Martin, Elizabeth to Robert Hall 8-2-1865 (no return)
Martin, Elvira to John R. Dun 4-3-1849
Martin, Emalin to Thomas Martin 11-29-1865 (12-30-1865)
Martin, H. P. to J. M. Loving 11-4-1876 (11-5-1876)
Martin, Hixey A. to Jacob C. Barr 4-28-1854
Martin, Jane E. to M. J. Tinsley 7-17-1849 (no date)
Martin, M. M. to R. C. Hays 9-19-1860 (9-20-1860)
Martin, Mahala A. to Henderson A. Edge 8-20-1855 (9-2-1855)
Martin, Margarett A. to B. S. Turner 4-13-1861 (no return)

Martin, Margat J. to Wm. A. Gilbert 12-18-1874 (12-19-1874)
Martin, Martha A. to James Gibbs 12-16-1872 (12-18-1872)
Martin, Martha Jane to Archibald D. England 12-16-1850 (12-17-1850)
Martin, Martha T. to John Hendrickson 7-9-1859
Martin, Mary A. to Wm. H. Vaughn 5-25-1859 (6-2-1859)
Martin, Mary E. to N. E. Brady 3-14-1865 (no return)
Martin, Mary to E. W. Taylor 11-29-1866 (11-30-1866)
Martin, Mary to James Hatfield 7-21-1864
Martin, Nancy to John M. Tinsly 12-20-1868
Martin, S. J. to William Bullard 9-26-1867
Martin, Sarah J. to L. S. Rolland 9-29-1872
Martin, Sarah to A. R. Stipes 8-16-1877 (8-19-1877)
Martin, Sarah to C. Robinson 12-25-1864 (no return)
Martin, Sarah to Even W. Weble 11-6-1851
Martin, Syntha to Wm. Bates 1-16-1851
Martin, Virginia L. to James C. Hailes 4-7-1874 (4-9-1874)
Marton, Boneta to W. D. Dingno? 12-9-1877 (12-12-1877)
Marton, Callidone to H. C. Taylor 3-18-1878 (3-21-1878)
Marton, J. to James M. Biba 1-9-1878 (1-12-1878)
Masior, Martha to Phinas Bozarth 6-1-1869
Mason, Catharine to Wilson Taylor 4-9-1852 (4-11-1852)
Mason, Faving? to N. E. Cantrell 7-9-1870 (7-10-1870)
Mason, G. A. to J. M. Snow 1-2-1869 (1-3-1869)
Mason, Martha A. to Richard? Meaks 8-15-1860
Mason, Martha to Wm. Redman 4-22-1865 (4-23-1865)
Mason, Mary E. to James Turner 9-12-1867 (9-15-1867)
Mason, Mary to Thomas Hays 7-11-1867 (7-18-1867)
Mass, Sarah to Jasper Garenhier 1-7-1867 (1-10-1867)
Mass, W. A. to J. H. Farell 12-23-1874
Massie, Jane to John Moss 6-11-1851 (no return)
Mathey, S. C. to J. R. Dodd 7-8-1876 (7-9-1876)
Maxfield, Eliza to Benjamin H. Glover 8-29-1868 (8-3?-1868)
Maxwell, Amanda M. to Doctor A. Davis 3-15-1860
Maxwell, Frances to Francis M. Dewese 11-19-1859 (11-23-1859)
Maxwell, Frances to James Robinson 5-13-1858
Maxwell, Sitha J. E. to G. W. McCulley 6-5-1879
Mayge?, M. M. to John C. Foster 11-30-1864 (12-2-1864)
Mayge?, M. M. to John Foster date omitd (exec.12-2-1864
Maynard, Eveline to Hardwell James 1-3-1866 (no return)
Maynard, Sarah J. to Joseph Earheart 6-20-1872
McAfee, Sarah to M. E. Adcock 10-10-1865
McAfee, Tolla to J. M. Gilbert 12-29-1866 (12-30-1866)
McCarter, Mary to W. A. Johnson 1-1-1880
McClelen, Martha J. to John H. Trammel 10-13-1853 (10-18-1853)
McClellan, M. E. to Lewis Crastie? 3-18-1866 (no return)
McClellen, Amanda P. to L. Curtis 10-3-1866 (10-7-1866)
McClellon, Elizabeth F. to John R. Taylor 8-8-1874 (8-9-1874)
McClenen, Mary to J. A. Parsly 1-23-1879
McClenon, Frances M. to Chesley Taylor 1-5-1854 (5-14-1854)
McClure, Frances A. to Wm. M. Glen 7-18-1873 (7-20-1873)
McCray, Mary J. to Wm. B. Moss 8-1-1870 (8-15-1870)
McCullough, Elizia to R. H. Buckner 10-14-1872
McCullough, Matildy F. to F. M. Allen 2-9-1874 (2-12-1874)
McCullough, Rachael to Saml. Warford 5-25-1872 (5-26-1872)
McDaniel, Eliza A. to John H. Minton 12-25-1864 (no return)
McDaniel, Polly Ann to John Fisher 2-20-1859 (no return)
McDole, Sissy to Wm. Steel 10-6-1848 (10-5?-1848)
McDowell, B. A. to James Green 3-13-1876 (3-14-1876)
McDowell, Lucretia to Thomas E. Wright 9-30-1870 (10-3-1870)
McDowell, Nancy to S. C. Jones 12-29-1870 (12-30-1870)
McEntire, Lucy to M. F. Herenton 10-5-1878 (no return)
McFarlen, Margaret to Daniel S. Colvert 10-25-1855
McGee, N. C. to J. M. Gilbert 4-3-1879 (no return)
McGee, Susanah to Farney H. Stanford 12-9-1872 (12-12-1872) [B]
McGinis, Asenith to Johnathan Atnip 7-1-1863 (7-2-1863)
McGinis, Elizabeth to Gibson Maynord 10-11-1865
McGinis, Hixey to James Green 8-25-1870 (8-27-1870)
McGinis, Jane to Wm. Cantrell 11-7-1862 (no return)
McGinness, Catharine to Jeremiah Clemmons 10-11-1850 (10-13-1850)
McGinness, Mary Ann to Allen F. McDaniel 2-11-1851
McGuffey, Thursy C. to Wm. T. Winfrey 10-15-1872 (10-17-1872)
McGuines, Sallie to Toney Hill 8-22-1879

McGuiness, Rebecca to David Cantrell 9-13-1877 (no return)
McGuire, Charlotty to E. H. Winnard 5-23-1852
McGuire, Harriet C. to James Dearmon 11-25-1873
McGuire, Lucindy to H. L. W. Capshaw 12-29-1860 (12-31-1860)
McHood, Eliza J. to Tilman L. Foster 11-2-1872 (11-17-1872)
McInteer, Dulana to Francis M. White 6-30-1855 (7-1-1855)
McInteer, Elizabeth to Sidney Kelly (Kerley?) 9-21-1850 (9-23-1850)
McIntier, Luisa to W. H. Tramel 9-30-1865 (no return)
McIntire, Elizabeth C. to Wm. B. Fish 7-7-1860 (7-8-1860)
McIntire, Martha to John Murphey 1-4-1873 (1-5-1873)
McIntire, Sarah M. to John Etherage 1-2-1873
McInturff, Mandelia to Richard Atnip 2-4-1858
McJulin, Luraney to John Tramel 5-19-1861 (no return)
McKisic, Milly to Nelson (Robinson) Vantrease 3-29-1877 (no date)
McKisseack, Anna to Thomas Belcher 12-15-1879
McLaine, Parly to Ned Betty 4-14-1875 (4-15-1875)
McLellan, F. M. to E. A. Coggin 3-12-1862 (3-13-1862)
McLellan, H. A. to James A. Nesmeth 11-9-1858 (12-23-1858)
McManas, Sarah Ann to Tilmon Adcock 11-2-1854
McMillan, Sarah to Tomas H. Vantreas 10-5-1874 (no return)
McMillin, Salley to Wm. Mass 8-2-1876 (exec. no date)
McMillon, Martha to Isaac A. Eaton 9-5-1874 (9-6-1874)
McNaimer, Margarett A. to Wilson Turentine 6-5-1878 (6-6-1878)
Measels, Catharine to John Vernatta 7-30-1857
Measels, Virginia A. to J. H. Fite 10-17-1874 (no return)
Meash, S. T. to T. H. Fite 3-28-1874 (3-30-1874)
Measle, Matildy to A. B. Hicks 9-1-1873 (9-4-1873)
Measle, Tennie to H. H. Jones 2-9-1870 (3-10-1870)
Measles, Alice to ----- Lynam 8-21-1878 (no return)
Measles, Harriet to James McMillon 12-10-1851
Measles, Julia E. to Moses A. Evans 2-22-1860 (2-23-1860)
Measles, Sarah to McAdoo Vanatta 3-13-1853 (3-15-1853)
Meazels, Elizabeth to Samuel Vanatta 2-20-1878 (no return)
Meazles, Eliza to Robert J. Givan 8-27-1850 (9-5-1850)
Medley, Amanda to Carls Robinson 1-8-1870 (1-9-1870)
Medley, Charity to John Raney 7-13-1870 (7-15-1870)
Medley, Eliza to John Oston 2-1-1875 (2-4-1875)
Medlin, Lotta Susan to James Munro Bozarth 12-15-1874 (12-17-1874)
Medlin, M. C. to Owen Elrod 12-21-1878 (no return)
Medlin, Mary to George Dildein 9-4-1864 (9-5-1864)
Megerson, Helen to Harvey Pettigo 11-9-1878 (11-10-1878)
Meggerson, Calaferna to Wm. R. Culwell 1-1-1870 (no return)
Meggerson, California to Wm. R. Culwell 1-1-1870 (1-12-1870)
Meggerson, Jane to J. W. Roberts 8-9-1863 (no return)
Meggerson, Louisa to Watson Martin 2-11-1880 (2-13-1880)
Meggerson, Matilda C. to Willis Ford 9-21-1861 (9-22-1861)
Meggerun, Elizabeth to John Hill 4-19-1862
Meggeson, Isabella to James Green 4-21-1869 (no return)
Meirs, Catharine to Thomas Fisher 9-1-1859 (no return)
Melton, Elvira P. to Partemas Pack 3-19-1860
Melton, H. to Jack Braswell 10-20-1876 (10-22-1876)
Melton, Mary J. to Henry C. Edwards 4-20-1854
Melton, Sallie to John Johnson 6-24-1872
Melton, Sarah A. to Samuel Liles 3-16-1861 (3-17-1861)
Melton, Susan B. to Eliga C. Self 11-8-1873 (11-9-1873)
Melton, Thona to Riley Durham 9-10-1874
Mercer, Jane to Isaac Jones 2-14-1874 (no return)
Merett, Frances R. to Philip N. Lowery 10-2-1871 (10-8-1871)
Mergerson, Mollie to J. C. Jones 12-18-1875
Merit, Elizabeth to Eli Conger 7-24-1856
Meritt, Josephine to Solomon W. West 4-6-1868 (4-8-1868)
Meritt, Virginia to Robert H. Buckner 6-12-1867 (6-13-1867)
Merritt, Jane to John Johnson 12-17-1860 (12-23-1860)
Migget, Jane to Wm. Oakley 12-2-1869 (12-3-1869)
Miller, Elizabeth J. to James A. Neasmith 1-8-1868
Miller, Mary Ann to Robert Johnson 11-24-1860 (11-25-1860)
Miller, Sarah to Wm. C. Gilly 9-8-1860 (no return)
Miller, Stacy to E. O. Underhill 2-9-1869 (2-11-1869)
Milligan, Samantha to Henry Crips 2-26-1879 (3-2-1879)
Milligan, Sarah to George Herd 8-31-1872 (no return) [B]
Mills, Louisa C. to John M. Dyer 11-17-1852 (11-18-1852)
Mills, Susan Anna to J. L. Mills 9-16-1875
Miner, Luisa C. to James A. Yergan 4-17-1850 (4-19-1850)

Mires, Kanzada to James Malone 11-15-1849 (11-18-1849)
Mires, Mary A. to Marion Rice 6-18-1870 (6-16?-1870)
Mitchal, Mary to John Love 3-29-1873 (3-30-1873)
Mitchel, Jane to G. T. Coleman 2-19-1869 (no return)
Mitchel, Jane to Joseph Williams 10-17-1874 (10-18-1874)
Mitchel, Josiphene T. to William K. Adams 9-24-1874
    (no return)
Mitchel, Josiphene T. to Wm. K. Adams 9-24-1874 (no return)
Mitchel, S. E. to C. M. Williams 9-14-1874
Mitchel, Sarah F. to J. B. Moss 1-3-1879 (1-5-1879)
Mitchel, Sarah J. to Wm. G. Stewart 9-5-1872
Mitchel, Tulina O. to George W. Neell 5-29-1858 (no return)
Mitchell, Jane to G. T. Coleman 2-19-1869 (2-22-1869)
Mixen, Isibella to James Ford 11-25-1869
Mohatha, Mary to Jefferson Braswell 8-8-1865 (no return)
Monard, Matilda to E. L. McGinnis 12-3-1860 (12-5-1860)
Mooneham, ElizabethWilliams to I. S. Smith 3-18-1879 (solmnzd?—
no date)
Moore, Adline to Simo Preston 11-10-1870 (no return) [B]
Moore, Elizabeth R. to James E. Bratten 6-19-1849 (6-20-1849)
Moore, Martha to James Cantrell 10-12-1853 (10-13-1853)
Moore, Mary T. to John F. Casty 9-6-1877 (no return)
Moore, Matilda to Luke Neel 2-23-1859 (2-24-1859)
Moore, N. E. to S. R. Young 8-8-1878
Moore, N. L. to G. J. Foster 12-27-1875
Moore, Nancy J. to Isaac M. Hayse 10-17-1872
Moore, S. B. to F. M. Cantrell 1-27-1875
Moore, Sarah to Charley Foster 6-17-1876 (6-18-1876)
Moris, Emaly to James M. Chehane 9-30-1861 (10-9-1861)
Morison, Edith to Spencer Gowins 2-11-1859 (exec. no date)
Morris, Elizabeth to Shemp Wisdom 2-8-1872 (2-13-1872) [B]
Mortain, Elizabeth to Jackson Rogers 5-14-1880 (5-15-1880)
Moses, Palina F. to Thomas D. Herren 2-11-1851 (no return)
Mosier, M. C. to F. C. Cantrell 10-20-1875 (10-21-1875)
Mosier, Parmelia to Wm. Yeargin 2-2-1871
Moss, Arcances to Wm. Kelly 9-7-1878
Moss, Elizabeth to Joseph H. Love 6-29-1861 (no return)
Moss, Elizabeth to Silas Stinebridge 12-31-1868 (1-6-1869)
Moss, Martha J. to Charles T. Mitchell 2-6-1861 (2-11-1861)
Moss, Sarah J. to B. F. Howell 7-4-1872
Moss, W. A. to J. M. Cantrell 11-28-1874 (no date)
Mottley, Matta to Dock Burks 5-18-1878 (5-20-1878) [B]
Mozier, Martha A. to Sampson Braswell 1-16-1864 (no return)
Mozier, Nancy J. to John T. Smitson? 12-19-1862 (no return)
Mulican, Allis to James Sams 4-25-1878 (5-7-1878)
Mulican, Haret to M. C. Green 2-28-1868 (3-1-1868)
Mulican, M. L. to R. L. Page 7-24-1876 (7-26-1876)
Mulican, Melvina to Bartimas Hays Pack 3-30-1867 (3-31-1867)
Mullenax, Omesa to N. B. Bethel 12-19-1856 (12-25-1856)
Mullican, Betty to Mc. Trapp 9-21-1872 (9-22-1872)
Mullican, M. F. to J. R. Jones 10-28-1876 (11-1-1876)
Mullican, M. P. to E. N. Allen 8-29-1872
Mullican, Nancy to Washington Taylor 4-29-1857
Mullican, Samantha T. to John Parsley 4-9-1872 (4-11-1872)
Mullican, Victory to Frank Vaughn 5-18-1880 (5-?-1880)
Mullin, Nancy to Barnibas B. Johnson 7-8-1861 (7-9-1861)
Mullins, C. A. to P. G. Cantrell 12-4-1877 (12-6-1877)
Mullins, Elizabeth to Wm. J. Rankhorn 2-6-1879 (no return)
Murdoc, Dianna to W. Bennett 4-12-1876 (4-16-1876)
Murdock, Mary to Pleasant Cantrell 9-5-1857 (9-8-1857)
Murdock, N. C. to P. F. Cantrell 8-8-1860 (8-9-1860)
Murfrey, Elizabeth to John F. Roberts 11-27-1862 (no return)
Murphey, M. M. to Wm. H. Buck 2-20-1878 (2-2?-1878)
Murphy, Caroline to Isaac Bozorth 3-23-1860 (3-28-1860)
Murphy, Ester to James H. Liles 12-12-1861
Murphy, Mary J. A. to Wm. P. Evins 1-16-1873
Murphy, Rachel to Enoch H. Banks 11-10-1853 (exec. no date)
Myers, Mattie to J. H. Schurer 1-20-1872 (1-23-1872)
Narceny, Mary to Joshua Haynes 7-26-1861
Narros?, Elizia to Alaxander Rich 9-26-1873
Natale, T. J. to John Crook 11-25-1865 (11-29-1865)
Neal, Charity to David Brock 6-10-1879
Neal, E. O. to E. Turney 12-7-1876 (12-10-1876)
Neal, Frances Helen to Isam Davis 9-10-1872 (9-12-1872) [B]
Neal, Hariete to George Close 7-28-1876

Neal, Julia to Purtilas A. Hale 3-27-1878 (3-31-1878)
Neal, Margaret J. to Wm. Whaley 4-2-1849 (4-4-1849)
Neal, Mary S. to Wm. Pinager 6-25-1869
Neal, Narcissa to James Johnson 2-24-1876 (2-25-1876)
Neal, Sarah Hane to Ephriam Clayborn 7-25-1872
Neal, Sarah to George Deling 7-22-1868 (7-25-1868)
Neale, Jane to Robert Duncan 8-2-1872 (no return) [B]
Neale, Mary A. to Littleton B. Sonellin 1-22-1873 (no return)
Neale, Nancy to Thomas Johnson 8-14-1868 (no return)
Neale, Sarah to Wm. D. Evans 8-11-1871
Neasret?, Rinda to Phillip J. Pledger 12-27-1876
Neel, Jane to Wm. Preston 11-15-1854 (11-14?-1854)
Neel, Jocy to Monsol Brient 2-23-1878 (2-24-1878)
Neel, Malissa to James J. Bennette 2-5-1856
Neel, Malissie to David H. Hale 10-14-1853 (no return)
Neel, Margret to James Terney 4-5-1879 (5-6-1879)
Neel, Martha Ann to Nicholas Truxton 7-13-1849 (7-15-1849)
Neel, Samantha to W. P. Young 8-30-1877
Neele, R? to J. R. Newman 1-27-1863 (1-29-1863)
Neil, Elizabeth to Wm. F. Gandy 12-31-1862 (no return)
Neil, N. E. to John Vernatta 9-2-1867 (9-4-1867)
Neill, Hester Ann to Ezekiel T. Rose 9-16-1856 (9-18-1856)
Nelson, Martha J. to W. M. C. D. Watson 1-3-1857 (1-4-1857)
New, Elizabeth F. to Thomas J. Finley 10-17-1849 (10-30-1849)
New, Leatha to Eli Winfrey 1-17-1878 (1-20-1878)
New, Martha to John O. Awlguire 10-5-1858 (10-8-1858)
New, Mary F. to John F. Kerr 2-22-1854 (2-23-1854)
New, Nettey to H. L. Hardcastle 2-2-1874 (2-15-1874)
Newby, Parzada M. to Wm. P. Vicus 3-20-1863 (no return)
Newly, Mary to W. B. Drury 12-30-1868 (12-31-1868)
Newson, Candis to N. M. Bennet 10-2-1865 (10-5-1865)
Newson, Narcissa to James G. Robinson 1-20-1852 (1-21-1852)
Nicholas, Elender C. to Richard Parsley 10-23-1854
Nicles, Elizabeth to Alfred Jones 2-16-1850 (2-24-1850)
Night, Margret to W. C. Yeargin 1-10-1877 (1-16-1877)
Night, Nancy to Isaac B. Aldridge 4-10-1873 (4-13-1873)
Nixon, Martha to John S. Roberts 5-30-1855
Noakes, Martha to John F. Keef 1-12-1876 (1-15-1876)
Noaks, Susanah to Isaac Alexander 9-12-1862 (9-3?-1862)
Nole, Mary to Anderson Will 4-18-1871 (no return)
Nollener, Elizabeth A. to Milus J. Starnes 6-19-1872 (6-17?-1872)
Noris, Rebecca to Solomon Wamack 10-22-1855
Noris, Tabitha to John H. Walker 1-8-1868 (no return)
Norman, Hattie to Robert B. West 6-10-1874 (6-11-1874)
Norris, Lucinda to Winslow Allen 7-11-1854 (7-13-1854)
Northcutt, G. N. to Lewis John (6-22-1865)
Norton, Elisabeth to L. T. Moore 7-10-1868 (7-12-1868)
Norton, Nancy to William Pace 7-21-1865 (no return)
Norton, P. F. to Aaron Braswell 11-15-1877
Norton, Sarah to A. J. Hale 1-23-1849 (1-22?-1849)
Nova, Elizabeth to Wm. B. Latamore 8-21-1856 (8-22-1856)
Oakley, Carolin to Wm. Jackson 1-10-1866 (1-11-1866)
Oakley, Elizabeth to J. W. Reynolds 12-6-1867 (12-8-1867)
Oakley, Fannie to F. D. Helm 1-3-1877 (1-4-1877)
Oakley, Josephine to Jessee W. McDonald 5-30-1872 (6-2-1872)
Oakly, Lizzie to Ness McClelon 6-25-1866 (6-30-1866)
Oames, Maggie to P. T. Shores 4-18-1877
Odins, Eliza to Allen Reasonover 3-4-1868 (3-22-1868) [B]
Odom, Samantha to James S. Robinson 4-29-1871 (4-30-1871)
Officer, Hennie to Bethel Bryson 7-25-1878 (7-27-1878)
Olburd, Rebeca to Moses Rigsby 9-4-1868 (9-6-1868)
Oliver, July E. to D. B. Madget 7-18-1860
Overale, Jennie to P. C. Adams 3-24-1871 (3-30-1871)
Overall, Canny to W. A. Whaley 9-9-1876 (no return)
Overall, L. L. to F. W. Reaton 8-12-1867 (8-13-1867)
Overall, L. L. to W. H. Keaton 8-12-1867 (no return)
Overall, Tennessee to James Ownes 12-28-1875 (12-30-1875)
Owen, Aulina to Daniel Starks 12-28-1875 (12-30-1875)
Owens, Mary to Wm. Steel 8-9-1879 (8-12-1879)
Pack, Cenith to John Clarke 8-12-1869
Pack, Eliza J. to Wm. H. Rhody 3-30-1880 (4-4-1880)
Pack, Eliza to John Webb 5-13-1856 (2?-14-1856)
Pack, Elizabeth to Bartemius Pack 10-27-1871
Pack, Elizabeth to John Pack 12-31-1858 (1-3-1859)
Pack, Elizabeth to Robert Person 5-25-1855

Pack, Emaline to John Pack 11-14-1867
Pack, Hannah to John Johnson 2-20-1858 (no return)
Pack, Lutisia to John Sandlin 10-9-1861 (no return)
Pack, M. B. to James T. Liles 9-21-1878 (9-23-1878)
Pack, M. E. to J. H. Mahattin 2-4-1865 (2-5-1865)
Pack, M. J. to T. J. Ballard 12-22-1869 (12-23-1869)
Pack, M. to J. R. Liles 2-5-1865
Pack, Malinda P. to Wm. Ervin 12-29-1867
Pack, Malvina to Henry Johnson 9-12-1871
Pack, Margaret to John S. Pack 2-14-1859
Pack, Martha to J. J. Ingram 9-10-1867 (9-11-1867)
Pack, Mary to Isack W. Batts? 12-21-1865 (12-24-1865)
Pack, Matilda to James Parsons 12-21-1855
Pack, Matilda to John Hayse 7-10-1852 (7-11-1852)
Pack, May to Henry Neale 11-26-1872 (11-28-1872)
Pack, Nancy to James Ferrel 12-21-1865 (no return)
Pack, Nancy to John Laxiter 2-3-1863 (2-4-1863)
Pack, Nancy to Penal Stewart 5-19-1866 (no return)
Pack, Nancy to Willims Harris 4-10-1856
Pack, Nancy to Wm. Alexander 3-4-1864 (exec. no date)
Pack, P. F. to Phillip Bandy 8-17-1876
Pack, Parthena F. to P. C. Pack 3-7-1877 (3-8-1877)
Pack, S. E. to James A. Taylor 8-12-1869
Pack, Sarah Jane to John Colwell 2-9-1860
Paddy, N. B. to J. T. Pheahane? 9-11-1878 (9-12-1878)
Page, A. P. to Wm. Pope 9-13-1877 (no return)
Page, Artemeri to Jephthah McGiness 7-13-1850 (7-14-1850)
Page, Elizabeth J. to Wm. M. L. Agee 8-9-1879 (5?-18-1879)
Page, F. T. to D. H. Trammell 2-1-1878 (2-3-1878)
Page, Lewisa to Hesakiah Allen 10-19-1853 (10-20-1853)
Page, Luisa to Wm. Davis 8-28-1867 (8-29-1867)
Page, Mary Ann to Thomas W. Lawrence 11-8-1856 (11-13-1856)
Page, Mary to John Allen 12-27-1855 (12-29-1855)
Page, Matilda to E. C. Walker 7-16-1879
Page, Milbery to John Casey 11-9-1850 (11-10-1850)
Page, Rebecca to H. F. Love 10-12-1867 (10-13-1867)
Page, Reney to Alexander Miller 8-5-1879
Page, S. A. H. to Barney Page 5-19-1868 (5-20-1868)
Page, Sarah E. to Wm. Cripes 5-8-1878
Pain, Mary J. to Joseph Oakley 9-13-1865 (9-16-1865)
Pain, Mary Jain to Joseph Cabery? 9-13-1865 (no return)
Pain, Mary to Dopson Johnson 2-12-1864
Pain, Mary to Dosson Johnson 2-12-1864 (no return)
Palmer, Mary A. to J. E. Burton 4-5-1880 (no return)
Panther, Pheby to John McCool 12-11-1849 (no return)
Parck, Mary to M. B. Thompson 8-6-1873
Parcly, Ellen to Jessee Green 9-6-1876 (9-7-1876)
Parelli, L. J. to Wm. Warren 5-18-1876
Parish, Elizabeth to Haywood Upchurch 12-16-1859
Parish, Josephine to Wm. Hardin 8-15-1872
Parish, Kizy to H. S. Hathaway 1-29-1858
Parish, L. to Wm. Adcock 4-8-1877
Park, Elizabeth to Harvey Malone 10-21-1875 (10-24-1875)
Parkenson, Nancy to D. E. Taylor 3-12-1877 (3-13-1877)
Parker, Adline to Alford Marks 8-2-1871 (8-8-1871) [B]
Parker, Alunda to Mallocki Roberts 8-11-1866 (8-12-1866)
Parker, Elenor to Wiley Martin 12-26-1855
Parker, Elizabeth to B. R. Judkins 5-12-1869
Parker, Elizabeth to Wm. B. Farler 1-18-1864 (no return)
Parker, Ellen to John Sanders 5-9-1859 (no return)
Parker, Fanny to Mathew J. Crook 12-26-1852
Parker, J. A. to T. G. Bratton 7-19-1878 (no return)
Parker, Laura to Samuel Burton 4-25-1878
Parker, M. E. to Yancy Maloane 12-27-1877 (12-30-1877)
Parker, M. J. to G. W. Smith 12-16-1869
Parker, Malindy to Wm. Vandeigrift 8-6-1873 (8-7-1873)
Parker, Manervy to James Hayes 5-27-1876 (5-28-1876)
Parker, Martha to Thomas J. Martin 1-9-1866 (1-10-1866)
Parker, Mary Ann to Washington Roberts 1-27-1858 (1-28-1858)
Parker, Mary C. to Abner Martin 11-27-1850 (11-28-1850)
Parker, Matildy E. to George Martin 9-22-1870 (1-3-1871)
Parker, Molly M. to Wm. H. Hayes 6-2-1868
Parker, Nancy J. to J. W. Crook 10-6-1869 (11-2-1869)
Parker, Sarah Ann to Alvis Thomason 2-12-1857
Parker, Sarah E. to John Bain 12-22-1869 (12-23-1869)

Parker, Susan to Taylor Campbell 12-27-1877 (12-28-1877)
Parkerson, Bettie to Monroe Willowby 3-2-1876 (4-6-1876)
Parkerson, Carolina to Levi McGuffin 7-16-1850
Parkerson, Elizabeth to J. S. Hicks 7-2-1867 (7-3-1867)
Parkerson, Malvina to Tilmon Crook 5-8-1855
Parkerson, Mary E. to Alexander Norten 4-25-1874 (no return)
Parkerson, Mary to Manson Payne 8-20-1879 (8-21-1879)
Parrish, Mary to Joseph Hammons 5-12-1853 (12-7-1853)
Parseley, Rebeckey to James M. Bullen 8-11-1870 (8-14-1870)
Parsley, Adline to Marsillis Smith 1-19-1869
Parsley, Amanda to James A. Moores 1-1-1867
Parsley, Armetta to Jasper Green Bullard 12-1-1874 (12-4-1874)
Parsley, Dorkus to B. A. Cantrell 1-23-1872
Parsley, Elizabeth to Timothy Smith 11-20-1850 (11-21-1850)
Parsley, Haraett to D. W. Potter 4-5-1869
Parsley, M. P. to Monroe Blair 11-13-1875 (11-14-1875)
Parsley, Marry F. to Andrew J. Stewart 12-25-1867 (12-26-1867)
Parsley, Martha Ann to Edmund Warren 12-21-1870
Parsley, Parlee to Geor. M. Campbell 2-22-1879 (2-23-1879)
Parsley, Sarena to J. S. Foster 12-18-1875 (12-19-1875)
Parsly, Eveline to Francis J. Duvault 9-19-1861
Parsly, Semantha to R. W. Banks 3-1-1865 (3-2-1865)
Parsons, Malejing? to James Morris 9-26-1870
Partlo, Martha J. to James P. Southeran 12-19-1873 (12-29-1873)
Pattager?, Molly to Mathew Patterson 2-3-1873 (2-6-1873)
Patten, Missouria to J. M. Anderson 9-11-1875 (9-12-1875)
Patterson, Bette to J. W. Tompson 10-7-1869 (10-13-1869)
Patterson, M. P. to S. M. Foster 6-21-1868 (6-22-1868)
Patterson, Martha C. to Thos. Pack 10-23-1862 (10-25-1862)
Patterson, Mary Ann to Isaac Borum 2-21-1874 (no return)
Patterson, N. A. to F. J. Bluhm 1-3-1880 (1-4-1880)
Patterson, Nancy H. to Plesant Watts 4-9-1869 (4-11-1869)
Patterson, Sarah E. to Jasper N. Hayse 5-13-1856
Patton, Amondy to B. L. Estis 1-?-1873 (1-9-1873)
Patton, Elizabeth to Green Taley 3-27-1871
Patton, July An to James M. Kidwell 8-14-1855 (8-16-1855)
Payne, Martha A. to Levi B. Hunt 8-14-1851
Pedago, M. F. to W. J. Parcly 9-28-1876 (9-1?-1876)
Pedigo, Elizabeth C. to John H. Mainor 12-21-1864 (12-25-1864)
Pedigo, Jane to Joshua L. League 4-13-1853? (4-13-1854)
Pedigo, Jane to Wm. James 5-25-1859 (5-26-1859)
Pedigo, Martha to Travis Pursley 11-24-1857 (12-5-1857)
Pellum, Dulsena to Jackson Jones 1-2-1852 (1-6-1852)
Pendleton, Mary to Lenard Cantrell 2-2-1864 (2-4-1864)
Penegar, Catharine to Foster F. Rigsby 2-26-1875
Penegar, Sarah Jain to Lawson Hutchings 7-27-1866 (no return)
Penia?, Marigath P. to John C. Vandegrifth 1-6-1866 (1-7-1866)
Pennager, Martha J. to John B. Adcock 2-14-1861 (2-17-1861)
Peples, Adeline to James Martin 7-25-1877
Perry, M. M. to A. W. Lee 3-8-1876 (3-9-1876)
Pertle, Mary E. to James T. Moore 12-11-1858 (12-12-1858)
Petigo, Mary E. to W. R. Medley 3-3-1879 (solmzd no date
Petress, Sarah J. to Rufus Petress 6-17-1874 (6-18-1874)
Pettey, Milbary to A. R. Johnson 2-7-1880 (2-8-1880)
Pettigo, Polly to Isaac Brown 7-24-1871
Pettigoe, Martha A. to Jefferson Bozarth 12-22-1879 (no return)
Petty, Ellennora to Isaac Young 12-23-1871 (12-24-1871)
Petty, Linda J. to A. D. Starnes 8-4-1868 (8-8-1868)
Petty, Louisa to R. V. Presley 10-4-1876 (exec. no date)
Petty, M. A. to J. M. Drew? 8-9-1866
Petty, Martha to C. G. Pineger 9-4-1876 (9-6-1876)
Petty, Mary to Wm. Karr? 5-21-1860
Petty, Samantha to Harman Kisshower 12-22-1869
Petty, Zany to Thomas M. Young 10-21-1867 (10-27-1867)
Phelps, Amanda M. to J. D. Watkins 10-3-1840 (no return)
Philips, Amanda to Cain League 10-6-1868 (10-?-1868)
Phillips, Julia to George Millar 11-10-1877 (no return)
Phillips, Martha to Wm. Reed 10-11-1879 (10-13-1879)
Phillips, Nancy to Charles Teague 2-23-1866 (no date) [B]
Phillips, Sarah to James K. P. Adcock 3-13-1872 (3-14-1872)
Picke, Mary J. to Henrey Adcock 2-13-1873 (2-15-1873)
Pickett, E. J. to W. M. Johnson 2-24-1865
Pickett, L. E. to B. L. Massey 4-28-1871 (no return)
Pigg, Polly to Watson Cantrell 4-20-1861 (no return)
Pike, Malisa J. to Daniel Lasitor 8-11-1855 (8-12-1855)

Pinager, Elizabeth to John F. Young 7-22-1871
Pine, Sarah to James Vernatta 9-7-1868
Pineager, Mary to Rufus Adcock 10-24-1868 (10-25-1868)
Pinegar, Louisey to David Rigsby 12-2-1870 (12-4-1870)
Pinegar, Sarah to Isaac Pinegar 7-3-1879
Piniger, Rachell to Jasper Cantrell 1-11-1864 (1-12-1864)
Pipkins, Bell to George Alexander 9-6-1878 (9-7-1878)
Piram, Lucy Ann to Isaac Colwell 10-17-1854 (10-18-1854)
Pistol, Annie to H? N. Mathis 7-4-1866 (7-5-1866)
Pistol, Frankey to Daniel Mathis 12-10-1867
Pistol, Sarah Ellen to Willis M. Caldwell 6-19-1872
Pistole, Catharine to Samuel Fuson 5-8-1853
Pistole, Dora to P. J. Mangum 2-10-1873
Pistole, Elenor G. to John B. Martin 3-29-1849 (4-1-1849)
Pistole, Frances to John Span 9-?-1877 (no return)
Pistole, Jane to Elijah Hathaway 6-19-1860 (exec. no date)
Pistole, Kalhael to Bluford Mathis 1-10-1861 (1-13-1861)
Pistole, Leona to Jeff Sims 6-20-1874 (6-21-1874) [B]
Pistole, Mary P. to Spencer King 8-29-1871
Pistole, Nancy to Hiram Bethel 12-14-1848
Pistole, Paralee to Sebastin Williams 12-15-1862
Pistole, Sarah to W. L. Evans 9-15-1876 (9-17-1876)
Pitman, Anny to Elijah H. Dunham 2-26-1852
Pitman, Mahaly to Levy Hathaway 10-9-1870
Pitman, Margaret to John Dunham 8-15-1849
Pitman, Nancy to Benjamin Cantrell 8-30-1849
Pitman, Sarah E. to J. A. Nixon 3-17-1876 (3-19-1876)
Pitman, Susan to C. Hill 2-4-1867 (2-6-1867)
Pitmon, Elizabeth to David Pain 7-14-1875 (7-18-1875)
Pitmon, Mary J. to John G. Close 2-16-1864 (no return)
Pittey, Dortherly to William Bullerd 1-23-1872 (1-25-1872)
Pittman, Sophrona to James Davis 12-10-1879 (no return)
Pitts, Nancy to Peter Taylor 8-14-1865 (no return)
Pitts, Susan to James Marimon 7-15-1868 (7-16-1868)
Pleager, Jain to Peater Brown 12-25-1866 (2-7-1867)
Pleager, Jaine to Mark Brown 12-25-1866 (2-1-1867)
Pleger, Sarah M. to Nuton Hodge 12-28-1865 (no return)
Plenner, Evaline to Judy Owen 6-20-1874 (6-21-1874) [B]
Plumber, Allice to Mason Bass 6-27-1874 [B]
Plumlee, Matildy to Eligiah Oakley 12-11-1872 [B]
Plumly, Mary to Wood Fuston 6-21-1873 [B]
Plunkett, Eliza to Wm. McDaniel 10-31-1862 (no return)
Pollard, Elizabeth to Christerfer C. Helton 12-30-1868
Pollard, Thursey to John Bain 12-19-1868 (12-20-1868)
Ponder, Mariah to John C. Winchester 1-19-1867
Ponder, Marinda to Jake Sandlin 4-29-1876
Pope, Alice J. to Elias Fuston 2-1-1879 (2-2-1879)
Pope, Lucinda to C. Hill 9-24-1868
Potter, A. to L. R. Webb 10-8-1866 (10-10-1866)
Potter, Aiseneth to P. G. Bins 2-19-1866 (2-20-1866)
Potter, Delia to Julis Cantrell 1-12-1876 (1-13-1876)
Potter, Elizabeth to B. C. Wilkerson 3-23-1859 (3-24-1859)
Potter, Elizabeth to Calvin Parrish 7-14-1860 (7-16-1860)
Potter, H. A. J. to O. D. Byars 12-15-1874 (no return)
Potter, Hannah to John B. Wilkerson 11-30-1853 (12-19-1853)
Potter, Josephine to B. F. Lancaster 3-28-1867
Potter, Josephine to George A. Bing 9-23-1871 (9-24-1871)
Potter, Kizey to L. B. Givans 3-2-1857 (3-4-1857)
Potter, Laura to Isaac Adcock 8-11-1858 (8-12-1858)
Potter, M. E. to B. H. Wamack 2-5-1855 (2-8-1855)
Potter, Martha to M. H. Cantrell 1-17-1877 (no date)
Potter, Mary J. to Wm. F. Deadman 10-23-1867
Potter, Mary to Melvin Davis 10-17-1864 (no return)
Potter, Mattie to L. W. Potter 9-29-1870 (9-30-1870)
Potter, Mourning to Green Cantrell 12-17-1868
Potter, Recey to Frank Cantrell 7-31-1878 (8-4-1878)
Potter, Sallie to Josiah L. Lock 10-30-1873
Potter, Simantha to Isaac Cantrell 11-30-1868
Powel, Kissie to D. D. Driver 8-9-1877
Powell, Delia to T. J. Lamberson 1-28-1877 (no return)
Pratt, Nancy Jane to James Scott 6-6-1852 (6-15-1852)
Prentice, Elizabeth to Wilson Jackson 10-6-1848 (10-8-1848)
Prentis, R. J. to L. R. Taylor 2-12-1869
Presley, Frances M. to T. J. Mitchell 9-28-1857 (9-29-1857)
Presley, Marthan to L. D. Lafeaver 1-11-1877 (1-22-1877)

Presley, Mary to Charles Denney 3-27-1878 (3-28-1878)
Presley, Mary to Kelly Lamb 2-10-1869 (2-11-1869)
Presley, Nancy R. to John C. Coggin 3-5-1856 (3-6-1856)
Pressley, N. C. to Wm. A. Moss 9-3-1872 (9-10-1872)
Pressley, Silvey J. to George H. Murdock 9-12-1872
Pressly, Nancy C. to Danial Baker 6-13-1874 (6-14-1874)
Prestley, N. A. to W. W. Maxwell 2-15-1866 (2-18-1866)
Preston, Eliza to Thomas Floyd 4-12-1876 (4-15-1876)
Preston, Lizy to Tobe? Doss 3-11-1871 (3-12-1871)
Preston, Mary to James Cope 4-15-1876 (4-20-1876)
Preston, Matilda E. T. to Dewitt C. Lamberson 3-11-1851 (no return)

Preston, N. E. to T. J. White 11-15-1876 (11-19-1876)
Preston, Sophia to Wilson Denbey 9-27-1866 (10-4-1866)
Price, Easter to Wm. J. Lasater 9-12-1867 (9-13-1867)
Price, Mary T. to Wm. E. Jones 10-31-1862 (11-7-1862)
Prichard, E. J. to B. F. Scuders 10-11-1868 (10-14-1868)
Prichard, E. J. to B. H. Presley 8-30-1866 (no return)
Prichard, M. E. to Isaih D. Fite 12-20-1876 (12-21-1876)
Prichard, Mary E. to F. B. Nolner 2-23-1859 (2-24-1859)
Prichard, Nancy A. to W. D. Boss 3-29-1871 (3-30-1871)
Prichard, Neoma E. C. to Joseph G. Maxwell 11-19-1872 (11-20-1872)

Pridy, Narcissy to Jackson Garrison 11-8-1848 (no return)
Printes, Rachel to Joshua Neel 10-12-1854 (10-13-1854)
Prowel, Hannah to Thos. Viss 8-7-1858 (8-8-1858)
Puckett, Caladonia to Edmond League 10-5-1857 (10-6-1857)
Puckett, Cyrena to John Walker 12-22-1870
Puckett, Martha to Joseph Bozarth 5-29-1866 (5-31-1866)
Puckett, Nancy to John J. Burton 8-18-1869 (8-19-1869)
Pugh, Ellice to James E. Adamson 8-11-1864
Pullem, Lucy to M. H. McGuinness 2-3-1879 (2-6-1879)
Purkins, Amanda J. to Solomon Driver 8-31-1859
Purkins, Martha to Thomas Bennette 7-10-1856
Purtle, Martha to A. J. Thomason 10-22-1856 (10-23-1856)
Purtle, Nancy G. to Banjamin Redmon 1-19-1852
Purtle, Stacy to William Certain 2-22-1850 (2-21?-1850)
Putman, Betsey to Wm. Pain 5-8-1877
Qualls, Sallie to Hiram Heagon 10-11-1872 (?-11-1872)
Quillin, Mary Ann to Thomas F. Holder 12-17-1852
Rackley, Mary to Green B. Ford 11-29-1852 (12-2-1852)
Rady, Julia A. E. to Cantrell Bethell 2-5-1862 (2-6-1862)
Ralley, Alaminta to James L. Fite 8-9-1850
Rankhorn, Angalina to John B. Webb 10-14-1852
Rankhorn, E. H. to William Tipett 2-14-1857 (2-15-1857)
Rankhorn, Emaline to Thomas Page 8-20-1873 (8-29-1873)
Rankhorn, Matilda to Joseph Rankhorn 11-24-1879 (no return)
Rankhorn, Susan to J. L. Manning 10-4-1876 (10-5-1876)
Rankhorn, Susan to Rufus Heath 11-15-1853 (11-16-1853)
Ray, Adline to Wad Huddleston 8-21-1879 [B]
Ray, Elizabeth J. to U. M. Blunt 12-27-1859
Ray, July to F. H. Hayse 11-7-1865 (11-9-1865)
Ray, Luisa V. to Joseph B. West 9-12-1854 (exec. no date)
Ray, Mary Jane to Moses A. Ford 1-2-1850 (1-3-1850)
Ray, Sarah to J. J. Ingeram 11-20-1848
Ray, Tildy to John Maning 9-1-1869 (exec. no date)
Read, Elizabeth to L. H. McGinniss 8-6-1864? (no return)
Read, Nancy E. to P. J. McGinis 7-8-1863 (no return)
Readman, Smith to W. R. Parrish 8-27-1864 (8-31-1864)
Readmon, M. J. to M. D. Adcock 12-19-1871 (12-20-1871)
Readmon, N. A. to T. E. Arnel 1-15-1876
Readmon, Sarah to John Cantrell 5-10-1872 (5-12-1872)
Reaves, Parlly to W. G. Ethridge 3-22-1877 (no return)
Redman, Arteta to Elial Cantrell 3-9-1853 (3-10-1853)
Redman, N. J. to E. F. Cantrell 5-10-1866
Redman, Susanah to Henry Beshears 6-8-1867 (6-9-1867)
Redmon, Alice to W. H. Martin 11-19-1879 (no return)
Redmon, America to James Delong 2-7-1861
Redmon, Charlotta to Calvin Holt 12-27-1878 (no return)
Redmon, Charlotta to John Hendricks 8-14-1856
Redmon, Elizabeth to J. D. Guinn? 12-4-1862
Redmon, Frances to John C. Goodman 12-30-1856 (12-31-1856)
Redmon, Jane to Hiram Dunn 2-8-1851
Redmon, L. E. to Daniel Webb 11-25-1876 (no return)
Redmon, Laura to John Bran 12-25-1878 (12-26-1878)

Redmon, M. J. to Samuel Barks 12-18-1865
Redmon, Martha J. to J. C. Fowler 11-27-1860 (no return)
Redmon, Roceana to A. L. Jones 12-23-1874 (no return)
Redmon, Sarah Ann to John J. Cantrell 3-2-1854
Reeder, Sarah L. to Preston F. Cantrell 1-17-1864
Reeves, Elizabeth to U. E. Cantrell 10-26-1854 (10-27-1854)
Reeves, Kizeah to John W. Gann 7-19-1866
Reeves, Mary to Joel Adamson 10-3-1874 (no return)
Reeves, Rebecca to Abraham Cantrell 9-6-1855
Reivs, E. J. to J. P. Martin 5-22-1858 (5-26-1858)
Revis?, Sarah to Thu? Bradford 12-2-1860
Reynolds, Elizabeth P. to Wm. B. Robinson 2-6-1856 (2-8-1856)
Reynolds, Emily to John Jones 2-26-1850 (no return)
Reynolds, Lean to Wiat F. Floyed 4-5-1869 (4-8-1869) [B]
Reynolds, Martha to John D. Sullivan 7-6-1874 (7-12-1874)
Reynolds, Mary to H. J. Watson 12-30-1869
Reynolds, Narcissa C. to Morgan Lawrence 11-3-1849 (11-8-1849)
Reynolds, Sarah Jane to James Vantrease 9-30-1851 (10-11-1851)
Reynolds, Sarah to Richman Stokes 3-17-1866 (3-18-1866)
Rhody, Mary to J. P. Pistole 1-18-1870 (1-19-1870)
Rice, Anna to Burgis Dowel 2-5-1866 (no return) [B]
Rich, Adlin to James Skerlock 12-29-1866 (12-31-1866)
Rich, Caroline to George Kithcart 1-27-1870
Rich, Delila Frances to James T. Haile 2-26-1875 (2-28-1875)
Rich, Eliza to W. C. Presley 12-4-1879
Rich, Hannah to James Rich 9-8-1874 (9-9-1874) [B]
Rich, Jane to John Millstead 4-18-1871
Rich, Mary to B. F. Hale 10-27-1869 (10-28-1869)
Rich, Sarah J. to A. C. Parker 10-24-1879 (10-26-1879)
Richard, Amanda E. to Wm. R. Lamberson 2-18-1867 (2-21-1867)
Richardson, Harriette J. to John B. Luble 3-18-1851
Richardson, Hellen to George Spurlock 7-13-1870 (8-21-1870)
Richardson, Mary E. to James H. Camoren 2-7-1880 (2-8-1880)
Richardson, Syntha to A. H. Sneed 3-18-1857
Richardson, Virginia to James T. Hayes 11-30-1867 (12-1-1867)
Richman, Sallie to F. M. Robinson 11-15-1870 (11-20-1870)
Richmon, Lyda to James L. Barnes 6-21-1853
Rigsby, Anna to Joseph Jones 3-18-1866 (no return)
Rigsby, C. J. to F. C. Hargis 5-20-1876
Rigsby, Callidonia to F. P. Parrish 7-10-1874 (7-15-1874)
Rigsby, Harriette to John W. Meador 7-15-1878 (7-18-1878)
Rigsby, Luizee J. to Winfield S. Sailers 7-31-1874 (8-2-1874)
Rigsby, Rutha to Thomas Stimerage 10-14-1875 (10-17-1875)
Rigsby, Sarah to Silas Gregory 7-6-1854 (7-12-1854)
Rigsby, Ziggy to Elisha Luny 12-10-1851 (12-11-1851)
Roady, Sarena A. to Epps M. Rich 8-14-1851 (9-10-1851)
Robards, E. V. to W. P. Evans 7-27-1879 (7-31-1879)
Robards, Mary to Amon Henly 7-28-1869 (no return)
Roberds, Jane to Allen Hendricks 7-25-1849 (7-26-1849)
Roberds, Katherine to John Bennett 4-24-1864 (4-25-1864)
Roberds, Nancy A. to L. M. Jones 1-31-1868 (no return)
Roberson, Frances to John Carter 2-14-1864 (2-15-1864)
Roberson, Nola to Manuel Stokes 6-15-1867
Robert, N. M. to J. J. Presly 7-5-1867 (no return)
Roberts, Elizabeth to Burrel Coggins 10-21-1867
Roberts, Elizabeth to Wm. J. Mullican 9-2-1862 (9-11-1862)
Roberts, Jinney to Sidney Brown 8-11-1866 (8-12-1866)
Roberts, M. E. to R. S. Evans 9-26-1876 (9-29-1876)
Roberts, Mahala to Jacob Starnes 6-25-1859 (no return)
Roberts, Mandy P. to John A. Driver 6-4-1870 (6-5-1870)
Roberts, Martha to Wm. Crook 7-1-1858 (7-3-1858)
Roberts, Nancey to John Presley 10-10-1866 (no return)
Roberts, Sarah to Thomas D. Driver 12-27-1857
Roberts, Syntha to William Elliott ?-7-1851 (8-7-1851)
Robertson, A. to R. Kelly 4-3-1866 (4-29-1866)
Robertson, Areanah to Richard Kelley 4-29-1866
       (no return) [B]
Robinson, B. Z. to W. W. Walker 4-29-1876 (4-30-1876)
Robinson, Barbery to James M. Baker 3-22-1854 (3-20?-1854)
Robinson, Callidoney to Zack T. Judee 8-1-1872
Robinson, Clary to George Turney 11-25-1868 (11-26-1868)
Robinson, D. A. to Wm. M. Summers 1-21-1878 (1-23-1878)
Robinson, D. J. to J. S.? Ayars 4-10-1869 (4-1?-1869)
Robinson, E. J. to James Maxwell 11-17-1864 (no return)
Robinson, Eles to Leroy Cubins 1-26-1875 (no return)

Robinson, Eliza H. to Isaac Hayse 12-18-1852 (12-23-1852)
Robinson, Elizabeth to Peter Garner 8-10-1870 (8-11-1870)
Robinson, Elizabeth to Robert J. Anderson 2-21-1857 (2-24-1857)
Robinson, Elizia to James Irvin 10-10-1872 (no return)
Robinson, Fanney to Nels Sneed 11-15-1877 (no return)
Robinson, Frances to W. C. Redmon 11-9-1878 (11-10-1878)
Robinson, Jane F. to Benjamin Prichard 4-21-1856 (4-22-1856)
Robinson, Jane to George Stokes 3-17-1866 (3-18-1866)
Robinson, Jane to W. B. Harrison 5-1-1871 (5-3-1871)
Robinson, Laura to Sampson Stokes 7-28-1871 (7-29-1871) [B]
Robinson, Louisa to Mariun Reynolds 9-26-1854
Robinson, Lucy to Wilson Taylor 3-27-1858 (no return)
Robinson, M. A. to J. W. Camp 1-13-1868 (1-19-1868)
Robinson, M. J. to W. R. Thomas 9-12-1876 (9-28-1876)
Robinson, Maggie to David Molone 3-25-1873 (3-27-1873)
Robinson, Malissa to Eli D. Hutcheons 10-11-1854 (10-12-1854)
Robinson, Manervy A. to W. D. Prichard 12-23-1867 (1-9-1868)
Robinson, Manorvey to James N. George 3-5-1855
Robinson, Marcy A. to James R. Jones 9-28-1870
Robinson, Margaret to Ezekiel Watson 8-26-1854 (8-31-1854)
Robinson, Margret to George Anderson 12-19-1876 (12-16?-1876)
Robinson, Martha F. to Wm. F. Robinson 9-8-1855 (9-9-1855)
Robinson, Martha to Sidney Prichard 11-7-1870 (11-10-1870)
Robinson, Mary C. to Joseph Ray 8-19-1875 (8-22-1875)
Robinson, Mary E. to J. N. Turentine 1-1-1873 (1-2-1873)
Robinson, Mary J. to Dr. A. S. Redmon 3-1-1859
Robinson, Mary J. to James Reynolds 12-9-1854 (12-10-1855?)
Robinson, Mary L. to D. P. Sorsey? 9-11-1856
Robinson, Mary to Asa Carter 1-16-1873
Robinson, Mary to John Dodson 12-8-1868 (12-10-1868) [B]
Robinson, Matilda A. to S. Haim 10-24-1865 (no return)
Robinson, Nancy to James Taylor 1-24-1857 (3-5-1857)
Robinson, Nancy to Monroe Blythe 11-13-1873 (11-15-1873)
Robinson, Roxy to P. T. Haggart 12-27-1879 (1-5-1880)
Robinson, Samantha J. to Wm. C. Hendrixson 12-26-1872 (1-2-1873)
Robinson, Sarah J. to F. H. Love 1-22-1863 (no return)
Robinson, Sarah J. to Joseph H. Lane 2-18-1863 (no return)
Robinson, Sarah to Hezekiah Allen 12-12-1857 (12-13-1857)
Robinson, Sarah to Moses Simpson 7-10-1854
Robinson, Sary J. to John A. Bass 10-15-1866 (10-18-1866)
Robinson, Susan to Hiram Childress 4-27-1870 (no return)
Robinson, Susan to Jesse Robinson 2-12-1880
Robinson, Tabitha to A. J. Yergan 11-20-1849 (11-22-1849)
Robinson, Tennessee to T. J. Davis 12-4-1879
Rodgers, Bathena to James M. Hull 6-17-1854 (6-18-1854)
Rodgers, Sophronia N. to Martin George 12-28-1853 (no return)
Rody, Mary to Jesse M. McGee 11-16-1864 (11-17-1864)
Roland, Laury to Lenard Hathway 2-9-1864 (2-11-1864)
Rolax, Mary to R. B. Love 3-29-1866 (3-30-1866)
Rolland, Mary to Tilman Haney 10-1-1862 (10-2-1862)
Rollins, Bethenia P. to M. P. Hearn 11-17-1873 (11-23-1873)
Romine, Julia to J. G. Swihar? 9-24-1852 (9-27-1852)
Rose, Evelin to Wm. J. S. Eam 5-21-1857 (5-22-1857)
Ross, Chance P. to P. H. Bennett 7-13-1860 (7-17-1860)
Ross, Lucy to David Ross 3-17-1866 (3-28-1866)
Rowland, Arena to Wm. Greeb 8-18-1874 (8-19-1874)
Rowland, Belvina to F. M. Foutch 4-1-1876 (3-2-1876)
Rowland, Juley A. to J. C. Marler 1-13-1873 (1-14-1873)
Rowland, Tennessee to Wm. Truett 3-20-1872 (no return)
Rowton, Elizabeth to John W. Brown 7-29-1854 (7-30-1854)
Roy, Amanda to P. L. Wood 11-6-1866 (11-8-1866)
Roy, C. L. to P. L. Wood 3-9-1861 (3-14-1861)
Roy, Elizabeth to Thomas L. Compton 1-3-1857 (no date)
Roy, R. J. to James W. Hutson 8-8-1874 (8-9-1874)
Rugle?, Elizabeth to George Cates 12-3-1870 (12-4-1870)
Rule, Anna to Abraham Blair 5-24-1869
Runels, Frances to Henry Davis 6-8-1864
Runnels, Frances to Henry Dunn 6-4-1865 (no return)
Rusan, Rebecca to John Etheridge 9-25-1859 (9-26-1859)
Rush, Ana to Joseph Pack 11-30-1865 (no return)
Russell, Udora A. to John L. Young 12-30-1872 (12-31-1872)
Russell, Udora A. to John Young 11-6-1872 (12-3-1872)
Rutland, Florence to Charles T. Yearigin 2-25-1871 (2-26-1871)
Rutledge, Sallie to A. E. Hibdon 3-16-1871 (3-17-1871)
Ruttan, Carolina to Randolph Smart 3-17-1856 (3-19-1856)

Rynolds, Malvina to Wm. H. Adams 11-?-1852 (11-3-1852)
Rynolds?, Malvina to William H. Adams 11-?-1852 (11-3-1852)
Sanders, Mison to William Bennett 11-10-1875
Sandin, Josephine to Wm. McDonell 7-25-1864 (12?-26-1864)
Sandlin, Candis to H. R. H. Newsom 8-23-1862 (no return)
Sandlin, Elizabeth to James Bly 1-30-1864 (no return)
Sandlin, Hannah to Jas. M. Bennett 10-14-1857 (10-19-1857)
Sandlin, Jan? to Manson B. Scott 11-10-1851 (no return)
Sandlin, Lucinda to Stephen C. Beshears 7-22-1858
Sandlin, Luisa to William C. Bennette 10-21-1855 (10-22-1855)
Sandlin, Mary to John B. Claiborn 1-4-1872
Sandlin, Mary to William Bennet 1-29-1854
Sandlin, Mary to William R. Bennette 3-31-1852
Sandlin, Melissa to Leonard Scott 12-29-1853
Sandlin, Pheby C. to Berry Driver 10-16-1867 (10-18-1867)
Sandlin, Tennessee to W. J. Ponder 4-29-1876
Sandlin,   to B. W. Butcher 4-11-1864 (no return)
Saunders, Mary to Thomas Fisher 12-16-1851 (12-19-1851)
Savage, Elizabeth to H. R. Torbit 4-2-1861
Scott, C. to James Bly 5-11-1850 (5-12-1850)
Scott, Catharine to Wiley Snow 5-15-1850 (5-16-1850)
Scott, E. M. to W. L. Fannes 1-21-1867
Scott, Eliza to Columbus Jones 6-23-1864 (no return)
Scott, Elizabeth to Henry Snow 9-3-1850 (9-4-1850)
Scott, Elvira P. to James Carter 3-1-1861 (3-3-1861)
Scott, Martha H. to Isaac Johnson 9-18-1867 (9-19-1867)
Scott, Mary H. to Benjamin Chapman 3-14-1874 (3-15-1874)
Scott, Mary to Josiah Shehan 9-8-1868 (no return)
Scott, Mesane to John Parker 3-17-1875 (3-18-1875)
Scott, Nancy J. to Wm. Scott 2-10-1853 (2-13-1853)
Scott, Peggy to Thomas Howard 8-10-1876
Scott, Phebe to John Hale 12-26-1860 (12-25?-1860)
Scott, Roweana to James Bley 4-22-1866 (no return)
Scott, Susanah to Josiah Griffith 7-22-1855 (7-26-1855)
Scribner, Susan to Joal D. Hale 1-24-1854 (1-26-1854)
Scurlock, Elizabeth to Isaac N. Murphy 9-11-1857 (9-12-1857)
Scurlock, Mary to J. Walston 7-25-1863 (no return)
Scurlock, Mary to John Wooddist 9-28-1870
Sea, Martha to Wm. L. Hathaway 10-17-1864 (10-19-1865?)
Seawel, Lizza to G. F. Dyer 5-15-1877
Seay, Amandy to Charles E. Crane 4-29-1861 (5-2-1861)
Seay, E. W. to J. W. Lambertson 2-1-1860
Seay, Elan to Henry H. Kidwell 1-6-1862 (1-12-1862)
Seay, F. to Henry Segraves 5-24-1862 (5-25-1862)
Seay, Mary Ann to Joseph T. Lawrence 8-28-1851 (9-2-1851)
Self, Anerilas to Levy Nickson 4-19-1875 (4-22-1875)
Self, C. A. to Edward Guthard 2-25-1870 (2-26-1872?)
Self, Charrity to Josiah Youngblood 9-22-1871 (9-24-1871)
Self, Isibell to J. H. Roberts 1-17-1867 (1-20-1867)
Self, Mary A. to Henry H. Taylor 5-1-1872 (5-2-1872)
Self, Nancy C. to Wm. Nesmith 1-7-1865 (1-8-1865)
Self, Nancy to Henry Adcock 1-27-1880 (no return)
Selff, Malinda to Francis M. Close 5-30-1867 (6-2-1867)
Sellars, Dave C. to Frank S. Moore 7-4-1874 (7-5-1874) [B]
Sellars, Martha to James Fusan 12-25-1864 (12-24?-1864)
Sellars, Mollie to J. F. Elledge 1-16-1880 (1-18-1880)
Sellars, N. C. to J. S. Jennings 8-10-1869 (8-11-1869)
Sellars, Shelata to Davis Calicut 3-19-1866 (3-20-1866)
Sellars, Tera to James M. William 10-27-1865 (10-29-1865)
Sellers, Cansady to Leroy Williams 8-8-1849 (no return)
Sellers, Jane to Isaac M. Smith 12-21-1857 (12-24-1857)
Sewel, Sarah to Olever Farkirson 10-17-1855
Sewell, A. J. to G. M. Bain 1-8-1863 (2-25-1863)
Sewell, F. J. to Gill Bates 1-31-1863 (no return)
Sewell, Julan to Larkin? McGinniss 9-3-1853
Sexton, Mavinia to David Rowland 3-16-1871
Shane, Silvy to Andy Terry 2-16-1867 (2-20-1867)
Shanis, Louisa Ann to Samuel K. Baker 4-6-1861 (4-7-1861)
Shaw, Elizabeth to Wm. Puckette 10-14-1876 (10-15-1876)
Shaw, Sallie to Caswell Tunny 8-10-1871  [B]
Sheahon, Nancy to John Mullins 9-23-1853 (9-25-1853)
Shehan, Sarah to Daniel Johnson 1-4-1869 (1-6-1869)
Shehorn, O. E. to Wm. Braswell 11-2-1853 (11-3-1853)
Shields, Jennie to Wade Hudleston 12-4-1871  [B]
Shields, Lucy to H. C. Marton 9-22-1877 (no return)

Shields, Nancy E. to James Hicks 10-16-1875 (10-17-1875)
Shields, Sarah to Wm. Frazier 10-6-1877 (10-7-1877)
Short, M. J. to H. C. Burton 8-14-1878
Simeril, Etily to Charles Neel 2-10-1857 (2-12-1857)
Simes, Elizabeth to Jacob Lawrance 11-2-1871 (no return) [B]
Simpson, Eliza to Aaron Williams 6-20-1869 (7-12-1869)
Simpson, Eliza to David Hendrickson 1-31-1855
Simpson, Emiline to Archabald Hunt 9-1-1852 (9-2-1852)
Simpson, Micy to Thomas J. Davis 10-15-1868 (10-?-1868)
Simpson, Orpha to John W. Williams 4-12-1853 (4-14-1853)
Sims, Ann to John Owens 4-11-1870 (4-14-1870)
Sims, Delila to Samuel Fouch 3-4-1850 (no return)
Sims, Emeline to Wm. C. Malone 3-6-1849 (3-8-1849)
Sims, Harriett to Tom Allen 8-25-1872 (9-2-1872) [B]
Sims, Paralee to John W. Hulet 11-17-1856 (no return)
Simson, Liza to Andrew Thomas 3-16-1878 (3-19-1878)
Skerlock, Sarah to J. G. Evanes 3-4-1866
Skurlock, Martha J. to James Smitson 9-13-1865 (no return)
Smith, Allice to Obediah Hollinsworth 1-2-1874 (1-3-1874)
Smith, Amanda to Joseph M. Pack 6-27-1868 (6-28-1868)
Smith, Angeline to W. H. Garner 4-7-1873 (4-15-1873)
Smith, Ann H. J. to John J. Callicoat 10-11-1854 (10-13-1854)
Smith, Barthena to Wm. Bain 12-30-1865 (12-31-1865)
Smith, Bettie W. to Thomas Mazab 11-8-1879 (11-11-1879)
Smith, Betty to Allen Reasonover 6-26-1878
Smith, Betty to Milus Northcut 6-27-1878
Smith, Catharine to Davis Smithson 9-16-1851 (9-17-1851)
Smith, Clara to William Brann 7-7-1858 (7-8-1858)
Smith, Corilee to Bunk Hoskins 10-27-1875 (10-28-1875)
Smith, Delia A. to Joseph Beaseley 5-7-1870 (5-12-1870)
Smith, Elizabeth W. N. to William P. Bennette 12-23-1858 (exec, no date)
Smith, Elizabeth to Elias Davis 12-10-1851
Smith, Elizabeth to Jessee Haggard 3-23-1859
Smith, Elvira to Benj. Thompson 8-8-1862 (8-20-1862)
Smith, Elvira to Harmon Alcorn 6-7-1856 (6-8-1856)
Smith, Ema C. to James A. Barrett 6-6-1867 (6-7-1867)
Smith, Frances R. to Huston S. Gill 9-20-1878 (9-22-1878)
Smith, Frances to Thomas Durham 11-2-1878 (11-3-1878)
Smith, Hariatt to Serss? Bass 3-17-1866 (3-18-1866)
Smith, Helan C. to Albert V. Meritt 6-22-1863 (no return)
Smith, Hellen to Nathaniel Parker 7-2-1873 (7-5-1873)
Smith, Huldy Ann to Robert Smith 1-15-1864 (1-17-1864)
Smith, Jane N. to James Vanover 7-31-1855 (8-2-1855)
Smith, Josephine to A. L. Reynolds 7-31-1872 (8-4-1872)
Smith, Julia A. to J. S. Hutchins 8-29-1876 (no return)
Smith, Katherine C. to Wm. Robertson 9-7-1859 (9-8-1859)
Smith, Leathey to John Garner 1-2-1871 (1-5-1871)
Smith, Lucinda to Thomas R. Goodson 2-11-1857 (2-12-1857)
Smith, Luisa to Thomas Garrett 1-29-1866 (no return)
Smith, M. A. to Haris McGuire 10-9-1869 (10-10-1869)
Smith, M. E. to S. J. Huggins 2-5-1865 (no return)
Smith, M. to James Bailey 10-22-1876
Smith, Mahaly to Thomas R. Harris 9-5-1849
Smith, Margaret to John E. Robinson 12-13-1854 (12-14-1854)
Smith, Marinda to Tilmon Foster 12-19-1877 (12-20-1877)
Smith, Martha A. to H. L. Hall 8-21-1876 (exec. no date)
Smith, Martha J. to Wm. Fugerson 6-29-1860 (7-1-1860)
Smith, Martha to Francis West 2-9-1850 (no return)
Smith, Mary B. to Isaac T. Vandergrift 12-31-1879 (no return)
Smith, Mary E. to Ezekial Taylor 11-27-1860 (11-28-1860)
Smith, Mary E. to James Crickenson 5-22-1865 (no return)
Smith, Mary E. to W. B. Wood 12-16-1875
Smith, Mary J. F. to W. J. Grindstaff 10-4-1879 (10-5-1879)
Smith, Mary to George Stiles 9-3-1868
Smith, Mary to J. H. Dodd 1-23-1866 (1-25-1866)
Smith, Mary to J. P. Lewis 4-8-1863
Smith, Mary to James K. Boyatt 7-20-1854 (7-21-1854)
Smith, Mary to Lamon Adamson 9-4-1865 (9-6-1865)
Smith, Nancy C. to John L. Crips 2-1-1854 (2-2-1854)
Smith, Rebecca to Richard Hendrickson 8-3-1864
Smith, Sarah A. to Wm. Sellers 8-4-1858 (8-5-1858)
Smith, Sarah E. to Wm. G. Ivins 4-3-1865 (4-6-1865)
Smith, Sarah to Monroe Maynard 12-13-1871
Smith, Tennessee to George Griffith 12-22-1877

Smith, Teresa to David Dunham 12-26-1868 (12-30-1868)
Smith, Vina to Jackson Owens 12-26-1877 (12-28-1877)
Smithson, Emeline J. to Thomas A. Tracy 11-2-1870 (9?-2-1870)
Smithson, Margaret to Wm. L. Roady 1-30-1864 (no return)
Smithson, Martha T. to George W. Ratliff 9-4-1872
Smithson, Mary A. to Simpson Estridge 11-13-1861 (no return)
Smithson, Mary M. to Wiley P. Eastrage 3-19-1853 (3-24-1853)
Smitson, Bettie to Wm. E. Ferrill 2-4-1876 (2-9-1876)
Smitson, Delia to John Bird 8-24-1878 (9-8-1878)
Smitson, Emaly J. to Josiah Magee 7-26-1864 (no return)
Smitson, L. C. to W. J. Stoner 9-26-1868 (no return)
Smitson, Mary A. to James Magee 7-26-1864 (no return)
Sneed, Cynthia A. to John W. Pitts 8-14-1850
Sneed, Eliza Ann to William Smith Patty 11-26-1850 (11-28-1850)
Sneed, Fannie to Rubin Phillips 11-20-1878 (11-21-1878)
Sneed, Harriette A. to Yandle Wood 2-5-1850 (2-13-1850)
Sneed, M. E. T. to G. W. Briggs 7-9-1850 (7-11-1850)
Sneed, Malissa to Yance Limb 4-27-1855 (ret.not exec.)
Sneed, Parilee to John W. Calvin 3-31-1863
Snider, Mary to Isham Ethridge 1-7-1851 (1-9-1851)
Snider, Nancy to Wm. E. Ethridge 6-14-1867
Snow, Amandy to Jasper Bullard 1-30-1873 (2-2-1873)
Snow, Elizabeth to G. C. McInteer 11-3-1849 (11-4-1849)
Snow, Elizabeth to George Styles 6-5-1873
Snow, L. E. to D. P. Mosier 2-14-1880 (2-15-1880)
Snow, M. E. to P. B. Blughus 1-28-1878 (1-29-1878)
Snow, Parilee to S. R. Rich 11-27-1875 (11-28-1875)
Spence, Betty J. to Bird E. Bates 12-13-1871
Spence, Parilee to Chesly Taylor 7-11-1860 (7-12-1860)
Spurlock, Delia to Jacob Webb 6-13-1880 (no return)
Spurlock, Elisabeth to L. D. Hollinsworth 1-23-1875 (1-24-1875)
Spurlock, L. F. to Christopher E. Adamson 1-25-1867 (1-31-1867)
Spurlock, L. J. to Thomas Brown 6-4-1877 (no return)
Spurlock, Mary Jane to Ammon Parsley 9-7-1854
Spurlock, Narcissus? to David C. Hardin 3-9-1871 (3-23-1871)
Stacy, M. J. to J. H. Williams 7-13-1878 (7-14-1878)
Stacy, Mary G. to Wm. E. Bartlet 9-16-1857 (9-17-1857)
Staley, A. E. to J. H. Cannon 9-4-1868
Staley, Volka? to Washington Moore 9-18-1870
Stalks, Mary Ann to J. M. Starnes 1-25-1866 (no return)
Staly, Elizabeth to Wm. Moon 1-21-1874 (1-22-1874) [B]
Standford, Hellen to Jerrymiah Fisher 10-25-1871 (10-26-1871)
Standlin, P. E. to W. J. B. Bernet? 1-2-1866 (1-4-1866)
Staner, Adaline to Calvin Kersey 9-17-1862 (9-18-1862)
Stanford, Elizabeth F. to Horrace L. Farmer 5-9-1874 (no return)
Stanford, Elizabeth to Francis M. Parkerson 7-19-1852 (no return)
Stanford, Martha Jane to Abner Luck 7-28-1854 (7-30-1854)
Stanley, Elizabeth to R. J. Stanley 2-21-1857 (no return)
Stanley, Mahala to Wm. Kinnmon 2-19-1857
Stanly, M. S. to G. W. Robinson 10-2-1876 (10-5-1876)
Stark, Alice B. to W. H. Robinson 1-8-1878
Stark, Charrity F. to George H. Anderson 9-4-1872 (9-5-1872)
Stark, Mary to Richard Anderson 12-20-1870 (12-29-1870) [B]
Starke, M. A. to John Gleson 3-21-1870 (3-23-1870)
Starke, Martha to John Crouder 12-16-1868 (12-17-1868) [B]
Starke, Nancy E. to James S. Perryman 3-1-1870
Starkes, Thema to Peter Barnes 7-4-1876
Starks, C. to Wm. Glenn ?-?-1866 (9-6-1866)
Starks, Childa to Wm. Glenn 8-25-1866 (no return) [B]
Starnes, Adaline H. to Wm. J. Isbell 7-27-1867 (no return)
Starnes, Mary to John J. Nixon 5-15-1879 (5-16-1879)
Statton, America L. to Wm. Adcock 2-26-1852
Steel, Bettie to John H. Dyer 1-1-1879 (1-2-1879)
Steel, M. J. to Newton Bilings 4-10-1875 (4-11-1875)
Steel, Mary L. to B. F. Foster 7-22-1857 (no return)
Steele, Amanda to B. J. Trulove 11-29-1866 (no return)
Stenson, Genarvie? to Charly Floide 3-25-1875 (3-27-1875)
Stephens, Ellet to John Kerby 3-22-1870 (3-28-1870)
Stephens, Mary J. to Harris Sullivan 6-22-1867 (6-25-1867)
Steps, Malinda to J. M. Gilbert 9-5-1874 (9-6-1874)
Stern, L. J. to Thomas J. William 6-23-1849 (6-25-1849)
Stewart, Mary A. to F. M. Hendrixson 4-9-1872 (4-11-1872)
Stewart?, N. A. E. to Wm. G. Fitts 12-23-1868 (12-24-1868)
Stiles, J. E. to W. A. Gilbert 11-14-1877 (11-15-1877)
Stiles, Margrett N. to Wm. C. Mullicen 3-12-1872 (3-14-1872)

Stocklin, Liza to Albert Johns 1-8-1878 (1-10-1878)
Stocklin, M. L. to W. W. Johnson 12-24-1877 (12-26-1877)
Stokes, Ann to Dennis Miller 7-15-1868 (no return) [B]
Stokes, Callie to L. M. Markum 10-23-1876 (10-26-1876)
Stokes, Darthula to Berry James 12-23-1872 (no return) [B]
Stokes, Elizabeth to Wm. Heflin 10-10-1877 (10-11-1877)
Stokes, Emley to James M. Crowder 1-3-1873 (no return) [B]
Stokes, Fanney to Elias Tubb 1-26-1876
Stokes, Hannah L. to James N. Calhoon 11-10-1858 (11-11-1859?)
Stokes, Harait to Andrew Philips 12-7-1870 (no return) [B]
Stokes, Hattie A. to Wm. A. Brian 5-27-1862 (6-10-1862)
Stokes, Izibel to Ned Tubbs 5-26-1877 (5-29-1877)
Stokes, Malisa Jane to William T. Hoskins 11-10-1855 (11-11-1855)
Stokes, Mariah to John Stokes 3-17-1866 (3-18-1866)
Stokes, Martha Jane to P. L. Powel 6-22-1859 (no return)
Stokes, Q. V. to Peter Robinson 1-7-1874 (1-10-1874)
Stokes, Sallie to George D. McNelly 12-23-1872 (12-24-1872)
Stokes, Silvey to Thornton Stokes 3-17-1866 (3-18-1866)
Stokes, Susanah to Nicholas Balis 9-21-1866 (9-2?-1866) [B]
Stokes, Tennessee to Licurgus Driver 11-3-1873 (11-4-1873)
Stokes?, Charlotty to W. B. Newbey 12-21-1866
Stoks?, Carline to Alex Tubb 1-25-1869 (1-26-1869) [B]
Stone, Laura to J. P. Bostick 3-30-1878 (3-31-1878)
Stone, Narcica to W. J. Delong 9-3-1877
Stoner, Jane to Benjamin H. Liden 10-22-1872
Stoner, Liddy to George Mitchell 10-21-1872 (10-22-1872)
Stoner, Nancy W. to Wm. V. Jones 8-29-1859
Stoner, Siller to George B. Rutledge 8-24-1859
Storm, Ann C. to G. M. McGee 8-1-1871
Stout, Mary to Hillis D. Cantrell 8-9-1871 (8-10-1871)
Stout, Oma to F. P. Knowles 2-7-1876
Stover, Eliza to Teral Maynard 3-6-1850 (no return)
Stricklin, Miley to Benjamin Taylor 1-15-1859 (no return)
Strong, Elizabeth to Thomas Leek 6-20-1856 (6-29-1856)
Strong, Mary P. to James M. Pistole 10-30-1850
Strong, Rachel to Wm. Sadler 10-26-1848
Strong, Susan R. to Levi B. Steel 12-30-1854 (12-31-1854)
Strowd, Nancy to George W. Jones 3-22-1850 (3-23-1850)
Stuart, R. J. to B. P. Martin 3-26-1872 (3-28-1872)
Stuart, Sallie E. to J. B. Davis 5-28-1870 (5-31-1870)
Styles, Sarah E. to Mathew Johnston 12-9-1878 (12-11-1878)
Sullens, Manervy to M. P. Ferrel 11-20-1858 (11-21-1858)
Sullins, Juley A. to Henry Bullard 3-18-1871 (3-19-1871)
Sullivan, Matilda J. to David J. Deeks 11-4-1852
Swearingin, Rebecca to Hiram Truett 4-7-1866 (no return)
Sweet, Elizabeth to Line Robinson 4-7-1849 (not exec.)
Swinford, Frances to John Chambiss 12-26-1853
Sykes, Cathrine to Wm. H. Baker 1-5-1857 (2-25-1857)
Talley, Fanie to J. T. Ashworth 10-24-1870
Talley, Martha to George W. Martin 11-22-1873
Tamel, Annis M. to Barzela Taylor 5-3-1861 (5-9-1861)
Tanbersan, M. J. to John G. Reynolds 3-10-1866 (3-11-1866)
Tate, Margaret to Elias C. Bowens 6-15-1854 (6-5?-1854)
Taylor, A. B. to George Robinson 3-2-1876
Taylor, A. B. to Thomas Smith 12-23-1868
Taylor, Ann to John W. Sanders 6-26-1859 (6-27-1859)
Taylor, Elizabeth A. to Jesse Arnold 3-25-1868
Taylor, Elizabeth A. to Wm. Sniders 10-28-1861
Taylor, Elizabeth to Henry Hendrixon 7-13-1861 (7-18-1861)
Taylor, Erlina? to Jdavid C. Taylor 3-22-1855
Taylor, Frances to Dempsey Taylor 12-23-1878 (12-24-1878)
Taylor, Frances to Wilson Hendrix 8-8-1866 (8-9-1866)
Taylor, Hannah to Josiah W. Taylor 9-20-1871 (9-24-1871)
Taylor, Hicksey to Samuel L. Walker 3-3-1879 (solemzd?)
Taylor, Jane to Abner Self 12-2-1851
Taylor, Kezy J. to Ruben K. Atnip 5-17-1855
Taylor, Kizamore to Allen Trusty 10-28-1871 (10-29-1871)
Taylor, Lida to William Turner 9-16-1858 (9-19-1858)
Taylor, Lizie to Isaac Taylor 9-9-1879 (9-7?-1879)
Taylor, Lucretia J. to Joseph W. Banks 1-25-1864
Taylor, Lucritia to Henry R. Taylor 12-1-1859
Taylor, Lucy to G. W. Spencer 1-9-1867 (1-12-1867)
Taylor, Malinda to Ezekial Taylor 1-4-1865 (no return)
Taylor, Manda to Wm. Merett 3-13-1867
Taylor, Martha J. to Isaac Parker 9-18-1878 (9-19-1878)

Taylor, Martha to Pleasant Robinson 10-13-1852 (10-14-1852)
Taylor, Mary A. to Francis M. Green 8-21-1860
Taylor, Mary Ann to Alexander A. Hendrixson 11-5-1865 (11-10-1865)
Taylor, Mary E. to Jordon Fish 7-28-1864
Taylor, Mary F. to A. D. Walker 12-19-1873
Taylor, Mary J. to Samuel Walker 8-2-1871 (8-5-1871)
Taylor, Mary to Alexander Neele 9-28-1848 (10-8-1848)
Taylor, May to Chester Turner 9-3-1853 (10-31-1853)
Taylor, Nancy C. to John H. Knowles 12-13-1869 (12-14-1869)
Taylor, Nancy J. to Thomas J. Taylor 9-13-1872 (9-22-1872)
Taylor, Nancy to T. N. Smith 4-15-1878 (4-19-1878)
Taylor, Rachel E. to James M. Gay 12-13-1872 (12-15-1872)
Taylor, Rhacal to David Robinson 11-27-1878 (11-28-1878)
Taylor, Rhoda E. to Horrace Trusty 12-11-1873
Taylor, Sarah Ann to Wm. Manning 10-9-1864 (no return)
Taylor, Sarah C. to James L. Mullican 10-7-1857 (no return)
Taylor, Sarah E. to William B. Tramol 3-3-1873 (3-6-1873)
Taylor, Sarah to Jeremiah Hendrixon 10-5-1861 (10-6-1861)
Taylor, Sarah to John Winfree 4-1-1858
Taylor, Sarah to Joshaway Neele 8-6-1877 (no return)
Taylor, Sarah to Levi Robinson 4-14-1850 (4-18-1850)
Taylor, Sarah to T. P. West 7-29-1879 (7-30-1879)
Taylor, Sarah to William Taylor ?-26-1853 (7-27-1853)
Taylor, Spica to Joseph Hammons 9-25-1858
Taylor, Tresa to Isaac Smith 10-13-1855 (10-14-1855)
Taylor, Visa to Mathew Johnson 5-10-1854 (5-11-1854)
Tayson?, Samantha to Mason Pain 8-11-1875 (8-12-1875)
Teen, Elizabeth to Wm. Curtis 9-25-1850 (no return)
Terney, Sarah C. to Wm. J. Hambleton 4-15-1871 (4-16-1871)
Terrey, Cordelia T. to Henry E. Staley 5-15-1873
Terry, Lucy to Edmond League 1-8-1857
Terry, M. J. to R. H. Watson 3-2-1878 (3-3-1878)
Terry, Margaret O. to B. M. Merrett 4-18-1870 (4-21-1870)
Terry, Mary to A. V. Lee 5-5-1859
Terry, Sarah S. to John F. Woodsides 1-13-1857 (1-14-1857)
Terry, Sarah to F. H. Smith 3-26-1860 (3-29-1860)
Thomas, Elizabeth to John Kerley 11-14-1855
Thomas, Fanny to Joseph Irvin Hill 10-17-1874 (no return) [B]
Thomas, Sallie to Benjamon Grindstaff 11-27-1876 (12-7-1876)
Thomas, Sarah J. to H. B. Reynolds 9-17-1878 (9-19-1878)
Thomason or White, Eliza J. to Lafayette Griffin 12-30-1850
Thomason, Mary C. to Wm. P. Allen 8-12-1854 (8-15-1854)
Thomkins, Sallie J. to J. F. Mason 10-3-1870 (10-8-1870)
Thompson, Ann E. to David Gorden 1-10-1874 (no return) [B]
Thompson, Martha V. to W. M. Linder 1-20-1880 (no return)
Thompson, Mary F. to Jon J. Spurlock 2-8-1873 (2-9-1873)
Thompson, Mary to James P. Stoner 12-14-1872 (12-18-1872)
Thompson, Parilee to James Merfey 11-26-1865 (no return)
Thompson, Sarah to Samuel Bennett 11-11-1850 (11-12-1850)
Thompson, Susan J. to S. A. Osburn 3-12-1879 (3-13-1879)
Thornberry, Elizabeth to Franklin Sims 8-10-1852 (no return)
Threwet, Malina Jane to Giles Driver 11-25-1849 (11-25-1849)
Thrue, Emaline to H. P. Adcock 11-28-1874 (11-29-1874)
Thurman, Lena to James Stephens 7-5-1875
Thurman, Malissa to Samuel T. Looney 2-1-1872 (2-8-1872)
Tibbs, Nancy A. to H. Taylor 5-29-1879
Tibs, Nancy M. to Wiley Congo 6-15-1859 (6-16-1859)
Tillmen, Elizabeth to Wm. Malone 1-25-1867 (1-26-1867)
Tinsley, M. A. to F. D. Warren 12-8-1869 (12-9-1869)
Tinsley, Rutha to Alexandria Warren 11-6-1872
Tippet, Mary Ann to John Rigsby 9-19-1850 (no return)
Tippit, Ciynthia A. to John McBride 11-30-1878 (12-1-1878)
Tisdal, J. S. to John Bates 11-8-1874
Title, Lucindy E. to Woodson C. Spurlock 1-27-1873
Titsworth, America to Edward Pollard 11-2-1868
Titsworth, Fanna to F. P. Sanders 3-2-1878 (3-3-1878)
Titsworth, Lesita to Champ Goodson 5-12-1862
Titsworth, M. J. to T. M. Reynolds 3-30-1872 (3-31-1872)
Titsworth, Martha E. to Tilmon Cantrell 10-23-1855
Titsworth, Nancy to G. P. Kelly 2-28-1879 (3-2-1879)
Titsworth, Palina to W. D. Womack 8-9-1864 (8-12-1864)
Titsworth, Rachel to Arch Bain 3-26-1864 (no return)
Tittle, Edney to George T. Moris 3-26-1869 (3-28-1869)
Tittle, Julia to George Hall 1-28-1876

Tittsworth, Mary Jane to Champion Goodson 11-14-1853 (11-24-1853)
Todd, Anna to Amno Green 11-6-1877 (11-7-1877)
Todd, Nancy to Wm. Thompson 9-13-1879 (9-14-1879)
Tomblin, Perthenia to John Banks 9-30-1874
Tramal, N. C. to Wm. Bane 10-7-1870 (10-9-1870)
Tramel, Elizabeth to William R. Hill? 8-29-1855 (8-28?-1855)
Tramel, Martha E. to James R. Hill 9-6-1871 (9-7-1871)
Tramel, Martha E. to Wm. L. Walls 1-13-1871 (1-18-1871)
Tramel, Mary E. to James Dale 10-2-1866
Tramel, Nancy to Albert McClenon 1-26-1854
Tramel, Sarah J. to Stephen Waldon 7-25-1874 (7-30-1874)
Tramel, Susan E. to Isaac N. Vanhooser 7-12-1855
Tramell, Margret to W. A. Moris 7-21-1871 (7-22-1871)
Trammel, Eveline to James G. Fuson 11-21-1874 (11-22-1874)
Trammel, Mary to Pleasant Hill 9-2-1856
Trammel, Parilee to Isaac Johnson 10-19-1865 (10-29-1865)
Trammell, Anis Mahaly to John Hoss 10-5-1864 (no return)
Trammell, Anisa M. to John Hill 7-25-1864
Trammell, Louisa to Seburn Page 5-11-1850 (5-12-1850)
Trammell, Mary B. to W. M. Trammell 11-12-1878
Trammell, Perelee to Porter Peak 7-17-1878 (7-18-1878)
Tramol, Susanah to George Evins 1-4-1873 (1-5-1873)
Trane?, Juda to A. T. Scrivner 11-20-1872 (11-21-1872)
Trapp, Amanda A. to Arwine Page 2-23-1857 (2-3?-1857)
Trapp, Dora to Jno. Taylor 3-1-1876 (no return)
Trapp, Elizabeth to John L. McClellon 8-19-1851
Trapp, Luisa to John Cripps 3-2-1866 (no return)
Trapp, M. A. to R. Cantrell 11-30-1877 (12-2-1877)
Trapp, Martha Ann to Elisha L. McGinnis 5-7-1856
Trapp, Nancy O. to James L. Atnip 8-30-1855 (8-23?-1855)
Trapp, Nancy R. to S. W. A. Hooper 10-26-1867 (10-21?-1867)
Trapp, Rebecca T. to Edmon Judkins 12-11-1868 (12-13-1868)
Trapp, Rebecca to Martin T. Bonhan 11-26-1865
Trapp, S. J. to Isaac Denton 2-24-1876
Trapp, Tennessee to Wm. A. Allen 3-16-1865
Traswell, Calista to William Eaton 1-24-1871 (1-25-1871)
Tree, Nancy to M. T. Martin 1-20-1857 (1-28-1857)
Trewet, Tennessee to Henry Smith 1-18-1867
Treysand, Amanda to Elisha Atnip 8-11-1866 (9-17-1866)
Trice, Adline to Henry Stokes 7-4-1874 (7-5-1874) [B]
Troglin, America J. to George H. Wright 10-29-1873 (10-30-1873)
Tromull, Rutha to Jermiah Keel 3-27-1878 (no return)
Trpp?, Susan to J. J. (G?) Pedigo 8-25-1859
Truett, Parthena C. to Wm. Adamson 8-2-1861 (8-4-1861)
Truette, Mary to Thomas Grooms 3-27-1855 (3-28-1855)
Truette, Nancy to Wm. Measles 10-2-1858 (exec. no date)
Truitte, Carolina to William Clark 11-19-1849 (2-2-1850)
Trustee, Martha A. to Samuel Caplinger 2-26-1864 (no return)
Trusty, E. M. to Henderson Bass 8-6-1876 (8-20-1876)
Trusty, Elizabeth to John Caplianeo 11-7-1865
Trusty, Margrett to David Taylor 12-15-1871 (12-17-1871)
Trusty, Mary J. to William Tates 8-9-1860
Trusty, Parlee Francis to F. F. Love 9-10-1874 (9-9-1874)
Trusty, Thena A. to Wm. Davis 3-29-1879
Tubb, Amandy to Amos Green 4-20-1872 (no return) [B]
Tubb, Carolina to L. D. Fite 8-3-1849 (8-9-1849)
Tubb, Conny to Fern. Smart 7-21-1879 (7-24-1879) [B]
Tubb, M. A. to John Stokes 1-7-1874 (1-8-1874) [B]
Tubb, Malisa to C. M. Williams 2-3-1873 (2-13-1873)
Tubb, Malissa to T. J. Trammel 2-9-1875 (2-10-1875)
Tubb, Paralee to Eli Sullins 1-15-1856 (1-17-1856)
Tubb, Setty to John Everett 6-3-1869 (7-4-1869)
Tubbs, Ann to Ben Bogle 12-27-1870 [B]
Tucker, Parmilea to Walter Anderson 2-13-1869 (2-14-1869)
Tucker, Rebecca to Wm. Austin 6-7-1854 (6-8-1854)
Turner, A. E. to W. C. Duff 10-20-1875 (10-21-1875)
Turner, A. T. to W. H. Adcock 10-16-1875 (10-17-1875)
Turner, C. L. to John Pinegar 9-6-1879 (no return)
Turner, Caldonia to O. D. Cantrell 7-19-1879 (7-20-1879)
Turner, Clarsey to Richard Officer 2-1-1870 (2-3-1870)
Turner, Eliz. J. to Thomas D. Bass 1-16-1861 (exec. no date)
Turner, Huldy B. to Jessee F. Hollis 3-10-1860 (3-11-1860)
Turner, J. C. to R. M. Dood 11-16-1878 (11-20-1878)
Turner, Kenie to J. H. Overall 2-15-1870 (2-16-1870)

Turner, Lucindy to Charles H. Bulington 11-11-1868 (11-12-1868) [B]
Turner, M. J. to Ed Young 10-29-1874 (no return)
Turner, Martha Ann to L. B. Richardson 4-17-1858 (4-18-1858)
Turner, Mary A. to John Mathes 10-18-1878 (solmzd--
    no date) [B]
Turner, Mary E. to Levi Pinegar 1-9-1871 (1-10-1871)
Turner, Mary J. to Almon D. Young 3-1-1873 (3-2-1873)
Turner, Mary J. to Levy Pinegar 8-19-1873
Turner, Mary Jane to John Pinegar 9-19-1864 (9-22-1864)
Turner, Mary Lee to L. N. Davis 5-2-1876 (5-3-1876)
Turner, Mary to Edly H. Gilings 3-15-1871 (3-16-1871) [B]
Turner, Mary to James B. Eledge 2-6?-1849 (no return)
Turner, Mary to Richard Paul 4-26-1873 (4-27-1873) [B]
Turner, Mary to Wels Allen 5-7-1866 (5-23-1866) [B]
Turner, Mattie to W. H. Sellars 9-22-1878
Turner, N. C. to G. M. Groomes 7-24-1879
Turner, Nancy V. to John C. Looney 1-24-1868 (1-26-1868)
Turner, P. to Eliol Simpson 1-11-1875
Turner, Rachel C. to John W. Bass 3-10-1849 (no return)
Turner, Rutha to James Pitman 10-12-1869 (10-13-1869)
Turner, Sarah to Charley Stout 4-3-1875 (4-4-1875)
Turner, Sarah to Matthew Braswell 2-5-1856 (2-6-1856)
Turner, Sinrellia to Marion Spencer 2-22-1866
Turner, Susan to Edward E. Woods 5-8-1856
Turner, Susan to Thomas C. Manning 9-15-1864 (9-18-1864)
Turner, Zantry P. to Hiram Hendrixson 8-17-1870
Turner?, Sucilla? to Marion Spencer no dates (w/1864 entries
Turney, Bathena C. to Thomas G. Ward 8-3-1857 (8-5-1857)
Turney, Catharine to John C. Cooper 8-19-1854 (8-20-1854)
Turney, Elizabeth J. to John W. Hayse 1-24-1855 (1-25-1855)
Turney, N. C. to J. C. Ford 12-13-1869 (12-16-1869)
Turney, Rebeca to Milton C. Dodd 9-28-1858 (9-29-1858)
Turney, Rebeca to William Trewett 7-16-1867 (7-18-1867)
Turney, Sarah to Jim Staley 5-24-1869 (5-27-1869) [B]
Twoney, Nancy to Wesley Ward 11-14-1876 (11-25-1876)
Tyree, Ellen to Jessee Frazier 12-31-1873 [B]
Tyree, Martha M. to James L. Calvert 1-14-1858
Tyree, Mary A. to Charles S. Frazier 1-19-1871
Tyree, Sophy to R. H. Grissam 1-7-1863 (2-18-1863)
Tyree, Susan E. to Henry Mandlebaum 10-4-1854 (10-5-1854)
Tyree, Vina to John Whitely 11-13-1875 (11-14-1875)
Tyson, Bethena to P. J. Lee 10-17-1870 (10-19-1870)
Underhill, M. S. to George W. Ratleph 7-10-1868 (7-12-1868)
Vanatta, Helen to T. M. Given 12-11-1879 (12-24-1879)
Vandegriff, M. L. to Wm. J. Parker 3-21-1876 (3-23-1876)
Vandergrift, Mary A.. to A. C. Dennis 1-28-1873 (1-30-1873)
Vandgrift, Martha C. to John G. Goggin 12-21-1872 (12-22-1872)
Vanhooser, Elizabeth to G. W. O. Kerby 10-6-1873 (10-9-1873)
Vanhoozer, Nancy to James Dodd 9-11-1862
Vannatta, Cansada to James M. Duke 8-6-1866 (8-4?-1866)
Vannatta, Caroline E. to John Alexander 1-7-1860 (1-8-1860)
Vannatta, Elizabeth to Berry Driver 6-19-1861 (no return)
Vantreace, Caroline to Noah Bowndes 11-15-1877
Vantreace, Lectes to James Neale 2-21-1875 (2-22-1875)
Vantreace, M. J. to W. Neale 8-3-1871 (8-6-1871)
Vantreace, T. M. to Gramison Baty 8-23-1876 (8-24-1876)
Vantrease, Armelda to Wm. R. Robinson 7-20-1851 (7-22-1851)
Vantrease, C. to I. Lawrence 10-29-1878
Vantrease, Catharine to Reuben B. Hale 8-17-1853
Vantrease, Emaline to John Malone 1-5-1872
Vantrease, Evalina A. to Fredrick E. Buckner 6-25-1850 (no return)
Vantrease, M. L. to Landon Reynolds 8-24-1877 (8-26-1877)
Vantrease, Martha J. to Zackariah Parker 3-7-1870 (3-10-1870)
Vantrease, Mary to Jacob Tubb 5-23-1878 [B]
Vantrease, Mary to Wm. Vantrese 4-9-1877? (no return)
Vantrease, Nancy to W. L. Adamson 12-20-1875 (6?-20-1875)
Vantreese, Julia A. to James P. Doss 1-14-1858 (1-20-1858)
Vaughn, Ireny F. to James Young 2-22-1868 (2-23-1868)
Vaughn, Martha Ann to David W. Luney 9-2-1852
Vaughn, Rebecca J. to Elisha Luna? 8-25-1874
Vaughn, Rena to James Smitson 9-4-1869 (9-5-1869)
Veer, Elizabeth to George W. Durham 12-11-1856 (12-15-1856)
Venon, Sarah to J. E. Moores 3-8-1873 (3-9-1873)
Vernon, M. A. to J. T. Wood 2-13-1872 (2-14-1872)
Vick, Amanda F. to John W. Grooms 1-12-1864 (exec. no date)

Vick, Eliza Jane to J. W. Griffin 7-24-1860 (not endorsed)
Vick, Frances to Johnson Adams 5-7-1866 (5-16-1866) [B]
Vick, Frances to Johnson Adams 5-7-1866 (5-7-1866) [B]
Vick, K. to Thomas Fite 11-?-1866 (no return)
Vick, Liza to W. G. Rowland 1?-16-1878 (no return)
Vick, Margat R. to Thomas Fite 11-5-1866 (no return)
Vick, Mary Josefine to Wm. D. G. Carnes 11-15-1859 (11-17-1859)
Vick, N. A. to H. G. Roy 11-25-1867 (11-26-1867)
Vick, Salina to Robert Yergin 3-5-1852 (3-9-1852)
Vick, Sarah C. to J. G. Squires 5-8-1873
Vickars, R. J. to H. S. Mosier 1-7-1878 (1-10-1878)
Vickers, Martha to George Parsley 1-4-1879 (1-5-1879)
Vickers, Sarah E. to Jackson Smith 11-14-1871
Vier, Delpha to J. C. Williams 10-26-1859 (10-27-1859)
Vier, Mary to William Braswell 10-10-1864 (no return)
Viers, Parilee to Wm. C. Murfey 11-1-1864 (11-2-1864)
Viesz, Catherine to Henry Hancock 6-3-1866
Vine, Martha to John Hale 2-21-1865
Vine, Parthena to Wm. S. Smith 8-30-1862 (no return)
Vistal?, Nancey Ann to Richard N. Mathes 7-4-1866 (no return)
Wade (Sadler), Harriet to Sampson Braswell 12-25-1858 (no return)
Wade, Susan to L. Y. Davis 7-4-1863 (no return)
Wailes, Mary Asilian to Richard Taylor 5-7-1869
Waker, Mary to John Warren omitted (7-12-1838)
Waldon, E. H. to B. H. Pressly 2-11-1867 (no return)
Waldridge, H. C. to L. Spurlock 11-4-1876 (11-5-1876)
Walker, Anna to Isaiah Bain 4-1-1861 (4-2-1861)
Walker, Frances to Dennis C. Julian 5-13-1856 (5-14-1856)
Walker, Frances to Thomas Jones 2-17-1865
Walker, Hanah to B. B. Page 7-5-1879 (7-8-1879)
Walker, Jane to Danial W. Cantrell 6-17-1874 (6-18-1874)
Walker, M. J. to J. W. Denney 10-12-1876 (no return)
Walker, M. L. to J. E. Wall 10-30-1876 (11-1-1876)
Walker, Nancy to James E. Moon 12-22-1864
Walking, Anny to Henry W. Taylor 12-14-1858 (12-19-1858)
Wall, Maring to Ozious D. Griffith 1-9-1868 (1-12-1868)
Wallace, Martha to James Prichird 9-21-1870 (9-22-1870)
Wallen, Sarah to John G. Norice 1-2-1850
Waller, P. E. to C. M. Neel 7-24-1878 (no return)
Walls, Eliza J. to Barnabas R. Page 3-11-1870 (3-12-1870)
Walls, Margrett M. to J. L. Tramel 6-25-1879 (6-26-1879)
Walls, Rebecca to J. F. Jackson 9-24-1862 (no return)
Walls, Roannia to W. G. Thriek 5-13-1875 (no return)
Wamac, Mary to Jas. F. Turner 3-3-1880
Wammac, Matilda to Abner Tumblson? omitted (3-14-1865)
Wanford, Louizia E. to John Wooden 5-15-1873
Wanford, Malvina M. S. W. to James H. Roberts 7-21-1873 (no
    return)
Wanford, Nancy E. to Wm. M. Driver 8-28-1869 (no return)
Ward, Carolin to Lewis Stuckrath 6-23-1860 (no return)
Ward, Elizabeth to J. F. Youngblood 9-9-1876 (9-10-1876)
Ward, N. A. C. to Wm. H. Fanes? 4-22-1869
Ward, S. S. to E. G. Griffith 9-23-1878 (9-26-1878)
Ward, Sarah E. to J. L. Smith 3-3-1875 (3-4-1875)
Warde, M. J. to J. E. Evans 12-25-1876 (12-28-1876)
Ware, Mary to Isaac Ware 1-1-1866 (2-3-1866)
Waren, Fanny to Franklin Lafever 6-17-1858 (6-20-1858)
Warfon, Sarah to C. C. Yergan 1-20-1849 (1-5-1849)
Warford, Amand to Bransford Burnett 7-22-1855 (7-24-1855)
Warford, Delililia F. to Isaac Bates 8-8-1872 (8-9-1872)
Warford, Milly E. to Thomas Adams 12-3-1864 (no return)
Warford, Milly E. to Thos. Adams 12-3-1864 (no return)
Warford, N. P. to Jeremiah Reasonover 8-10-1865 (no return)
Warner, Maliss to W. W. Calwell 3-20-1866
Warren, Amanda to R. J. Montgomery 12-5-1877 (no return)
Warren, Elizabeth to George Warren 1-25-1857
Warren, Elizabeth to John Elrod 1-1-1868
Warren, Fancy to Henderson P. Farley 5-5-1856 (no return)
Warren, Louisa to M. J. Durham 1-14-1876 (1-15-1876)
Warren, Mary to Wm. Fuston date omttd (exec 4-30-1839)
Washer, Becca to Thomas Foutch 8-8-1876 (8-10-1876)
Washer, Caroline to Bethell Williams 9-22-1869 (9-23-1869)
Washer, Dorainis to Yance Maylone 8-27-1866 (8-29-1866)
Washer, Mary to A. C. Williams 12-19-1877 (12-27-1877)
Washer, Ronea to James P. Tubb 10-20-1879 (10-23-1879)

Washer, Sarah to John A. Fouch 3-10-1852 (3-14-1852)
Wasker, M. F. to F. W. Hobson 12-5-1865 (12-6-1865)
Wats, Mary to N. Mullican 4-12-1856 (4-13-1856)
Watson, B. Z. to Elijah Hale 10-2-1877 (10-8-1877)
Watson, Feby to Elem Edge 12-23-1853 (no date)
Watson, Julia Ann to Thomas Ebre 6-25-1853 (6-26-1853)
Watson, Mary to Ira Nelson 8-28-1854
Watson, Mary to Isaac Vandegrift 9-2-1870 (9-22-1870)
Watson, Susan to John Underhill(Loranhill) 11-23-1859 (no return)
Watts, Susannah T. to Jacob Atnip 3-26-1851 (3-27-1851)
Webb, Emsy to Benjamin F. Hicks 1-2-1869 (1-3-1869)
Webb, Eugenia to E. J. Evans 6-22-1875 (6-23-1875)
Webb, Mary Ann to Wiley Kerklin 6-23-1855 (6-24-1855)
Webb, Mary to L. D. Furgerson 5-7-1877 (5-9-1877)
Webb, Morning to Isaac Cantrell 7-22-1852
Webb, S. C. to H. J. Sneed 12-29-1877 (12-30-1877)
Webb, Susan to Littleton Horton 9-8-1852
Webster, Sarah F. to John H. Pitman 8-5-1872
West, Adah E. to W. C. Youngour 1-20-1873 (1-23-1873)
West, Allis to C. F. Marler 12-19-1877 (exec. no date)
West, Amanda to James Love 11-4-1856 (11-6-1856)
West, Eliza Ann to George Wilbern 9-22-1867 (no return) [B]
West, Fimantis? T. to F. P. Potter 12-6-1865
West, Helen to J. P. Barry 2-9-1875 (2-11-1875)
West, Julia E. to John S. Harrison 12-22-1856 (exec. no date)
West, L. C. to James L. Dinwiddie 5-14-1873 (no return)
West, M. C. to J. T. Kennedy 12-28-1869 (12-29-1869)
West, Mallie to H. B. Wilkinson 1-3-1878
West, Martha D. to Russel Eskew 12-21-1854 (12-24-1854)
West, Martha to U. M. Neal 12-7-1879 (no return)
West, Mary P. to James Jones 12-11-1855 (12-12-1855)
West, Mary T. to John B. Wheeler 12-19-1849
West, Mary to James W. Adcock 8-13-1853 (8-14-1852?)
West, Mary to Wm. F. Vantrease 4-2-1874 (4-9-1874)
West, N. E. to W. E. Rich 11-19-1867 (no return)
West, Sarah to William Vick 4-8-1851
Whaley, Bettie B. to P. T. Shares 3-20-1872
Whaley, Eliza to R. F. Jones 3-15-1878 (3-17-1878)
Whaley, Elizabeth to Hyram Neale 2-5-1866 (2-15-1866)
Whaley, M. E. to J. P. Stark 9-25-1874
Whaley, M. E. to L. J. Potter 1-4-1877
Whaley, Martha A. to Joseph Clark 8-7-1874 (no return)
Whaley, Matilda to James R. Beckwith 3-27-1849 (no return)
Whaley, Nancy to E. D. Burton 3-13-1849 (3-15-1849)
Whaley, Nancy to J. J. Foster 2-13-1849
Whaley, Rachel to Nathan Tubb 2-5-1866 (no return) [B]
Whaley, Talitha to Abraham Witt 4-3-1866 (exec. no date)
Whaly, Sarah to Thomas Given 5-5-1866 (5-6-1866)
Wheeller, Emma to J.? E.? Warren 7-20-1871
Whilliby, Sarah B. to James B. White 4-6-1867 (4-10-1867)
White, Drucilla C. to Wiley Conger 11-10-1870 (no return)
White, Elizabeth C. to Wm. P. Overall 7-31-1856
White, Elizabeth to W. F. Malone 8-22-1867 (8-25-1867)
White, Louisa to James Davis 9-22-1857 (9-20?-1857)
White, Malinda to Lee Lafever 2-11-1864 (no return)
White, Mary A. to John B. Self 5-19-1858 (5-20-1858)
White, Mary F. to James D. Calvert 2-11-1879
White, Mary H. to Mathew Green 2-3-1863
White, Mary N. to Calvin Garrison 1-16-1856 (2-7-1856)
White, Mary to Joseph B. Caskey 7-24-1855 (7-25-1855)
White, Rachel to Francis B. Warford 2-5-1849 (1?-11-1849)
White, S. D. to Joseph Turner 1-29-1874
Whitley, Lucy A. to O. W. Roberts 4-20?-1860 (exec. no date)
Whitley, Mary A. to Henry Sisk 5-23-1867
Whitley, Mary to Christofer P. Sartean 3-6-1854 (3-7-1854)
Whitley, Salley Ann to Thomas Christon 4-12-1854 (4-13-1854)
Whitlock, Alice to Ed Norman 3-29-1879
Whitlock, Rody to Benjamin Cantrell 6-26-1862 (6-27-1862)
Whitly, Empy to Rufus Rackly 2-24-1850 (2-25-1850)
Whitman, Allis to Isaac Hutchins 7-6-1868 (no return)
Whitten, Sarah E. to R. B. West 11-2-1869 (no return)
Wilder, Elizabeth to Wm. Evans 3-9-1854
Wiliams, Jane to Josiah Herriman 8-9-1865 (no return)
Wilkerson, Artemisa to J. P. Cotten 9-25-1858 (10-1-1858)
Wilkerson, Drusilla to David L. Dunham 1-12-1856 (1-17-1856)

Wilkinson, M. E. to J. H. Waldredge 2-4-1878 (2-5-1878)
William, Darcas to Owen Paisley 3-7-1861
William, Jane to Jacob Adcock 7-5-1867 (no return)
Williams, A. M. to Peter Davis 12-18-1865 (12-21-1865)
Williams, A. to James Hollensworth 1-28-1878 (1-29-1878)
Williams, Alyin to Alexander Hildreth 4-2-1866 (no return)
Williams, Armetine to Thomas J. Curtis 10-24-1866
Williams, Canzada to Jacob Adams 5-5-1879
Williams, Caroline to S. M. Crowder 10-4-1867 (no return)
Williams, Delila to B. S. St. John 3-20-1857 (3-22-1857)
Williams, E. J. to John Richardson 8-25-1866 (no return)
Williams, Elizabeth to A. J. Fusan 2-25-1864 (no return)
Williams, Elizabeth to F. C. White 11-20-1872 (11-21-1872)
Williams, Fally to R. E. Simpson 10-10-1878 (10-15-1878)
Williams, Felby to W. J. Payne 5-10-1873 (5-11-1873)
Williams, Haxa? T. to Wm. D. Trapp 1-5-1857 (1-6-1857)
Williams, Hellen to Alfred O. Allen 2-19-1874
Williams, Irena S. to Gustavus Ewing 4-23-1873 (4-24-1873)
Williams, Levina to Wm. D. Adamson 8-24-1853 (8-25-1853)
Williams, Lucinda to Joseph Sparks 6-14-1864 (6-19-1864)
Williams, Maggie E. to Oval Perkey 11-1-1859 (11-3-1859)
Williams, Malisa to A. P. Jones 9-28-1878 (9-29-1878)
Williams, Mandy to Mitchael Overall 3-17-1866 (3-18-1866)
Williams, Margaret to John Austin 10-13-1852 (10-14-1852)
Williams, Margaret to Johnathan Griffith 1-5-1874 (1-7-1874)
Williams, Margaret to Wm. Herrondon 10-4-1855
Williams, Margarett Jane to Elijah M. Brant 10-22-1859 (no return)
Williams, Martha E. to Abram S. Malone 9-13-1873 (9-21-1873)
Williams, Martha J. to Wm. J. Farmer 12-19-1879
Williams, Marthaan to W. R. Bryant 9-2-1875
Williams, Mary to A. R. Myers 5-1-1880 (5-2-1880)
Williams, Mary to Newton Reynolds 7-28-1869 (8-15-1869)
Williams, Mary to Stephen Goodner 3-11-1871 (3-12-1871)
Williams, Minnie to Albert J. Edwards 12-24-1873
Williams, Mollie to A. S. Yeargoin 2-20-1872 (2-22-1872)
Williams, N. E. to J. W. Naill? 8-10-1876
Williams, Nancy B. to J. M. Trapp 1-2-1861 (1-3-1861)
Williams, Nancy P. to James H. White 11-6-1865 (11-9-1865)
Williams, Nancy to S. M. Crowder 4-11-1874 (4-12-1874)
Williams, Paralee to Josiah L. Bass 3-12-1851
Williams, Parilee to Isaac Tumey 10-22-1866 (10-23-1866)
Williams, Rebecca L. to A. H. Robinson 1-6-1869 (1-10-1869)
Williams, Rebecca to James G. McIntire 9-21-1862
Williams, Sarah H. to John F. Foster 10-30-1879
Williams, Sarah to Matthew Jones 2-17-1849 (no return)
Williams, Sarah to Peter Hackette 6-21-1849
Williams, Sintha to George W. Springfield 7-29-1865 (no return)
Williams, Tabitha to Richard Lambrison 4-18-1874 (no return)
Willis, Drusila to Bracket L. Estes 2-3-1857 (2-4-1857)
Willis, Nancy Ann to Thos. J. Anderson 7-24-1851 (7-26-1851)
Willmoth, Eliza. to Wm. Jones 5-31-1854 (6-1-1854)
Willmouth, Sarah to Wm. Adcock 1-6-1876
Willoby, Vicktory to David Waford 6-23-1877 (6-24-1877)
Wiloby, Sarah to James B. White no dates (w/Jan)
Wilson, Edney to A. B. Hooper 9-22-1875 (9-23-1875)
Wilson, Elizabeth to John Tarply 7-9-1853 (7-10-1853)
Wilson, Hester to Frank Moore 1-11-1876 (1-13-1876)
Wilson, Kiziah to Wm. Ramy 2-11-1849
Wilson, Luvina to Parker Amonet 9-1-1859
Wilson, Malinda A. to James E. Jones 8-15-1861 (no return)
Wilson, Mary A. to Edmond Butterbough 7-21-1873 (7-23-1873)
Wilson, Mary A. to J. A. Shane 8-21-1867
Wilson, Mary Ann to Henry Hirendon 1-18-1871 (2-19-1871)
Wilson, Mary H. to R. W. Mason 10-24-1878
Wilson, Thursey to L. F. Moore 1-4-1864 (no return)
Wimaid, Eliza to Thomas Bailif 9-8-1875
Winchester, Jane to William Cantrell 2-7-1859 (no return)
Winchester, Mary Anis to George W. Null 10-1-1862 (10-2-1862)
Winchester, Tennessee to R. S. Love 4-27-1867 (4-28-1867)
Windham, Bell to Eurasta Smith 9-9-1872 [B]
Windham, Rebecca J. to Thos. A. Christian 2-26-1871
Wine, M. C. to N. G. Maddux 2-14-1865 (no return)
Wines, Malissa to Lafayette Hale 8-23-1854 (8-24-1854)
Winfor, Emandy to E. S. Bowers 12-21-1868 (12-22-1868)
Winfree, Achsah to Wm. Nixon 11-3-1851 (11-6-1851)

Winfree, Fanny to Thomas N. Christian 5-8-1854 (5-11-1854)
Winfree, Martha to Abner S. Harper 8-11-1856 (8-14-1856)
Winfrey, Eliz. R. to Thomas Garrison 12-15-1879 (12-16-1879)
Witt, Bettiniah to James Strang 7-24-1852
Witt, Nancy V. to James Martin 11-5-1873 (11-6-1873)
Womack, Rebecca to Peter Crips 9-6-1869 (no return)
Womackj, Caroline to Jerry Cantrell 12-31-1869 (1-1-1870) [B]
Wood, Della to J. F. Allen 10-14-1879 (10-16-1879)
Wood, E. J. to Joshua L. Bryant 11-17-1870
Wood, Frances R. to James R. Merrette 3-6-1850
Wood, Lue to Joseph Hancok 2-22-1878 (2-27-1878)
Wood, Lusetta J. to Archibald A. Jones 3-26-1850
Wood, Mary F. to W. W. Womack 2-14-1874 (2-15-1874)
Wooden, Delia to Henry Reynolds 4-29-1874 (5-3-1874)
Wooden, Luncindy to John Taylor 3-6-1869 (no return)
Wooden, Mary to Isaac Gibbs 1-24-1857
Wooderd, Kiza Ann to Matthew Hunt 10-22-1856 (no return)
Woodrell, Kizanie to John Reives 7-24-1858 (7-25-1858)
Woods, July E. to Wm. T. Moores 10-21-1871 (10-24-1871)
Woods, Mattie E. to W. D. Gowen 9-24-1873 (9-25-1873)
Woodson, Elizabeth to John S. Simpson 6-1-1850 (6-2-1850)
Wooldrage, Fannie to Robert Miller 9-6-1859 (?-7-1859)
Wooldridge, Martha Ann to Samuel J. Hildreth 3-13-1850
Woolridge, Luella to Wm. T. Hayse 12-11-1872 (12-12-1872)
Woolridge, M. J. to John A. Jones 12-16-1871 (12-17-1871)
Woolrige, M. E. to W. A. Johnson 8-27-1865
Worley, Kiah to Benjamin Orsben 5-25-1852 (5-27-1852)
Worley, Tennessee to James C. Pack 5-11-1876 (5-16-1876)
Worley, V. L. to H. H. Hildreth 11-16-1877 (no return)
Wouldred, Jane to H. Reynolds 11-25-1876 (11-26-1876)
Wouldridge, Sarah to Woodson Petty 11-4-1870 (11-7-1870)
Wright, A. P. to W. C. Oakley 10-9-1875 (10-12-1875)
Wright, Allis to James Mullins 12-31-1855 (1-2-1856)
Wright, C. A. to T. F. Bowman 2-24-1877 (3-1-1877)
Wright, Catharine to A. J. Cantrell 1-14-1879 (1-19-1879)
Wright, Ebaline to Anthony P. Adcock 11-15-1856 (11-16-1856)
Wright, Elizabeth to Samuel Williams 3-20-1869 (no return)
Wright, Fannie to Brown Ford 9-30-1879 (10-2-1879) [B]
Wright, Fannie to Lenard Cantrell 10-5-1878 (10-6-1878)
Wright, Frances to Lafayette Garrison 12-24-1864 (no return)
Wright, Harriett to Lafayett Banks 7-22-1871 (no return)
Wright, Jane to Benj. F. Wright 12-5-1878
Wright, Louisa to Ferdinand P? Fisher 2-8-1872 (no return)
Wright, Mary P. to James Picket 8-18-1853 (exec. no date)
Wright, Matilda to Jasper Rule 8-13-1868
Wright, Rebecca to Peter Goodson 3-22-1849
Wright, Roxa to D. Griffeth 10-6-1874 (10-11-1874)
Wright, Sarrah A. to John Cotten 10-1-1873
Wright, Susan to Joseph J. Fisher 11-15-1854 (11-161-1854)
Wright, Texas to Richard W. Landers 2-6-1873 (2-9-1873)
Wynns, Mary N. to Perry Adcock 10-1-1860 (10-2-1860)
Yeargan, Helan F. to J. F. Roy 2-21-1870 (2-24-1870)
Yeargan, Masey to Joshua W. Peckette 3-7-1849
Yeargan, Talitha to Isaac Cooper 11-15-1848 (11-20-1849?)
Yeargin, Saliny to George Hathaway 12-7-1868 (no return)
Yergan, Zade to Bence Miget 1-15-1880
York, Easter to George Gilbert 8-6-1879
Young, Elizabeth to Daniel Fowler 10-2-1866
Young, Elizabeth to Henry Joines 7-13-1877 (7-15-1877)
Young, Ellen to Ranse Green 10-16-1879
Young, Helen to Solley Louise 10-7-1878 (10-10-1878)
Young, Jane to Samuel Pettey 7-19-1879 (7-20-1879)
Young, Loucinda to J. M. Luny 5-24-1877
Young, M. J. to John West 7-27-1878
Young, Martha to Wm. Brimer 8-6-1859 (no endors.)
Young, Mary J. to John Keil 12-23-1861 (no return)
Young, Nancy to Jessee Haley 9-30-1870 (10-2-1870)
Young, Nancy to Layfayette Neal 2-24-1876
Young, Nancy to R. H. Ponder 8-21-1867 (8-22-1867)
Young, Prissey to Wm. Capshaw ?-2-1859 (11-3-1859)
Young, R. H. to J. M. Certain 2-8-1876 (2-9-1876)
Young, Rachel to Edward Pertle 4-2-1851
Young, Sarah to William R. Billings 11-6-1851
Young, Susan Jane to John L. Pirtle 3-8-1860 (not endorsed)
Young, Susan to Charles Rigsby 9-4-1876 (no return)

Youngblood, A. A. to A. J. Potter 1-16-1860 (1-17-1860)
Youngblood, Charity to Thomas Blackburn 6-16-1878 (6-23-1878)
Youngblood, Mary Jane to Hanable Kursey 7-26-1854 (7-27-1854)
Youngblood, Paralee to H. F. Hicks 12-26-1855
Zachary, Harrett to W. C. Zachary 11-27-1879 (12-3-1879)
, Rosy to Wm. Tubb 1-8-1876 (1-9-1876)
, to Thomas J. Eastus 5-31-1871 (no return)

www.ingramcontent.com/pod-product-compliance
Lightning Source LLC
Chambersburg PA
CBHW081341090426
42737CB00017B/3238